# The Moon Home

月

# The Moon Home

When a Psychotherapist is the Patient

by Suko Nagatani

Copyright ©2019 Etsuko Nagatani
All rights reserved.

No part of this publication may be reproduced, stored in a retrieval system, or transmitted in any form or by any means, electronic, mechanical, photocopying, recording, or otherwise, without written permission of the author.

Published in the United States by
Etsuko Nagatani
Playa Vista, California
TheMoonHome@yahoo.com

ISBN: 978-0-578-59054-7
Library of Congress Control Number: 2019916227

Book cover and interior design by
Katie Mullaly, Surrogate Press®

To Grandma and Donna - with your love,
I became who I am.

In memory of my father.

# Table of Contents

## PART I: Life Lessons

    ONE: One Mountain, One River, Two Houses.........2

    TWO: Musashi Miyamoto........................................31

    THREE: An Untamed Child ..................................50

## PART II: Working Through

    FOUR: The Beginning............................................76

    FIVE: Death, Compulsion and Secret ...................107

    SIX: New Home...................................................148

    SEVEN: Therapist................................................176

## PART III: Free Association

    EIGHT: Trouble to be Loved ................................208

    NINE: Empty Stomach and Empty Mind.............231

    TEN: Love ...........................................................257

    ELEVEN: Cuckoo's Nest........................................291

Acknowledgments .................................................309

If you or someone you know is in crisis, please call
the National Suicide Prevention Lifeline:
**1-800-273-TALK (8255)**

月

# Life Lessons

## PART 1

## CHAPTER ONE
# One Mountain, One River, Two Houses

During May in Hokkaido, the Kitoushi mountains are covered with lavender, the hillsides brushed with soft pink cherry blossoms and miles of narcissus, vivid yellow and milky white, contrasting with the deep green wild grasses that bring lively spirits to those who pass them on the sidewalks and streets below. The air smells as if I have just walked into a greenhouse, full of oxygen, and I breathe the scent in through my nose. I sense the essence of chlorophyll as it moves into my brain, and purifies my mind. In the early morning, the sky is not quite blue, the clouds are not quite crisp, there are drops of water on the surface of the leaves as if they produced tiny clear fish eggs during the night. The water is from condensation that was created during the transition from the cool night to the warmth of the morning sun. The wet grasses and wildflowers will dry before noon. Many of those wildflowers, even small colorless ones, are beginning to make their appearance on the ground. They are not intentionally seeded or planted, yet they show up in the same spots every year. They will continue to come back yearly. The familiar native species that I saw last year, and the year before survived through the winter. I am alive, but at

### — One Mountain, One River, Two Houses —

the same time, I am nothing, as I'm in zen state of mind. No noise except sounds from the distance of the cuckoo, and its coo bounces off the hills and echoes in my ears. The sounds of the cuckoo seem far away, so far away from where I live, where I am. When I was small, I learned that the cuckoo lays its eggs in the nest of a shrike. The cuckoo does not raise its own offspring; it allows the shrike to hatch the cuckoo's eggs and raise its birdling young. I wonder if my childhood was like that of a cuckoo's birdling. I again hear the cuckoo bird's sound from far away. Something is leading me to the sound, the sound from the land of the unknown.

Soon, May will be over. While most of Japan is drenched with rain in June, we have a whole month of sunny days in Hokkaido, the northern-most island of Japan; yet, the tip of Mount Taisetsu still has snow. During the spring, snowmelt streams run rapidly from the highest mountain in Hokkaido. I sense its snow is melting every second and bringing its water to the Chubetsu river to purifies the land for the summer. The water is fast moving, offered from Mount Taisetsu, father of the land, into the Chubetsu river, mother of the land, and the river is carrying the water for us to cleanse our souls. The water nurtures vegetables and plants on the island. The river runs dark green from the distance, the reflection of green grasses on the both side of the river, bringing the clean cold water we drink in the town where I live. The water also nurtures us, it's the mother of the land, the mother of water, and we are in the mother's womb. The water contains a lot of minerals, yet it is smooth with absolutely no taste. The things here are stark. Nothing means more than something. Like zen.

## - The Moon Home -

The house where I speak my first word and hold my first pencil has two stories and sits near a creek, surrounded by numerous bamboo leaves. Neighbors call it "a circle window" house because a large round window dominates the front from a distance. Coming through the bridges over the creek, thousands of small gray stones create the path leading to the house. A variety of shades of smooth and rugged gray stones are a nuanced monotone that creates calming metaphor of life. The small smooth stones are arranged in an oval lake-like shape in the middle of the garden. Lighter-colored gray rocks simulate water features, like a calm wave in the ocean. Stone arrangements and other miniature elements are used to represent mountains, rivers, and waterfalls. The selection and placement of rocks is the most important part of making a rock garden. For creating "mountains," they usually use volcanic rocks, rugged mountain rocks with sharp edges. Smooth, rounded rocks are used for the borders of gravel "rivers" or "seashores." The garden emphasizes the harmony of the composition. We call it a zen garden.

The first thing that catches my eye is a huge maple tree in front of the main entrance. There is a hammock between two branches so that Grandpa can take naps in the afternoons listening to the sounds of water from the creek next to the maple tree. My grandparents' house follows Feng Shui concepts in not having the bathroom and kitchen in the northeast corner, not placing fire-related objects on the north side, and making sure the sunset won't get into the house from the west. Great Grandfather, who passed away when I was 3 years old, designed it himself. It's made of a combination of red brick, concrete, and various woods. Traditional Japanese houses are

*— One Mountain, One River, Two Houses —*

not painted, so that the natural beauty of the wood remains exposed. Transparent lacquer covers the plain wood for protection. There are many sliding doors in this house. Grandma says that sliding doors are more convenient for this type of architecture, because sliding doors can expand space in a small room.

To the right of the main entrance is the large tatami mat room with a tokonoma, a recess in the wall that is one step higher than the floor. Here, a traditional vertical painting, depicting a scene from nature, is hanging on the wall. Grandma has placed a flower arrangement below the painting. The south side of the tatami room is all windows and it's facing the front yard. As I look out at the window, I see the zen garden. I smell the new tatami, which reminds me of rain-washed straw that was dried in the sun.

In front of the white and yellow chrysanthemum flower arrangement in the tokonoma recess, Grandma writes haiku and tanka poems using Japanese calligraphy. She brushes black ink mixed with water on the rectangular Japanese paper, and then she adds dried spring flowers from last year that she pressed between the pages of a book. The Japanese paper, called washi, is thin and soft but very strong. During the Edo period (beginning in 1600), in the case of fire, they dropped important documents into a well because washi survives in water. The tanka that she writes with dark black ink contrasts with the red, purple, and yellow pressed flowers, but they coexist perfectly on the white washi paper. Tanka uses similes, metaphors, and personalization. There are five lines in a tanka poem, containing 5, 7, 5, 7, and 7 syllables. Tanka express, love, sadness, and other strong emotions. This form of poetry dates back almost 1300 years. Grandma writes the tanka and gives it to me to use as a bookmark so that I can carry it with me every day.

*You are born in a home with honor and courage*
*You have no worries or confusion*
*You belong in a place close to my heart*
*Your home is somewhere inside of you*
*Be aware of who you are*

*Where ever you live*
*Whomever you're with*
*Whether you plan or are guided by fate,*
*Your endless path will take*
*Whoever you want to be*

Grandma makes a hole at the top of the tanka papers, and threads red and gold ribbons through the hole. She asks me to pick the ones I like for me to use as bookmarks. I pick two so that I can take one to school. Every time I open my textbook at school, I see grandma's tanka and colorful seasonal flowers.

Life in Grandma's house is tanka itself. The décor in each room and garden is haiku. Grandma's house stands poetically and exists rhythmically. When I'm in her house, everything around me becomes my tanka. I exist with poetry and rhythm, my life is in harmony.

During the Obon festival in July and August, Grandma decorates the tatami room with paper lanterns, called chouchin. They are made of thin bamboo frames and Japanese rice paper, which is foldable. They are usually designed with pictures or written words on them. They are also handy in lighting the pathway in processions. When I light the candles inside the paper lanterns, the images of lotus on the paper come alive. These images have different colors: yellow, red, blue, pink, and purple. I pick up a purple paper lantern with my left hand and unfold it. I hang the lantern near the tokonoma wall recess and lie down on the tatami. As I hold a pencil in my left hand, I start drawing two cranes as if they are dancing on the lantern. I'm humming as I hold the pencil. I'm allowed to sing, write, and draw the way I want. I'm free, I feel alive, I exist.

Grandma tells me that we decorate the tatami room with chouchin to honor the spirits of our ancestors, which are coming back to visit during the Obon festival. Grandma also places three white chrysanthemums in the bronze flower arrangement plate in the tokomona wall recess, and then three dead leaves in front of the bronze cup.

"You left some rubbish in the tokonoma, Grandma," I say loudly as I'm lying on the tatami drawing.

"I left them deliberately," Grandma says.

"I didn't clean it all up because it would be artificial if I cleaned perfectly. I left three dead leaves so that the tokonoma looks natural, like our garden outside. Beauty is imperfect, impermanent, incomplete, and irregular. Sometimes we deliberately create imperfection called 'wabi-sabi'." Grandma sounds confident.

I leave my drawings all over the tatami room and try to leave.

"You might want to pick up your papers if you are done drawing," Grandma says as she is sweeping the tatami floor with a straw broom.

## - The Moon Home -

I turn around. "I left the papers deliberately, it's called 'wasabi'," I say proudly.

Grandma's straw broom stops moving. She looks at me with her peripheral vision.

"That's called a mess." She smiles.

Grandma's house has very few furnishings. Very little furniture is placed in a traditional Japanese house. The room is divided by four panels of fusuma doors, which are made of paper like a paper-planed shoji screen; but fusuma doors are thicker and have designs on them. The four vertical rectangular panels can slide from side to side on wooden rails. These features flow into a spacious open great tatami room where a pair of full-height sliding fusuma doors flood the room with natural light, and provide an open airy feel, with plenty of bright sunshine. When we open fusuma doors, two rooms become one large room so that we can have a wedding or a funeral at home. Ancient Japan didn't have hotels or ceremony halls; they used their home for special occasions. Each fusuma door is divided into four side-by-side designs, which appear from left to right: Mt. Fuji, two white cranes with red heads and black beaks, two pots of bonsai trees on a large stone in a zen garden, and an old castle in the mountains. There are no paintings on the walls. The fusuma's images are enough, and wooden walls coated with lacquer expose the beauty of the grain, so that there is no need for paintings. Shoji screens cover the windows in the tatami room. The architecture itself constitutes the main decoration of the house. Grandma's tanka is everywhere in her house.

As the sun goes down, I hear a low hollow sound from distant drums. It's the annual Bon-Orodi and taiko drum festival.

## - One Mountain, One River, Two Houses -

A neighborhood association built a high wooden stage, where the men are beating drums. The stage is decorated with hundreds of chochin, and children form circles around the center stage tower. Bon-Odori with drums is performed during the festival – it was originally a dance to welcome the spirits of the dead.

I can't wait to go to Bon-Odori, but until then, Grandma and I dance in the tatami room. I wear yukata, made out of cotton, a casual version of a kimono worn during the summer. Unlike the junihitoe-kimono, a twelve-layer robe that is a set of formal complex kimono made of silk, yukata comes in a single layer of cotton. I can move easily. Grandma and I picked the fabric decorated with images of fireworks, and she sewed my yukata by hand. We both wear yukata and dance Bon-Odori. While kabuki is a classical dance drama which takes place in a theatre, Bon-Odori is more casual and we dance without special training. We casually walk in a circle, swinging our arms all around, moving our bodies to the music and drums. In the spacious tatami room with no furniture, I dance without worry. I'm free, I feel alive, I exist.

From the tatami room, I walk to the meditation room, where my ancestors' black and white photos have been placed on the wall, and a wooden cabinet is a Buddhist shrine crafted with doors that enclose a religious icon with a memorial tablet to family members. Grandma keeps in the shrine her deceased son's photos and his letters to her. In front of the shrine, there are zafu cushions on the tatami mat. Large yellow chrysanthemums and small white ones are arranged on both sides of the shrine. Grandma brings freshly cut flowers from her garden weekly, and arranges them on the shrine.

The meditation room is the only room on the north side of the house. The window in the room is small compared to the windows in the large tatami room, so that not much sunlight will shine into the room. Two long dark green incense sticks sit slowly burning in a bronze cup. The incense sticks are made out of cedar and cypress, and the incense creates a mild scent. All of the ashes fall into the bronze cup within eight to twelve hours. As incense is supposed to be food for dead people, we keep the ashes in the bronze cup forever.

Grandma lights the deep dark green sticks as she sits on the zafu cushion in front of the wooden shrine. The burning tips of the dark green sticks produce a small amount of white smoke, which rises with a lavender aroma. The thin white scented smoke moves over the shrine, then floats around the entire room, and finally spreads slowly around the entire house. Sunlight from the window gives the smoke a soft orange and yellow glow. It feels as if I'm surrounded by the spirits of my ancestors in the cedar cypress forest in the Kitoushi Mountains. When I'm with Grandma in her house, my tanka is always there.

In contrast to the zen garden in the front yard, the back yard is a natural garden filled with seasonal flowers along with vegetables and herbs. There are several Taxus Cuspidata, which have small ruby colored berries that I eat in the spring. Ainu, the native people who have lived on the island of Hokkaido since before the Japanese moved to the island, called the ruby berry tree Onko. I smell fresh green mint when Grandma waters her garden with water from the creek next to her house.

## - One Mountain, One River, Two Houses -

Betula Platyphylla, tall white trees that look as if they are covered by snow, are lined up east to west along the creek. There are short bamboo trees with large leaves all along the creek by the north side of the house. During the winter, bamboo and Betula white trees protect the house from snow and cold winds from the north.

In the backyard, Grandpa is feeding chickens with yellow chrysanthemums from Grandma's garden so that their egg yolks will become more yellow. So Grandpa says. All chrysanthemum flowers are edible, but the flavor varies widely from plant to plant, from sweet to tangy to bitter or peppery. It may take some experimentation to find flavors you like. Grandpa's chickens seem to like yellow ones because yellow chrysanthemums are sweeter than the others. Their stems, also known an shungiku have a mild flavor that lends itself well to stir-fry and tempura. Since we can use both the flowers and the greens of the Garland chrysanthemum, it's the most popular chrysanthemum for home gardens. Here, chickens and humans eat the same foods. Traditional Asian chrysanthemum tea is typically made from the yellow or white flowers of Chrysanthemum morifolium or Chrysanthemum indium. Grandpa washes yellow and white chrysanthemums, and places them on top of old newspapers to dry and make tea leaves. He wants to finish drying the flowers before winter comes so that we can have hot tea in the cold winter.

Opposite, through the hallway is a family room with a TV and a dining table. The family room floor is half tile and half wood. The round wooden dining table is the family gathering place. We sit on zafu cushions on the floor to eat and drink. The kitchen is not big, it's very simple, two gas stoves and a sink are surrounded by the kitchen counter. At the end of the hall, there is another kitchen with access to the back yard, and the back entrance door is never locked. In this kitchen, Grandma washes things other than rice and vegetables, such as meat products or her underwear.

Grandma's hair is piled up high in loops secured with a bamboo chop stick. The extra fabric of her kimono sleeves is tied back to keep it from getting wet. She is preparing a chicken dinner in the second kitchen. Grandma complains that Grandpa never kills his chickens so that she always has to ask a neighbor to kill one of Grandpa's chickens. We only have three chickens left in the little coop.

"We are going to dissect a chicken today," I hear Grandma says in the kitchen at the back entrance next to the bathroom.

I run to Grandma and say proudly, "Oh, oh, I know. I did that to a frog in my science class last month."

Grandma cleans the chicken's gut. She explains where the heart, liver, and eggs are inside of the chicken. She pulls out the stretched glowing yellow pre-eggs. "These are eggs," she says and stretches the different sized glowing yellow pre-eggs connected to a yellowish white amoeba-like substance.

"They could have been babies if we didn't kill her," I say indignantly.

"That's why we should appreciate it when we eat, and not waste their lives," Grandma says with a smile.

Grandpa walks in and asks "What are you doing here?"

"We scienced the chicken!" I shout.

Grandpa starts cleaning the kitchen without saying a word.

### - One Mountain, One River, Two Houses -

After Grandma and I dissect the chicken, Grandma dips sliced chicken in teriyaki source in a ceramic container, and we wait until the chicken is marinated. Meanwhile, Grandma and I take a bath together. The bathroom is right next to the back entrance where we can see Grandma's green garden. The fireplace looks like a wood-burning pizza oven filled with wood, and it heats the water that goes to the deep bathtub. It's Grandpa's job to calculate minutes, estimating the temperature of the water, readjusting as he goes along. The oval shaped tub is made from the Hinoki cypress tree, which infuses the bath water with a lemony fragrance. After long use, the wooden tub has turned the color of dark tea.

There is a large window next to the tub so that we can look at the vegetable garden while we sit in the Hinoki cypress bath. Some nights, we don't use any lights, moonlight is just right during our bath time. Under the moonlight in the Hinoki bathroom, Grandma gets into the tub and makes sure the water temperature is okay. I jump into the tub and the water overflows, it sounds like a waterfall. Grandma smiles and touches my wet hair. As we sing a song together, our voices echo in the Hinoki bathroom.

"Saita saita tulip no hanga. Naranda naranda aka, shiro, kiiro. Donohana mitemo kireidana" ("Blooming, blooming, tulips, red, white, yellow. All colors are different, but each of them is beautiful in its own way.")

After Grandma and I take a Hinoki bath on a hot summer night, I crawl into Grandma's futon bed in the tatami room. Grandma sleeps in a tatami room on the second floor, which is divided by the fusuma screens. When the fusuma screens are

## The Moon Home

open, I can see the kimono that she is planning to wear for the weekend tea party hanging on the large standing kimono hanger in front of the white wall on the other side of the room. The kimono is dark green silk embroidered with silver thread, showing rising white cranes, yellow peonies, and gold pine trees. The kimono colors contrast with the white shoji screens, and the kimono decorates the white wall so there is no need for a painting. My tanka is everywhere in the house.

One of my favorite things during summer vacation is staying at Grandma's house, because I'm allowed to have my own cat, Mimi. When Mimi stretches, her spine becomes like a camel, and she sneaks into Grandma's house. I'm not allowed to have pets other than hamsters and small fish at my parents, but here, I can have real animals. I snuggle into Grandma's bed with Mimi.

When Grandma turns off the light, we know it's story time. Grandma does not read me books at bedtime, but instead tells stories, using language that is more poetic than descriptive. Grandma tells each story with a few different arrangements, depending on my day and my moods. She always seems to know how to get in tune with my feelings. Her stories often start with "Once upon a time" and in a vague place such as on a mountain, in China, or in a village in Europe. Grandma's voice is no longer her voice. Her voice becomes a man, a woman, a child, or an animal. As her voice goes up and down, my heart beats up and down with her voice. The silent shafts of moonlight coming through the round window softly light Grandma's face. I'm fully awake and full of excitement. Without realizing it, I grab Mimi's ears and squeeze her ears hard. Mimi lashes out at my arm and runs away.

The stories are about princesses, witches, monsters, and evil stepmothers, and feature sadness, envy, jealousy, and happiness. Some of her stories are set in worlds distant in both time and space. The crises in the stories are exciting, yet not too terrifying, because they happen in the far away unknown land. When I do feel scared, I know that I can share my fears with Grandma. In this house, I feel safe and protected. While she tells a story, I hear the rhythmic sounds of frogs around the creek behind the house. The sounds of frogs do not stop until I fall sleep. Grandma's stories seep into my mind and dreams.

Again and again, throughout summer vacation, I ask Grandma to tell me the same stories. One of my favorite stories Grandma tells, "Kaguya-hime" (Princess Kaguya), has been passed down through the generations since the Muromachi era (1300-1500):

> Once upon a time, while walking in the bamboo forest, an old, childless bamboo cutter called Okina comes across a mysterious, shining stalk of bamboo. In the bamboo forest, the air is cooler than it is in the village. Even in the middle of the day in the summer, you feel chilly. There are countless bamboos in the forest, and the bamboos are twice as tall as Okina. You would lose your way if you are not familiar with the forest because the thousands of bamboos look the same everywhere.
>
> Okina sees something strange, a shiny bright gold light comes from a bamboo tree. He becomes curious and moves closer to the light. When he cuts the

bamboo tree open, he finds a baby the size of his thumb inside of it. He rejoices to find such a beautiful girl and takes her home. He and his wife name the little baby girl Kaguya, meaning "Shining princess of the supple bamboo," and raise her as their own child.

After Okina takes Kaguya home, he discovers that whenever he cuts down a stalk of bamboo, he finds a small nugget of gold inside. Soon, he becomes the richest man in the village. Kaguya grows from a tiny baby into a woman of ordinary size and extraordinary beauty. At first, Okina tries to protect Kaguya by keeping her away from outsiders, but over time, the news of her beauty spreads. Eventually, five princes come to Okina's home to ask for the beautiful Kaguya's hand in marriage. The princes finally persuade Okina to tell a reluctant Kaguya to choose from among them. Kaguya concocts impossible tasks for the princes, agreeing to marry the one who manages to bring her his specified item.

That night, Okina tells the five princes what each must bring. The first is told to bring her the stone begging bowl of the Buddha from India, the second a jeweled branch from the mythical island of Hōrai, the third the legendary robe of the fire-rat of China, the fourth a colored jewel from a dragon's neck, and the final prince a cowry shell born of swallows. Realizing that his task is impossible, the first prince returns with an expensive stone bowl, hoping that Kaguya would believe it to be Buddha's begging bowl, but after noticing that the bowl

*- One Mountain, One River, Two Houses -*

does not glow with holy light, Kaguya sees through his deception. Likewise, two other princes attempt to deceive her with fakes, but also fail. The fourth prince gives up after encountering a storm, while the final prince loses his life in his attempt.

Shortly after, Mikado, the emperor of Japan hears about Kaguya, he comes to see the strangely beautiful Kaguya and, upon falling in love, asks her to marry him. Although he is not subjected to the impossible trials that had thwarted the princes, Kaguya rejects his request for marriage as well, telling him that she is not of his country and thus can not marry him. She stays in contact with the Emperor, but continues to rebuff his requests and marriage proposals.

The following summer, whenever Kaguya sees the full moon, her eyes fills with tears. Though her adoptive parents worry greatly and question her, she is unable to tell them what is wrong. Her behavior becomes increasingly erratic until she reveals that she is not of this world, that she was sent to Earth for her own safety during a celestial war, and that she must return to her people on the Moon. The gold that Okina had been finding had in fact been a stipend from the people of the Moon, sent to pay for Kaguya's upkeep.

As the day of her return to the Moon approaches, the Emperor sends many guards around her house to protect her from the Moon people, but when an embassy of "Heavenly Beings" arrives at the door of Okina's house, the guards are blinded by a strange light. Kaguya announces that, though she loves her many friends on Earth, she must return with the Moon people to her true home. She writes sad notes of apology to her adoptive parents and to the Emperor, then gives her parents her own robe as a memento. She then puts a little of the elixir of immortality in with her letter to the Emperor, and gives it to a guard officer. As she hands it to him, her feather robe from the Moon is placed on her shoulders, and all of her sadness and compassion for the people of the Earth are apparently forgotten. The heavenly entourage takes Kaguya back to the Capital of the Moon, leaving her earthly adoptive parents in tears.

The parents become very sad and are soon put to bed sick. The guard officer returns to the Emperor with the items Kaguya had given him as her last mortal act, and reports what had happened. The Emperor reads her letter and is overcome with sadness. Then, he asks his servants, "Which mountain is the closest place to Heaven?" to which one replies the Great Mountain. The Emperor orders his men to take the letter to the summit of the mountain and burn it, in the hope that his message will reach the distant princess. The men are also commanded to burn the elixir of immortality, because the Emperor does not wish to live forever without being able to see her. The legend has it that the Japanese word for immortality became the name of the mountain, Mt. Fuji.

## One Mountain, One River, Two Houses

When I hear the story, I feel like Kaguya, fantasizing that I need to find a way to go back to the Moon to reunite with my real parents.

I'm standing in a dark hallway, and I run toward the stairs. I must run, I have to run. I reach a spiral staircase. And it's dark, pitch black—so dark I can't see the bottom, but I keep roaring down, as if my feet are sucked by a vacuum, skipping two or three stairs with great speed, unsure if my feet will land on the step or catch the edge and I'll slip without knowing how far I am falling. I wake up.

During the school week, I stay with my parents. Life in Mother's house has no tanka. The décor in each room and garden is not haiku. Mother's house has no poetry and no rhythm, but constant anger and fears. When I'm in her house, everything around me freezes. There is no harmony. My life is lonely and chaotic in this house.

The house is built close to the street; cars pass by day and night. The house is boxy like a Lego house. This is where I learned to play piano and to stop using my left hand and only use my right hand. The house has a separated garage. There is a concrete walkway, trees, and big stones brought from great grandfather's mountain. There are so many things in the small garden: plants, trees, bushes, stones, and a little man-made pond directly below our living room window in the middle of the small garden. Light orange and white koi fish, dark red and black koi fish, and many small orange goldfish swim in the pond. The beautiful colors of the koi mask the dirty water. During the winter, the water in the pond freezes, and the koi and goldfish hibernate under the ice. They start moving again when the ice melts in the spring.

The house is made of wood and clay. The entrance is a one-panel door made of fake wood, on a concrete porch. A small living room has white walls. Rooms in the house are like small boxes in a big box. It's uncomplicated. There are too many large pieces of furniture squeezed into the small spaces of the rooms like a sumo wrestler wearing an child's outfit. Lights are directed toward the round table in the front of a huge sofa made of brown and white micro fleece. The sofa back is covered by months of piled up clothes, and I can't see the clothes that are under the top layer. There is more clothing over a chair back. Stuff is forced onto every available space in the rooms until nothing more could possibly fit. My mind is jumbled like the piles of dirty clothes, and can't pull myself out. I should just stay buried in the dirty clothes until I become invisible. I look for my tanka but I can't find it here.

My room, next to Sister's, has one large window and one small window coved by shiny orange drapes. Who picked the red and black carpet? The walls in my room are covered by pastel pink rose wallpaper so that I won't draw any pictures on them. I've piled up gifts and souvenirs on the shelf on the wall. In the middle of the shelf, two plastic kabuki masks with white dust sit next to a stuffed panda bear. On the left side of the shelf, there is an empty basketball-sized beehive connected to a dead branch. The wall is very thin, and I can hear every word of my parents' arguments in the living room. Their voices are louder than the loud TV. The clutter of the house, the loud TV noise, and my parents' fight overwhelm my sense of peaceful solitude. It's loud. There is no simplicity and peacefulness. Nothing zen.

I hear loud TV sounds from the living room – the TV is on all day. Father is sitting in the massage chair in front of the black and white TV, watching the successful Apollo 11 mission. Man landed on the moon. They find no rabbits on the moon. A few weeks ago, Grandma told me a bedtime story about a rabbit and princess Kaguya on the moon. Father tells me not to believe what Grandma says. The moon's sky always looks dark even when the sun is above the horizon because the moon does not have an atmosphere. If I were on the moon, the sky would be dark both night and day. Am I a part of the sun or the moon? Is the moon a planet or a star?

I wake up early on the weekend, and ride my red bicycle to Grandma's house. Grandma's house is always unlocked, so I run upstairs to the tatami room on the second floor, where I see the green slope of Mt. Taisetsu. On the front of the second floor are the round window and two rectangle windows with 180-degree views, each with a sliding shoji screen door. The windows flood the room with natural light. In the spring, I can still see snow on top of the mountain until the end of June. In the fall, leaves from the maple trees outside the window cast moving patterns of light and shadow. No matter the season, I enjoy the views from this room.

Another tatami room on the second floor is used as a dressing room, with a lacquered 6-foot-tall bamboo hanger for Grandma's kimono. In front of a small window with a shoji screen, a folding three-panel mirror sits on top of a dresser so that Grandma can arrange her hair and put makeup on in the morning.

Before Grandma fixes our breakfast in the morning, she gets dressed and fixes her hair. Her black hair is piled high, with loops secured with combs. Grandma's daily kimono is made with a fabric called yuki-tsumugi, using the katsura method that samurai warriors used back in the 1600's. The fabric is very light and warm so that people who wear the kimono could easily move around and keep their body warm even in the winter. Yuki-tsumugi is usually not colorful, instead using darker tones. Grandma looks elegant even without a colored kimono.

I never get bored in Grandma's house because she always gives me things to do. Replacing a shoji paper panel can look like a somewhat difficult task, but it's quite a simple project. The task is simple enough that it's usually done by the women in the house. The paper renewal process is done in two stages. The first stage requires removing the old paper and allowing the wooden frames to dry. The second stage requires replacing the paper, trimming the paper, and then allowing the paper to dry. Using rice-based glue between the paper and the wooden frames to replace shoji screen seems like simple work, but using rice that is too thick, or too much glue, would destroy the shape of the screens. Grandma boils rice that's a day or two old with

## - One Mountain, One River, Two Houses -

extra water and mixes until the rice gets sticky like glue. It's all organic, and it's safe when the kids are around. The best part of the whole process for me is that I can destroy the old paper without being scolded, and this only opportunity comes only once in a few years. It's usually when Grandma finds a hole in the shoji screen caused by me or the house cat, Mimi. My sister Harumi wants to join me, so I have to share my panels with her. As I give her four panels, I get eight panels. Harumi takes one panel from me after she finishes her panels. I hit her hand with the broken wooden frame. She cries loudly. Yikes, she always cries and it gets me into trouble.

"Have you ever heard that the power of the pen is stronger than the sword?" Grandma asks without smiling.

"I don't have a pen to hit Harumi with," I say with anime triangle eyes.

"To write."

After we have worked hard fixing the shoji screen during the day, Grandma brings us tuna and salmon sashimi at the kitchen counter. It's time for a celebration of hard work. The best parts of tuna fish are the fatty parts, called toro. Grandma chooses a special knife to cut sashimi. It takes skill to cut sashimi, because it's easy to destroy the soft meat of raw fish. She has to cut the fish quickly. If she takes too long, bacteria can grow. Grandma removes cut pieces of toro from the wooden cutting board and places them on a white rectangular sashimi plate. Grandma carefully places the sashimi so that the reddish-pink side of the toro looks presentable on the plate. She slices daikon radish like thread, and places it next to the reddish-pink toro sashimi. Display is very important to Grandma. A half inch between pieces of food makes a difference on the display. I try to reach the toro with my chopsticks.

"Not yet," Grandma shouts.

She washes green shiso leaves from her garden, and places three of them next to the white thread radishes.

"A tip for presentation is to place garnish in three dimensions so that the plate won't look flat," Grandma says confidently as she moves her wooden chopsticks from the plate.

White thread radish and green shiso leaves are garnish, but they have meaning as well. Daikon radish helps digestion of fish proteins, and shiso leaves kill bacteria in raw fish. Garnishes are an important part of the dish for sashimi and sushi. Colors are vivid on the table and there is a smell of freshness. It's a time for a food celebration.

"Everything you place on the plate has meaning to it. In nature, there are no unnecessary creatures or plants." Grandma completes her talk as she competes her sashimi plates. Contrary to zen, everything on our plate has meaning.

The sashimi dinner is getting ready. We are waiting for Grandpa, but he is still in his garden, picking miyouga buds. Miyouga herb has spines, and each spine has 10 buds that turn into a flowers. There is something mysterious about the taste, perhaps because it contains a chemical called alpha pinene, which stimulates the part of our brain that maintains concentration and relaxation at the same time.

Grandpa slices freshly washed miyouga buds on a wooden cutting board, and separates them into three different batches. One is for putting on top of cold tofu, one is for tempura, and last one is for miso soup. I sit at the kitchen table while Grandpa fries tempura in the pan on the gas stove. Grandpa dries the sliced miyouga buds with towels and coats them with potato starch. He then places them into egg yolk, and after they are well coated, he uses wooden chopsticks to place them into the frying pan with the tempura. He takes out the tempura from the pan and places them on white paper on a large plate on the kitchen table.

We are seated at the round wooden dining table. When Grandma completes the sashimi display with colorful garnishes, she sits next me and whispers, "Let's eat." Grandma grabs chopsticks and starts eating salmon sashimi before the tempura is served. I raise up to my knees from the zafu cushion on the floor, and lean over to reach a bottle of soy sauce. While I'm pouring soy sauce on a little round ceramic plate, Grandpa stops me and then helps me to pour just a few drops of soy sauce on my plate. "Too much soy sauce destroys the flavor of the fish," Grandpa says.

Grandma takes a bite of a fresh ginger slice before she eats another sashimi. She says, "A slice of ginger cleanses the palate. It removes aftertastes of fish you just ate, so you can taste a different kind of sashimi without mixing two different flavors." I pick up some miyoga tempura with my short pink chopsticks, and dip it into the soy sauce.

"You don't know how to eat," Grandpa says as he pours his miso soup into his lacquered cup.

"You are tasting soy sauce, not the taste of miyouga. Each vegetable and herb has its own aroma and taste. Soy sauce will kill the aroma and taste. You don't need to use a lot of ingredients, food itself has flavor. If you use less, the quality comes up and you will enjoy it more." He sprinkles sea salt onto another plate and dips the tempura.

The texture of miyouga is crispy and fluffy at the same time. The salty taste brings sweetness into my mouth. Miyouga's natural sweetness comes out when I bite miyouga through crispy tempura.

I'm dreaming I'm standing in a dark hallway, and I run toward the stairs. I must run, I have to run. And I reach a spiral staircase. And it's dark—so dark I can't see the bottom, but I keep roaring down, my feet skipping two or three stairs with great speed, unsure if my feet will land on the step or if my foot will catch the edge and I'll slip without knowing how far I am falling. I can't stop. I still I can't see the bottom. I feel as if I'm stuck on a roller coaster, without fun or excitement. Each time I skip a few stairs my stomach jumps and I feel utterly horrified. I wake up.

I've never liked Sunday nights because I have to come back to my parents' house. My parents' house has a yunitto basu, which is just "unit bath" pronounced with a Japanese accent. In this factory-produced bathroom module, the walls, ceiling, bathtub, and floor are made of a continuous piece of plastic, so there is no concern about leakage. There are no windows, so I turn on the light. I have to take a shower quickly before I go to bed so

# One Mountain, One River, Two Houses

that my sister can take a bath. The clock is ticking, I have to hurry. I have to wash the entire unit with the shower spray when I am done.

"Dry your hair quickly. You have homework to do," Mother yells. She yells at me for everything. When I spill milk, she yells at me, when I can't find my socks, she yells at me, when my sister, Harumi cries, she yells at me, when Father drinks, she yells at me. It takes quite a while to dry my thick wavy hair. "Why is this child's hair not straight like Harumi's." Mother has one more complaint about me. Taking a shower is not relaxing in this house. My body is cold by the time I get out from the shower. My neck and shoulder are stiff, my feet are stretched tight, my body is tense. Until my wet thick wavy hair dries, I pretend to do homework by looking at the paper. I can't find harmony; there is no tanka in this house.

There is no ceremony room and no meditation room, but there is a karaoke room. I'm passing the karaoke room, looking at the blue bright light on the karaoke machine. I close my bedroom door, and make sure my Snoopy lies next to me. When I turn off my light and lie on my bed at night, I anticipate. Something. Always something that will happen. Always something that will happen before morning. My father is not home yet. I fall sleep with anxiety. My life is not in order.

I'm sitting on the couch in the living room, watching cartoons. A fearful pathetic rabbit with both ears up, is freezing. Her five senses are all alert. Her life is in danger. A lion watches the rabbit from a distance. Quietly, the lion gets closer. I turn around and tame the wild lion. Despite my fears, I talk gently to the lion and pull its weak body up. He closes his jaw, slowly unclenching it and loosening his muscles. Then, he goes to bed silently. As he goes to bed, I fall asleep on the couch with the TV on. Am I dreaming?

A taxi stops in front of our house, I hear him from a distance, I hear multiple men from a distance. Those men's voices are getting closer. A smell of cigarette burning. I wake up. Five or six men are smoking in the small karaoke room next to my bedroom, I can smell burning cigarettes through the shared wall. The singing gets louder as they drink more. The murmur of my father's co-workers' conversation and occasional bursts of laughter between their karaoke performances continue all night long. I cover my ears. I feel vibrations coming from four large speakers on the wall in the karaoke room. I get out of bed and take Snoopy with me, I can't abandon him. I open the closet, get into the closet with Snoopy, and close the door. I put Snoopy's black ears into my ears, but Snoopy and I can still hear the noise. I wrap clothes around myself, I wrap my arms around my legs and press my face into Snoopy's stomach. My feet seem a long away from me, as if my feet and head are separated. The clutter in the closet and the karaoke noise exacerbate my sense of uneasy solitude. The small Lego-like house vibrates with the booming base notes of the karaoke machine. I wait until the night is over, the loud long night seems never to end. There is no simplicity, but chaos. It's loud. Nothing zen.

I'm dreaming I'm in Africa. An untamed lion walks through me. The door is open. He got out? His mane touches my rib. Goose bumps rise all over my body. I have to put him in a cage—an empty cage. Then, I hear him growl. His canine teeth grow larger than my face. There's an extra claw on each front paw. They could slash me. I feel disgust and horror. Waking in the dark, my body goes through ice. I'm frozen. My father is drunk again. He's throwing oranges. It all begins when he drinks. The whites of his eyes become bigger than his irises. So many blood vessels in the white. He growls, he snarls, he lies down on the floor. Extra fingers, I have to cut them off.

In the morning, I see a sick stray cat on the yard, lying down. I must not be hostile, I must not be frightened, then I fool myself; I'm dreaming, I'm dreaming.

Grandma comes to visit on some weekdays to babysit Sister and me. When that happens, my heart beats with joy again. One Wednesday afternoon, I struggle with an intense urge to draw something when I see white eggs and white walls in my parents' house. I color each egg and distinguish them from each other by painting different flowers and stars – no two are identical. I carefully lay the colored eggs into a nest made out of towels on my bed. I cannot wait, one day they are going to hatch, and I'm hoping that the chicks will not all be the same. I fantasize that each chick has different patterns on its feathers like the yellow flowers or purple stars on the eggs. Drawing and painting eggs are not enough. With my left hand, I start drawing a picture of trees, a house, Grandma, Mimi, and me on the white wall in the living room. I'm free, I feel alive, I exist. I want to grasp the feelings, I want to keep Grandma on the wall while Grandma is not with me.

The garage door starts to open loudly. Mother is banging the doors as she enters the house. Each door that Mother opens and shouts from shakes the whole house. A yellow crayon falls off from my left hand. Quietly, I walk away from the wall I was drawing on. As if she were a samurai warrior, Grandma stands in front of the wall. When Mother opens the door and goes to the kitchen to put grocery bags on the kitchen counter, I'm not afraid anymore. Mother comes back to the living room, and she looks nastily at me and Grandma. Silently, Grandma and I are standing in front of the wall. Mother asks Grandma to sit on the couch; she refuses to sit. Mother looks behind Grandma and screams – she sees my drawing on the wall. My father has to paint the wall white again. My haiku and tanka are destroyed.

To get away from Mother's yelling, Grandma and I run to Grandma's house. Grandma holds my hand, takes a deep breath, and says, "You are a dragon, no one could kill a dragon's spirit." Grandma tells me that I was born in the year of the dragon. The dragon is the only mythical animal in the 12-year cycle of animals. In Chinese folklore, dragons are symbols of fearlessness, wisdom, strength, ferocity, and wealth, and they remain strong and survive whatever life throws at them. "You might not feel that you're a dragon yet because you're still little, but don't forget, you're a child of dragons, and someday you will be a dragon. Until then, keep this wooden seahorse with you." The Japanese word for seahorse (tatsuno-otoshigo) means "dragon's bastard child." Grandma drops the wooden seahorse keychain into my palm. I look at the dark green wooden "dragon's bastard child" in my left hand, and hold it tight.

## CHAPTER TWO
## *Musashi Miyamoto*

二

I'm standing in a dark hallway, and I run toward the stairs. I must run, I have to run. And I reach a spiral staircase. And it's dark—so dark I can't see the bottom, but I keep roaring down, my feet skipping two or three stairs with great speed, unsure if my feet will land on the step or if my foot will catch the edge and I'll slip without knowing how far I am falling.

I can't stop. I'm skipping a few steps rapidly. I still I can't see the bottom. I feel as if I'm stuck on a roller coaster, without fun or excitement. Each time I skip a few stairs my stomach jumps and I feel utterly horrified.

I wake. It's morning. I convince myself it was a dream, but my heart rate does not decrease easily. It's as if I just finished running a foot race. Soon, I feel a constant sense of emptiness in my gut.

Near the end of the first grade Mr. Abe, my teacher, calls my parents. Father is busy, so Mother has to come to my school. Mother worries that I did something wrong. She dresses in a black suit with a white collar. She puts on make-up. She puts me in the back seat and drives to the school. Mother and I enter through the main entrance, which is only for teachers and visitors. The entrance looks so official, clean and quiet. As we walk through the entrance, I hear the sounds of our shoes clicking on the green shiny tiles. I see a lady through the glass window of the side reception area. Mother tells the lady that we have an appointment with Mr. Abe at 4 pm. The lady asks us to come to the Principal's office so that other teachers won't be around and we can have a private conversation. Nothing good could come from the words "Principal's office." Mother and I remove our shoes and put on green plastic slippers that are lined up on the floor for visitors. They are one size fits all, but are too big for me. I drag my feet in the large slippers as I walk down the hallway. The slippers feel so heavy on my ankles, as if my ankles are chained with irons. My shoulders are down and my head is 6 inches in front of my shoulders. I walk as if I have served a death sentence, moving toward the gallows.

The teacher, Mr. Abe, tells Mother that the IQ score of her daughter does not match with her academic achievement. Mr. Abe sits on the chair and looks at Mother's reaction, but she has no clue what he's talking about, so he continues, "There is a huge discrepancy between her IQ score and her grades." Mr. Abe expresses his concerns about the daughter's poor academic performance in the class, and questions the parenting style of Mother.

After the meeting, Mother becomes like a Spartan warrior to prove to Mr. Abe that she can do her job. Mother makes sure that I write with my right hand every night before I go to bed.

## - Musashi Miyamoto -

Dozens of small pink cherry blossoms on the yellow silk notebook are covered by plastic, so my tears don't destroy the beautiful book – I'm in the 1st grade.

A round wooden table, with legs that are knee-high, is in the center of the kitchen. It's a gift from my grandparents when my parents purchased this house. We place zafu cushions on the floor and sit around the table to eat. Father is leaving the table, Sister is finishing dinner. Mother leaves the table and starts to clean up. I try to delay finishing foods so that I can avoid torture of having to write. I stay at the dinner table and pretend that I'm still working on the plate, holding chopsticks with my right hand. I swallow bitter vinegar, it's coming back up to my mouth – I can't spit. The only thing I know is that a time will come where no one will be able to rescue me. I hear her footsteps, and feel the vibrations in the floor. She takes everything from the table. Nothing left, but me. Mother starts cleaning dishes. I don't look up, but I hear dishes and pans banging together and making annoying sounds. The sounds are becoming louder and louder, like the finales of a Buddhist funeral. She is hurrying so that she can finish her work of correcting the composition in my diary. I want to disappear.

"You are so slow, how come this child is so slow to do anything." Mother's face becomes a dark shadow. I become smaller and smaller. I sit on the desk chair and lean forward with my head down so that no one will see my face and tears. The intense light hits the yellow diary. A sudden rush of coolness hits the left side of my body, Mother is coming from the kitchen to watch my writing. When Mother sits beside me, the frosty air seems to grasp my arms – I'm paralyzed. I feel the freezing air on my skin, and smell her salty breath. "Why are you using your left hand? Change it to the correct hand," Mother yells. "How come this child was born left handed, no one in the family is left handed," Mother says sternly. I grab the pencil with my right hand. I look down to avoid mother's face. "Why are you are writing just the facts? Why can't you write about your thoughts?" Mother yells again. I can't have good thoughts when I'm forced to use my right hand. I bite my lip so that I won't cry, but my tears drop on the page. As I erase my writing over and over again with an old cheap eraser, the white paper turns gray, and the wet paper rips. "Look what you did, you messed up the notes." Mother's voice comes out of her devil's horns. Nothing more can be written on the page. As the page is destroyed, my mind is destroyed. I lost my left hand and right brain.

My daily assignment is to write journals in the yellow silk notebook about what happened that day at school. The right hand writing practice continues every night until I finish the diary. By the time I get into bed, my body feels as if it's coming out from the freezer. All the warmth I have stored in my arms at Grandma's house is fleeting, completely gone. I'm violently pulled into opposite directions in a senseless black hall with no way out. The tyrannical leaning environment destroyed my existence. Sometime long ago, I did not talk, draw, or paint. I lost my voice, erased my existence and I was invisible until I became bad and existed as bad.

Grandpa never owned a house or a car, he never owned anything. So, Grandma lived in the house that my great grandfather built. While Grandpa lay on the hammock in the maple tree and played violin, Grandma worked seven days a week, and raised her three children, my father, my uncle, and my aunt. Grandma has never complained about her destiny, instead, she created a greenhouse in the south side of her back yard in front of two large storage rooms. Every morning and afternoon, she goes into the greenhouse and works for hours before she prepares meals for us. Grandma's meals are all organic and safe.

In early fall gardens are made of pumpkins, daikon radish, and corn grow. Fall gardens grow out of summer gardens. There are cabbage and spinach left over on the ground. The garden will be covered by heavy snow between December and March. This is the end of the entire year cycle. Grandma is picking corn in her back yard on a late Saturday afternoon. The sun is low and its light is weak, it's getting closer to the horizon. The horizon is covered by orange clouds – it might rain tomorrow. Grandma puts corn into a large cane basket that she had placed next to several overgrown Chinese cabbages. During the fall, most parts of Grandma's back yard are brown except the corn area. She does not pull the leaves and branches. The droppings and the unharvested vegetables are scattered over the garden's surface; they will soon provide nourishment for the soil. Her thick palm and short fingers pluck at the corn and its yellow hair. She pulls it off from the stem that has grown a lot taller than her.

I squat beside Grandma, reach out to the piled up yellow corn silk on the ground, and wrap my head with slender yellow corn silk. The soapy, waxy, bitter, sweetened, sticky corn silk is hanging from my head.

## The Moon Home

"Grandma look!" Grandma looks at me immediately, she has a look of surprise and humor at the same time.

"You are wearing a blond wig, like your doll," she smiles and speaks, "Those slender yellow silk things are called pistils." Grandma picks up dried stems from my head. "These are called petals and they give each flower and vegetable its unique shape."

"Why do you separate corn from the other vegetables?" I ask Grandma as I play with my blond corn hair.

"Plants like corn prefer warm sunshine around their roots. We don't put other plants around them, so that the ground around them gets enough sun," Grandma says. From the distance, Mimi sees me and comes forward me. Mimi often takes a nap in the wooden storage next to the creek. The wooden sliding door to the storage room is always open during summer. Mimi slowly gets close to me and sniffs the corn in my hand.

"Why do you have two large storage rooms in the back of your house? Nobody ever uses them," I say.

Grandma looks at me, surprised, glances around the garden and smiles. I see the large orange sunset behind her. Now, I can't see her face.

"People who used to live in your great grandfather's properties brought land tax and ground tax to us, sometimes in the form of rice or grain which would stored in the storage rooms. Now, those storage rooms have become your grandpa's junk yard," Grandma speaks slowly.

"Do you wish people would still bring land tax to you so that you could store rice in the storage room?" I ask.

Grandma laughs; she laughs loud. Her laugh echoes in the serene vegetable garden.

"Sweetheart, you shouldn't expect people to bring things to you. You shouldn't keep wishing to have something if you really want it. You just have to work hard to get the things you really want. That's the way life works."

It makes perfect sense, leaving old habits behind us and moving forward. Grandma always seems to know how to respond to my curiosity in a way I understand. I always understand what she means. I still wanted to tick her off because I also know she likes little challenges.

"Grandpa has never worked, and he waits until you get home to cook for him," I say.

Grandma is bundling bamboo sticks that were used to support tomatoes during spring. She wrings her hands and looks at me out of the corner of her eyes.

"Sweetie, he is very unique and a special person," she says triumphantly.

"The majority of people don't live like him." Then, her eyes become pale, and she looks away. As she is sweeping and pulling weeds from her garden, she starts talking again.

"It was rare to see this type of house back in 1940's. Our neighbors called this house Nagatani castle, but now it is rare to see this kind of crappy house in 1970's." We laugh out loud, bending our bodies. Grandma always knows how to lighten my mood. The sun is down. A combination of yellow and purple-pink clouds glow with the blue orange surface of the sky. I hold Grandma's hand tight.

## - The Moon Home -

During summer vacation, I stay with my grandparent, and work on my social studies research project. I'm more motivated to do because I'm with Grandma. Summer is almost over and I need to complete the school assignment. I look around the outside of the house to see if there are any interesting subjects or objects. I see birds, flowers, and insects, but I can't find something related to social studies. I find Grandma in the backyard cleaning.

"I can't find anything," I say to Grandma as I stand beside her with a notepad and a pencil.

Grandma squats and reaches and wraps her hand around a thick weed and pulls. "What would you like to do when you grow up, sweetie?" She asks.

"My mother wants me to be a pianist," I say.

"What do you want to do?" Grandma asks with a bold voice as she pats the dirt back down to fill the hole in the ground.

"I'll ask Grandpa." I ran to the front yard.

Grandpa is very much like zen. It's not as if he is deeply affected by the emphasis that Buddhism places on intuition, but his life style fits zen philosophy. He does not eat meat, but he eats cabbage and beans daily. He does not buy new clothes, but wears clothes that Grandma makes. He does not have any desire for wealth, he does not drink or smoke, he never looks at women other than Grandma. His only pleasure is taking naps in the hammock between the large maple trees in his front yard. Grandpa might be an interesting subject for my research project.

I see a pair of zories, flip flops made of rice straw, on the roots of a huge maple tree that Grandpa's father planted in 1932. Grandpa is lying down on the hammock between the

– *Musashi Miyamoto* –

maple trees rocking gently side to side. He looks as if he is in a safe cocoon. As his hammock swings, the maple tree's gray branches with green leaves swing, and they make sounds as the leaves rustle in the breeze.

"Why are you taking a nap, Grandpa?" I shout as I look up at the forty year old huge gray trunk maple tree.

"I'm not taking a nap. I'm meditating," Grandpa says with an annoyed voice. "Resting is important for working efficiently in the afternoon."

"What kind of occupation do you have, Grandpa?" I ask. "Why do you stay in the hammock every day? Why do you play the violin all day?" I don't stop asking.

"You ask too many questions."

"Why do we dance?"

"We just dance."

"Why are flowers there?"

"No meaning, they are just there."

"What is the meaning of the universe?"

"No meaning, it's just there," Grandpa asks and answers his own questions.

"We just live in the moment. In this world, you don't own anything. You are just borrowing. You will return everything you have when you die. All you have is this moment." When Grandpa stops talking, his hammock stops swinging.

Grandpa's skinny white legs climb down on each branch of the large maple tree. Grandpa gets out of the hammock, and goes back into the house. Then, he takes a long bath in the Hinoki tub. I go back to the back yard, and tell Grandma with curled lips and one lifted eyebrow, "Grandpa said he can't answer my questions."

"The ideas have to come up from you." Grandma hunches over and moves piles of dried corn husks on the ground into a large trash bag. Her arms are thick and tan. Sweat drips down her temples, and she grabs the dry white towel around her neck to wipe her entire face. I keep standing next to her as my face gets red. I am not quite convinced. I run into the house.

Next day, when I wake up, Grandma and Grandpa are not in the bedroom. I hear running water from the first floor, so I come down to the kitchen in my pajamas. Grandma asks me to get three eggs from the chicken coop for our breakfast. Before they have breakfast, Grandma and Grandpa do simple chores such as cleaning the yard, watering the plants, and feeding the animals. My job is to get eggs from the chicken coop. I put my feet into Grandpa's straw sandals and go out. Since the back yard is surrounded by thick bamboo trees, no neighbors can see me wearing pajamas.

While the morning sun softly shines on the zen garden in the front yard, the back yard is still shaded by the house. There is a barn next to the Onko trees in the back yard for Grandpa to keep an abandoned horse. In the back yard, there are also two separate storage buildings. Next to the storage buildings, Grandpa built a chicken coop by using left over wood he got from neighbors. Grandpa keeps his chickens in the coop during the cold nights. The whole coop is about ten square feet, the left and right side of the coop is not symmetrical. They don't need a bigger coop because Grandpa lets the chickens out of the coop to exercise during the day.

## - Musashi Miyamoto -

I put three fingers into a wire mesh door and slowly lean forward. The door makes noise. I close my eyes as I lean forward. My right foot and head move inside the coop. The ground of the coop contains dirt and sand so that the chickens can do dust bathing. I don't make eye contact with any of the chickens. Eggs are lying here and there on the dirt. I only need three eggs, I tell the chickens. Slowly and carefully, I pick them up. The eggs are bigger than my palms, they are still warm. Those chickens are not aware of my presence, I tell myself. I quickly leave the coop.

Grandma is waiting in the kitchen, I have to hurry. The third egg is between one egg in my left hand and one egg in my right hand, so I have to be careful to not drop it. The eggs have soft white feathers on their shells, and they swing as I carefully run. Suddenly, I hear the horse neigh. I stop and I look at the barn. Grandpa is feeding his horse.

When a horse becomes useless for racetracks, the owners give the useless horse to Grandpa. Grandpa takes all of the animals his neighbors want to get rid of, Grandma complains. Grandpa's useless horse is galloping in the back yard, its shadow is still longer in the early morning. The hair on his back moves left and right. His white legs look as if he's wearing a pair of white boots. He has no saddle or stirrups, so no one will get on him. Grandpa watches his horse and lets his horse come next to him. Grandpa gradually reaches his arms forward to lengthen the reins, to give the horse's head and neck more freedom, to give him the chance to find his balance. But he has to be careful. The horse wants to run. Everything in his breeding and training until a year ago tells him to run as fast as he possibly can.

## - The Moon Home -

It reminds of me of my puppy that got lost last year, and never came back home.

"The horse might leave and never come back to you," I say to Grandpa as I'm thinking of the puppy I found on the street. Grandpa slows the horse down to give him water.

"Once horses run the path, they won't forget how to get back. Once they experience, they remember," Grandpa says as he runs a large brush down the brown horse's hide.

I leave the three eggs on the ground. I pull a two carrots from Grandma's garden. The carrots come with wet dirt. I wash the carrots with water in a large bucket next to the barn. I give the horse a carrot. He takes the carrot from my hand. He bites quickly, chews slowly, and makes crunchy sounds. There is no dog food or horse food. We eat the same foods.

"The horse needs a new house, Grandpa."

"Fine horses never need fancy barns. No need for gold decorations or fancy stalls," Grandpa says.

Grandma calls me from her kitchen. I've forgotten the three eggs on the ground. I pick up the eggs and look at the horse. The horse looks beautiful as it is. I run into the house with the three eggs.

Later in the afternoon, I'm lying down on the tatami mat on the second floor in Grandma's bedroom. Summer vacation is my zen time. I can hide from all of the anti-left-handed prejudice. I've become right-handed in school and parents' house but ambidextrous in Grandma's house. On the second floor, in Grandma's kimono room, I'm holding a pen in each hand in case someone walks in, so I can drop a pen from my left hand. I'm writing my name with my left hand over and over again on the back of coloring papers. As if he were a ninja, Grandpa sneaks into the room. I quickly drop a pen from my left hand, and flip the paper.

"You are Miyamoto Musashi."

I freeze like a startled rabbit. Then, I realize I'm in Grandma's house.

"Who is he?" I lie down on the tatami looking up at Grandpa.

"Musashi was a warrior who invented a waza called NitenIchiRyu."

Grandpa tells me that practice forms are called waza, and Musashi used two swords with the kenjutsu technique called "NitenIchiRyu" ("two heavens as one"). Musashi's waza was different from other styles; his technique was sophisticated, efficient, and powerful, with no flashy or unwanted movements.

"I believe Musashi was left handed, which is possibly what led him to develop a two handed style, using swords in both hands," Grandpa says as he leaves the room.

I hold a pencil in each hand. I start writing with my left hand, feeling free with a happy heart. I've decided that my social studies project will be learning about Musashi's journey to find his real mother, as well as his struggles and his philosophy of life.

I'm standing a dark cold hallway, and I run toward the stairs. I must run, I have to run. And I reach a narrow spiral staircase. It twists and turns to the bottom, and another bottom, it seems to not end. And it's dark – so dark I can't see the bottom, but I keep heading down, my feet skipping two or three stairs with great speed, unsure if my toes will land on the step or if my foot will catch the edge and I'll slip without knowing how far I am falling. I wake up. Imprisoned in the hell of an endless, unchanging world of what is called Sadame.

Father does not inherit the zen life style from Grandpa. Father loves brand name clothes, nice cars, expensive audio, ski equipment, and expensive restaurants. He drinks beer, sake and whatever has alcohol, and he smokes like a chimney. Father is never home. He leaves for work early in the morning, and gets home late and drunk. When he is drunk, he becomes a loud and mean man. When he is home sober, which does happen a few times a year, he makes kind gestures to his daughters. He never raises his voice at me even if I drop expensive glasses and break them. It is confusing for me to decide whether he is a cold blooded asshole or an empathetic kind man. I am not quite sure how to interact with a sober normal man whom I only see a few time a year. Who is this man?

During winter vacation, Father takes me to Kitoushi mountain for ski lessons. I walk on the snow with a pair of heavy ski boots as I dig my ski poles into the snow. This is not a ski resort. No one is around. I push the heavy boot heel onto the ski. The click sound hits the mountain, and its echo reaches back to my ears. My first experience of skiing, learning how to carry my own skis, is the first lesson that I received from Father. I put my kid's skis on my left shoulder, and walk like a toddler to the mountain. The snow gets halfway up to my knees. Unlike a ski resort, the slopes are not smooth and perfect. The trees are on both sides of the slope, and some large stones are showing their dark heads through the snow. For some areas, it's quite rocky until the mountain gets more snow.

There is no one on the slopes except for Father and me. I loop my wrist into the black strap of my ski pole and start digging into the fresh snow. The ski poles make noise as if I were cleaning a shinny glass window. Father and I are making parallel lines with a pair of skis on snow where there were no lines. I avoid the rocks. The winter sun is too bright when if reflects off the few acres of fresh white snow. The frozen crust of the snow holds me for hours, then I collapse. I sit in the snow for a while and look at the hill side. I see some movements. Yellowish brown things moving in the area of the trees. Their ears are bigger than their faces, their tales are thicker than dogs'. A fox with her baby. I look at the foxes motionlessly, then I look at Father's face. The sun is blinding against his face, which becomes a shadow. I can't see his face. My eye turns to the foxes again. They stop, they stay, they look at us. I stop, I stay, and I look at Father. Father waits and whispers, "It's an Ezo red fox, and a kit fox." The baby fox seems to be well protected by her mom. After ten seconds of looking at each other, they start walking toward the forest. Father and I start moving as well. All day skiing in the wild mountain, I don't pay attention to how cold my hands get.

Day time in Hokkaido during the winter become very short. The mountain is getting darker quickly. Seeing the stars clearly in the sky is not unusual in the island because there are

## The Moon Home

no city lights in much of Hokkaido. On a clear moonless night in the island, I see a few thousand stars with my naked eye. The Big Dipper is visible throughout the year.

Father points out at the sky as he opens the door to the driver's seat. "Look at the Seven Stars of the Northern Dipper." When I look up the sky, the stars are everywhere. Too many stars, too bright, shine against the moonless dark sky. I look at the sky without knowing where to look.

"Locate the two stars that form the edge of dipper that's farthest from the handle. Draw an imaginary line straight through the two stars at either end of that edge, starting at the bottom of the dipper and extending past the top of the dipper. That imaginary line points to Polaris. The distance between Polaris and the star at the bottom of the dipper should be five times the distance between that star and the star at the top of the dipper," Father continues. I measure and count to five to find Polaris.

"If you ever get lost, look for the Seven Stars for the Northern Dipper. From the Northern Dipper, you can find Polaris. You will find the way to get back." Father is placing my skis on sky racks on the roof on his car.

"Look at those two stars on the handle of the Northern Dipper. Constellations are imaginary groups or outlines that look like a meaningful pattern on the celestial sphere. Those stars seem related to each other, but it just a pretense." Father always tells me things to destroy my fantasy.

After my fantasy is destroyed, a new fantasy comes alive in my mind. In the Milky Way, galaxy, planets' positions in the sky seem preordered by cosmic disposition. How did I end up being a daughter of my parents? Is it destiny that we are not in control of the arrangement? All the answers to my questions are registered in the galaxy. The majestic passage of the stars across the night sky stimulates my curiosity about the idiosyncrasy of life. I close my eyes against the sky in the cold winter night until Father calls me to get into the car.

It is the heaviest snowstorm this year in Hokkaido. This always happens in January. The train is held up all afternoon, and traffic is paralyzed. The rest of the schools in Japan have two weeks of winter vacation, but schools in Hokkaido have four weeks because they have a longer winter with a lot of snow. I have two more weeks until school starts, but I have to get ready for my tonsillectomy. Mother says that I get sick too often so that my tonsils have to be removed. Mother complains that I'm always trouble; I'm a sick troubled child.

The TV news says that there are eight people who went skiing and have not returned from Mt. Taisetsu. I hear blowing snow and wind from the windows and chimney. Skiing at Mt. Taisetsu is not a joke during the winter. Father went to Mt. Taisetsu with his team to rescue the missing people because he's been in a rescue team since he was young. He has not called since he left at 4 am this morning. Was he able to find the missing people? Was he able to come back this time?

Despite the snow, Mother drives me to the hospital to get prepped before my tonsillectomy. When Mother and I get to the hospital, a nurse escorts us to the nursing room next to the operation room. The room is cold and the windows are small. A white uniformed young nurse brings unfamiliar equipment on a metal plate. The ceiling lights are white, and they are reflected off the equipment on the metal plate. I want to leave, but Mother is next to me. Without any word, the nurse comes in with a syringe on her hand. It looks bigger and thicker than my arm. She says she is taking my blood in case I need a blood transfusion. She pushes the needle into my arm. A sharp pain sting my arm, the red blood starts showing in the glass syringe, but the blood does not come easily. The nurse struggles with a large needle in my vein. I cry like a baby monkey, but the nurse does not care. The nurse says that they need a full syringe of blood just in case I need a blood transfusion during the tonsil removal procedure. I say I need a transfusion now. My eyes are swollen from the tears, and the blood runs down into the huge syringe. No matter how much I cry, it does not end until the clear syringe becomes full. Finally my blood is taken away. They remove my soul before they remove my tonsils.

Then, the nurse requests one more thing after the tragedy. The nurse cuts my ear lobe to check my blood type, it turns out my blood is type A. The nurse asks Mother the parents' blood types. Both of my parents are type O. Mother tells the nurse.

"A blood type A child is not born from parents of type O blood," the nurse says with a confused face.

Mother calls Father, who is back home this time. Mother explains the blood type issue. "She is not my daughter," Father says on the phone. Today, he's saved eight people's lives on Mt Taisetsu. Doesn't he know how to save his own daughter? Mother screams and yells at Father for assurances. I sit next to Mother and look at her for direction but her eyes do not meet mine – she is busy yelling at Father. I am not crying anymore.

## - Musashi Miyamoto -

Finally someone is telling me the truth, my version of the truth, I now have proof, they are not my real parents. Father finally comes to the hospital and gets his blood type tested. It's Type A. Father seems content with the result, but I am disappointed.

After my tonsils, blood and soul are stolen, my time with Grandma is stolen as well by my school and daily homework assignments. Our exchange of letters becomes the only bonding time for us. In my desk drawers, I keep pink, lavender, orange, and purple papers with flower, animal and anime prints. Choosing paper for the letter is an exciting process and deciding what kind of scent to use on the paper is a major decision. Every day, secretly, I write the letter with my left hand. Grandma writes me back immediately. When she agrees with all my thoughts and ideas in the letter, my thoughts and ideas are growing bigger and bigger in my head. Writing letters with my left hand and exchanging thoughts and ideas with my Grandma protect my undesired feelings of chaos and disintegration in my life at my parents' house. I try to hold on to the feeling as much as I can, but the strong requirement of right hand use all day and every day, witnessed by teachers and mother, makes me want to give up my existence. I write my address as Milky Way galaxy, solar system, the earth, Japan, Hokkaido… Grandma lives so close, yet the time we are not together, I feel so far away from her and myself. Soon after, my letters to Grandma are few and far between.

## CHAPTER THREE
## An Untamed Child

Japanese kids are elastic, lazy and untamed wild animals just like kids in other cultures, but teachers use ceremony-minded discipline of mind and body to make kids become more serious and formal. Days start with ritual and discipline, and schools turn everything into a ceremony. A brief speech is presented by the school principal in the morning either outdoors or indoors with a great deal of ceremonial bowing to the principal. A bell signals the start and end of each class. The students engage in bowing when the teacher first arrives and again when the class ends. After the teacher arrives but before class starts, teachers let students work either cleaning their classrooms or gardening in the school yards. Eating, cleaning, gardening, and farming are all zen practices. All the students learn everything in the school.

Usually, fathers are the head of the household, and many of them are workaholics who come home late at night. They even go to work on weekends and holidays. Many fathers who work late get drunk after work to relieve stress. Some fathers don't make it home; they sleep in their office or sleep in a capsule hotel (a hotel with tiny rooms that look like capsules). Early the next morning, they buy cheap underwear, shirts and ties, and they go to work. Children don't get to see their fathers during the week because fathers get home after the kids go to bed and leave before kids wake up in the morning. During the weekends, fathers are so tired that they usually sleep all day, or get up at 4 am and play business-related golf. Many children grow up without seeing their own fathers for weeks, sometimes months. Many fathers don't have time to get involved in child rearing, and the family and society don't expect them to be a part of it.

Teachers are well respected in their society, their academic credentials are very high. If you want to be a school teacher, you have get good grades throughout your school years. Teachers have great salaries and benefits, like doctors and professors. Once they become teachers, they usually stay in the field until they retire. Parents and grandparents trust school and teachers to raise their children, and respect teachers' opinions and decisions. It is rare for parents to go to a school and complain or challenge the teacher's decisions regarding their children. Most importantly, kids know about the system, and they don't play games with school teachers, because parents won't buy kids' excuses.

The school year starts in April. The elementary school is surrounded by cherry blossoms, and after the blossoms are gone, I pick cherries and eat them without washing. They are all organic. The kids in the island eat whatever looks edible in their surroundings. On warm sunny days in May, many first through six graders are out on the playground. Some are running around, some are playing on the seesaw, and some are on the jungle gym or on the horizontal bar. The bell rings to signal the end of recess, and the children come back inside and run to their classrooms. They make sure they are seated and have their text books out from their backpacks before the teacher gets into the room. No kid is allowed to say a word. In Japan, it is prohibited to speak before your authorities initiate a talk. Verbalizing thoughts or asking questions are considered to be demanding.

Classrooms are usually assigned randomly at the start of every year, especially in elementary school. Students stay in one classroom, their homeroom, and it's the teachers that move around when the bell goes off, except for PE, science experiments, and cooking. The teacher comes into the classroom on time. The student on duty calls, "everybody rises, bows, and then sits," and the teacher starts the class. Students don't raise hands and speak in front of the class unless they are absolutely sure that they are correct because expressing unsure thoughts would be considered irresponsible and making mistakes would cause embarrassment. Students believe that teachers' opinions are worth much more than their own opinions, and they should follow and obey without questions; this causes students not to think on their own.

Japanese society values suppressing one's emotions. A disciplined body is a disciplined mind. No kids go to the bathroom during class – little kids are no exception. Japanese kids are expected to control their bowel movements, even if they are in the first grade. They are expected to be able to think ahead of time and arrange their bathroom breaks during recess. When kids get the urge to go to the bathroom, they do "Gaman," which means enduring physical and mental pain or hardship with patience and dignity. Not just to put up with it, but to

# An Untamed Child

find an acceptance, a love, or even happiness in intolerable situations. Of course, small kids sometimes have accidents. Those kids who pee in the classroom in front of other kids have trauma later because of the embarrassment and humiliation. Later in their lives, this feeling of shame is connected to the "losing face" phenomenon. Little children exercise and stretch their patience during the school years, but this is not all, it's just a beginning. This concept of Gaman and losing face haunts them throughout their lives.

Punishments in elementary schools in Japan are not always verbal or physical. If children are not paying attention, the teacher may place their desks next to the teacher in front of the classroom, and the children sit there all day. These seats are called "The seats of Gabacho." Mr. Inoue, who is a teacher, invented this punishment, took the name of the seat from a cartoon character, President Gabacho, in a show called "Unexpectedly Gourd Island," which was broadcast in Japan in the late 1960's. The show started with a school field trip. While the students and teacher were on the island for their field trip, a small piece of the land separated from the island because of a volcanic eruption. Then, the survival adventure of the teacher and the students begins. President Gabacho is supposed to be one of the student's nicknames. I was too small to watch that cartoon in the 1960's and never understood the meaning of the seat of Gabacho. However, I still don't like to be seated in Gabacho's seat, because then I am in a different seat from the other kids. This punishment makes many children feel humiliated for the entire day. In Japan, being different is bad, and being the same as everyone else is good.

Right before summer vacation in the 3rd grade, I end up in Gabacho's seat. I'm playing jump rope with the other girls. I don't want to leave the playground because I waited until everyone got a turn, and finally my turn came. I'm five minutes late for my class. The teacher is already in class and the other kids are seated. "Well, well, well, you have a lot of nerve to come to my class late," Mr. Inoue says with his finger pointed to the Gabacho seat. There are no explanations, no excuses, and no more time wasted for the other competent children. I quietly drag my desk next to Mr. Inoue's desk. Then, the discipline starts when I sit in Gabacho's seat in front of all the class for the entire day. At the end of the day, I feel bad, I am bad. The emotion goes far deeper to my experience of self. Once shame is instilled by self, how do we process through and move past the shame?

Another way to punish kids in the 1970's was to have children who misbehaved stand in the hallway until the end of class so that entire school such as teachers and students would know the kid did something wrong. The humiliation and embarrassment lead to the feeling of shame, which was what teachers and parents were trying to achieve. By the end of elementary school, most of the wild animals were completely domesticated. I learned how to sit, wait, and roll over as if I were a domesticated Chihuahua.

Negative self-judgment is learned within group settings in their early life, such as a Gabacho's seat. This is supposed to work for the rest of our lives. Shame is an emotion that is felt but never discussed; it is experienced at such a deep level of my existence. Now, they don't have to punish me, because I have already established negative self-judgment that I learned from sources such as parents and school. Unlike guilt, shame is a challenging emotion to address for Japanese because most them are unspoken about it and possibly unaware of it. Guilt is inward and shame is outward, some people say. The others say that shame may result from the awareness of guilt, and claim guilt is a factual state but shame is a natural emotional consequence of guilt and wrongdoing. I may feel shame within guilt through Gabacho's seat. I may feel shame and guilt at the same time, and also at different times. In that case, Gabacho's seat creates a double punishment. Japanese society and educators believe that if we don't welcome and honor our shame, we won't be able to change our own behaviors, and we will continually do things we know are wrong. Thus, we won't have the determination to stop our wrong behaviors. Shaming children is supposed to help them change their bad behaviors and make sure that they don't hurt others. That is the rationale.

Schools don't focus only on punishments; teachers spend many hours creating a variety of work for school children. According to zen, eating, cleaning, washing, farming, and gardening are zen practices. All students are responsible for doing their chores every day. Even elementary school children have daily multiple chores at the school. One of the important chores is erasing the blackboard after each class and cleaning the eraser and blackboard after school. Some kids are assigned to decorate the classroom. I'm in a flower arrangement unit, so I pick up wildflowers on my way to school and replace old ones in my classroom during the summer. Some children take care of class pets such as rats, mice, and birds by feeding them, cleaning them, and playing with them. Sometimes kids make mistakes and pets die. Kids cry and prepare for the funeral and bury the dead animals on school grounds.

Daily chores are not just at school. I have to clean the entrance area during the summer and winter vacations before I have breakfast. During summer vacation, I have to pull the weeds in the yard. As I pull out the weeds, my fantasy grows; I pretend that I'm Cinderella and my mother is an evil stepmother. Someday, a prince will rescue me and the evil stepmother will regret the way she treated me. Somehow, teachers and parents are on the same page all the time. There is no escape from discipline.

Schools are a kid's natural habitat, and their work habits inform self discipline. Self-discipline does not appear by itself, but is completed by competitions. Classrooms in elementary schools are very colorful. There are usually three blackboards in the classroom. One blackboard is in front of the room where teachers write during class. Another one is in the back, where kids put their art such as pictures, paintings, and Japanese ink brush calligraphy. The last one is on the side, where the teacher places a bar graph. Red, green, orange, blue, pink, purple, black, and yellow rectangular bars stand on the large white paper on the board. Lengths and heights are proportional to the value of self for the kids. Teachers use bar graphs for students' academic activities and create competitive environments in the classroom. Every day, by the end of the day, I either get or don't get stickers on the graph, which represents my value. A bar graph creates an easy way to see who is doing well and who is not. If I get no points, that means that others are ahead of me. No one helps

## - An Untamed Child -

me in the classroom. Kids don't help each other, but compete with each other.

Competition is not only in the classroom. Teachers also create competitive environments outside of the classroom. There are many tricks for training us domesticated animals to work more, study more, and play musical instruments better: they called these tricks "competition of garden beauty" and "competition of music appreciation." They create competition against other classes. In the spring, the school buys flowers and soil for each class, and has students work on their own garden. Students work during their break time and after school. Some of them have to come early in the morning to water the flowers daily. By the end of summer, teachers decide to give classes prizes if students keep their garden pretty enough. The school saves a lot of money by not hiring gardeners for the whole summer. No wonder Japanese gardeners are good at what they do. They've been practicing gardening since they were little.

Little by little, we animals are becoming less goofy and elastic. Once those wild animals become domesticated enough, we are ready to go to another grade. By the time the animals reach the fifth grade, we are responsible for cleaning our own classrooms, the hallway floors, and the toilets. After the students clean, teachers check the classrooms to see if students did what we were supposed to do. Mr. Masuda, a custodian, once ran into the entrance window and broke it into a thousand pieces because I cleaned the window too clean. He did not see the window. Children are very good at cleaning or anything that we are assigned to. We don't do a mediocre job.

## - The Moon Home -

There are no special programs for gifted or mentally challenged children in our school. I'm in a classroom that includes some kids who are doing extremely well in mathematics and other kids who are academically challenged. A little math genius Kubo sits next to Masayo who is mentally challenged. Masayo says something loud and leaves the classroom during math class, then goes to the playground with her pants down to her ankles and shouts something. Masayo's fair skinned butt presents quite a contrast with the pink cherry blossoms in the playground. Soon, a teacher chases and grabs Masayo to take her into the school building. Seeing Masayo's butt cheek is quite shocking for eight year old kids, but nobody explains anything about the incident. No children have any idea why Masayo acts the way she does, and no children are allowed to say a word. In Japan, it is prohibited to speak or ask when authorities start to talk. Laughing is totally unacceptable.

After the short summer, winter comes quickly in Hokkaido, and students are not able to play in the field except for skating and skiing. I'm the tallest girl in school, so I join a basketball team. There are many brand new basketballs in the brand new indoor activity building in the school. I feel vibrations of balls bouncing on the shinny wooden floor. I can smell brand new basketballs, but I'm not allowed to touch any balls. First, I have to run three kilometers. Then, do 50 squats. And then, two sets of 25 sit ups. Wax on, wax off. I get bored waxing on and off, so I'm goofing around with one of my girlfriends on the team. She and I poke each other laughing until we both get irritated. She runs after me, I run after her, I catch her, and I pull her pants down. The basketball coach sees me, and kicks me off

*- An Untamed Child -*

the team before I even touch a basketball. I am kicked out, forever. I learned that children who are not patient enough, who can't wax on and wax off, are not achievers. There is no second chance if they are unable to Gaman.

As the saying goes, the nail that sticks up gets hammered down. During the restroom cleaning, I check my hair on the mirror because teachers check "grooming standards," and I have to straighten my naturally wavy hair to fit in with my classmates who have mostly straight hair. After the morning meeting, students the turn on the classroom TV on for the morning meeting. The school principal speaks from the media room to all students, telling us what he expects us to do today, this week, and this month. Media club students report significant issues and plans for the week and the month. The teacher comes into the classroom anytime during the morning media conference. If someone is not sitting properly, he or she would get in trouble. Usually, one kid is responsible for telling us when he sees the teacher come close to the classroom. This student has to listen for the sound of the teacher's slippers, then quickly tell the class, "he is coming," then all the students sit up straight, show serious faces, and pretend that they are focusing on the media conference. Now, these animals still have a little spirit left for fighting back against authorities.

School is the mysterious time for children's transformation from wild animal to tamed, domesticated animals. Sometimes children act wild, but other times, they become tamed. For the most part, students obey rules without questioning. You will never know what they will be until they graduate from elementary school. Some kids argue between classes, but they stop arguing immediately when a teacher approaches; they respect authorities. As I'm becoming a tamed animal with some strategies and tricks, my daily right hand writing at home and school becomes natural and normal. It seems my left hand is dead. When my left hand and right brain are dead, no one is yelling at me. Until…

I'm standing in a dark cold hallway, and I run toward the stairs. I must run, I have to run. And I reach a narrow spiral staircase. It looks familiar twists and turns into the bottom, and another bottom without the end. And it's dark – so dark I can't see the bottom, but I keep heading down my feet skipping two or three stairs with great speed, unsure if my toes will land on the step or if my foot will catch the edge. I can't stop myself falling. I'm tired of having the feeling, so I wanted to end. I throw myself into the dark. Under the sudden drop, my eyes open. I am awake.

Terror, Thursday nights, Mother leaves to pick up Sensei Sasaki at the bus station near our home. I make sure my fingernails are short and clean. I polish the black Yamaha piano with a dry orange felted cloth and wipe my fingerprints off before Sensei gets here. Sensei Sasaki is a middle-aged woman with thick wavy black hair, wearing red lipstick and a long skirt. She never smiles. She limps when she walks.

## - An Untamed Child -

My parents put a black piano in my small bedroom, making the small space even smaller. While I'm waiting for Sensei Sasaki to arrive, I sit on the black piano bench looking at the piano. It looks even more shiny at night with the reflection of an orange light hanging from the ceiling. Then, I regret what I asked for. Mother says no to everything; but Father never says no. Knowing that Father would never say no to my requests, I asked him for a black grand piano for my birthday when I was five years old. One afternoon, a man from a store delivered a big box with my name on it. I was very excited. When I opened the box, it was a red toy grand piano, the size of my sister's training potty. I expressed my feeling by not talking to Father about the red toy grand piano when he got home. Months later, Father bought a real black grand piano on the condition that I take weekly lessons. I had no idea that expressing what I wanted would lead to the long-term terror Thursdays.

As I'm thinking about how I ended up taking piano lessons, the garage door start to open. I hear a stream gurgling and feel the sharp pinch of dry pine needles poking my hands. Mother and Sensei come in through the front door. I place the Hanon book on a board on the piano to make my piano area appear as if I have been practicing all day. I hear her foot steps. I sit straight. Sensei comes up behind me. To the right side of the piano bench, I stand up like a soldier. Sensei sits on the stool to my left like a drill sergeant. "Onegaishimasu," I step forward and bow to Sensei. Sensei is still. She keeps looking at the piano, and says nothing. I sit on the piano bench, on the front third to make sure my legs are bent at a ninety degree angle. I adjust up and down, back and forth to change the height of the bench for no reason. I check the angles of my arms and hands to make sure that my both wrists are not below the arch of my fingers. Sensei is watching and waiting for the first movement of my fingers, she knows I'm trying to delay the piano lesson. Silence. And then, there is nothing to do but play.

I hear the rapid speedy fast moving rhythm. My fingers move as my eyes move on the book of Hanon piano exercises. This finger exercise is supposed to improve my technical skill, speed, and precision stretching. My ten fingers are then exercised by moving up and down the octaves. Then, I lift the fingers high and with precision, play each note very distinctly. Sensei circles the exercise I completed with her red pen. I close the Hanon book, and open a Czerny book, which is far more known for its challenging works and techniques. Tunes are echoed in my small room, then turn into crescendo in the darkness.

Since my parents taught me little about the world, I had no choice but go to the library and read about different subjects. I read Carl Czerny at the library; he died in Vienna at the age of 66, never married and never had children. The black and white keyboard feels cool and smooth as if I'm petting my cat Mimi on a cold morning. I tend to think of something else while I'm playing piano. The moment that I become aware of the temperature of the keyboard on my fingertips, my left hand is slapped by Sensei's big thick exercised right hand. Sensei's hand reacts to it by instinct as if she has to kill an annoying fly with a fly swatter. I feel the weight and size of Sensei's hand. My left hand is no longer on the keyboard. When a silent anguished force, I realize that I hit a wrong note. She knows exactly which hand made the mistake. First, it comes as a shock, then becomes predictable. After getting hit for the twentieth time, I feel no pain. This is not my hand and the pain is no longer mine.

"Lessons are not for you to practice, lessons are for you to show what and how you've practiced and improved. Making mistakes knowing I will be here is very disrespectful," Sensei says in a deep tone of voice as she keeps staring at the Czemy book on the polished black piano. She does not look at me. I don't look at her. After my hands are slapped twelve times more, there is no hitting, no pain, but the pain of silence. The sharp silence with a deep sigh. She leaves the room without a word to me. I don't get an opportunity to play from the Sonatinen book. Sensei is disgusted, my playing is disgusting, I'm disgusting.

Sensei never played in front of me. She never said what went wrong or how I made a mistake. Based on the way she slaps my hand or sighs, I am supposed to know what my mistakes are and correct them. I'm not worthy enough for Sensei to play for me. I've never heard beautiful music from the shinny black piano. All I hear are my disgusting mistakes. If I want something, it's dangerous. The piano lesson is usually for one hour, but I felt as if I had ten years of torture in a dark dungeon with chains on my ankles secured to the metal at the bottom of the piano. I can't escape, but I'm not ready for the sacrifices, so I keep practicing the melody of worthlessness and rhythm of shamefulness. Forced right-hand writing in the yellow diary and practicing piano remain my daily activities. I no longer think about escaping from those punishments. If I stay quiet and hardly speak, the time would pass. If I don't exist, the pain would not be so bad.

- The Moon Home -

In the spring, rivers in Hokkaido are full of cold water from melted snow from Mount Taisetsu, the tallest mountain in Hokkaido. It almost seems as if it wants to sweat off our anger and pain from the autumn, and sorrow and misery from the winter. A variety of wild spring vegetation shows up near the Chubetsu river, and it whisper to us about the power of lives. Many school teachers take their students on fieldtrips for art class to paint because the nature on the island and weather are perfect for school children being outside for several hours. The 4th grade teacher takes us to the small hill overlooking the Chubetsu river. The river is below the road we walk on. A steep incline. Kids throw rocks, and they slide down and sink into the river. "Make sure we don't fall into the river," the teacher says loudly.

All the children bring their own wooden sketch boards and watercolors. They start finding their spots and sit in front of me, and put the rubber attached to the sketch boards over their necks. I don't hear them talking anymore. They are focusing on their sketching. Quietly, I sit on the grass at the top of the slope, far behind most of the children.

I open my paint box and put it beside me on the grass, staring at the blank canvas. I stretch my arms, take a pencil with my left hand, and press the tip of the pencil on the canvas as I look at the old closed-down factory beyond the river. I stop. I look around to make sure no one sees me using my left hand. I feel as if I'm hiding and peeing in the bush with an unbearable urge that probably, later, would become my dirty secret. In a

## - An Untamed Child -

moment of silence, I hear the flow of the river. When I imagine the murmuring of the creek next to Granma's house, I feel the fresh air and the canvas in front of me. Then my left hand moves on its own. I'm filling in the shape of the old wheels near the red brick building – they all look dusty and rusty. My left hand muscles are still in charge, the past is brought into the present. They have not died yet.

Since no one interrupts me, I finish sketching with a peaceful mind. I get up and look around at the other children and their paintings. We have one particular view from the hill overlooking the river, yet their paintings are all different. I take a plastic cup and go down the hill to the river to get water for my painting. When I reach the river, I look up at the sky and then glance around the area to compare the colors of my surroundings. As I scoop water from the river, I imagine how I will paint the rusty closed-down factories under the clear blue sky. When I feel the cold water on my hand, my heartbeat increases with excitement. My right brain spontaneously captures the colors of the nature, and the color images come to my mind automatically. As I walk up the slope, I'm ready to explore and play by mixing a variety of colors together on the canvas.

I come back and sit on the grass facing the river. I grasp the wooden brush and it leaves an imprint on my fingertips. The afternoon sun hits the metal part of the wooden brush when I hold the brush over the sketched canvas. The reflected sunlight from the gold part of the brush rises into the air as I'm holding the brush. I am with a fairy and see her holding a magic wand. Nothing is prohibited. After I spend another two hours painting with watercolors, the dead factories and old bricks come alive in the reflections of the river. I complete the painting during the field trip and turn it in. After my sense of self was destroyed by the terror of Thursday piano lessons, I found another opportunity to turn up my spirit. My left hand and right brain are still alive.

A few weeks later, I see my watercolor landscape painting on the wall, in front of the school principal's office, with a gold medal on it. I walk by the principal's office several times a day without any particular reason. Before summer vacation, on the last day of school, the teacher returns my paining to me. As I walk home, I think about putting my painting on my bedroom wall. When Mother gets home and asks me to show her my quarterly school report, I show my gold medal painting instead. She looks at my painting, and quickly looks away. "Where is your report card?" Mother demands with her determined voice. While I'm looking at the wrinkled skin between her eyebrows, I start to wonder if she knows that I used my left hand for the painting? Slowly, my painting becomes smaller and smaller as if my mind is shrinking. Next day, I throw it into the trash. No one has mentioned that my painting is in the trash. In the trash, the rusty closed-down factories in the painting look even more dead than ever.

After I give up painting, I lose interest in school work. Instead, I become interested in collecting things such as varieties of cicadas' cast-off shells. After school, I quickly run to a shrine in front of the school. The shrine is surrounded by many small stores, a kindergarten, and an elementary school. Outside the shrine, people are walking and I can hear children playing.

## - An Untamed Child -

Girls are playing with jump ropes, and boys are playing baseball on the school playground.

Once I step onto the grounds of the shrine, I am transported to a different world. A simple Torii entrance turns it into a small forest, and the Torii gate leads to a network of trails behind the shrine's main buildings. One trail will lead me to a forest of the sacred worship building, but I can't see any buildings from the main entrance gate. As I walk on a trail, I can't tell the time of day. Hundreds of pine, cedar, and fir trees surround the trail, sunlight doesn't reach the trail. The small forest has a buzz of thousands of cicada throughout summer. The constant buzz becomes a part of the small forest. I don't even notice the buzz as I become a part of the forest. Japanese call it the sound effects of summer, the voice of cicadas. There is a wooden worship building with an entrance, but the entrance is not for people. There is supposed to be a god (Kami) inside the worship building.

Shinto is a form of animism, which dates back to prehistoric times. Ancient Japanese saw and celebrated gods (Kami), everything from the sun, the moon to the stone. Many Japanese still visit a shrine on the new year's day in search of luck or happiness, but they don't consider themselves religious. In fact, many Buddhists and Christians visit Shinto shrines. Shinto has no scriptures or doctrine. It is a way of thinking or living.

The reason I run to the shrine after school is not to worship Kami, but to worship cicadas' cast-offs. I visit the shrine to collect cicadas shells. Most cicadas are on trees, but they leave their cast-off skin on the ground by the middle of August. Cicadas are active in the underground; they are not sleeping or hibernating.

## The Moon Home

After a long thirteen to seventeen years, cicadas emerge from the ground as nymphs. Nymphs climb the nearest available tree, and begin to shed their nymph exoskeleton. Cicadas live underground as nymphs for most of their lives. Most cicada die off within two weeks in the island.

Trees are growing off to both sides of the trail, and some curled leaves lie on the ground. I carry a plastic insect cage that has a green top, air holes, and a yellow strap on my shoulder. I believe they need air holes in their box to survive because I treat cicada shells as if were live creatures. I see a few cicadas' shell lying on the top of another curled leaf. As I squat down, the dry roasting heated air evaporates from the soil. I pick a cast-off shell up and drop it into my insect cage. I feel the curled warm crusty leaves in my hand as I pick up the shell. Children are fascinated with catching butterflies and beetles at the shrine in front of the school. It's easy for me to collect cicada shells because no children are interested in empty shells, but me. I keep my collection in my bedroom without my parents knowing. They are just empty shells. No one finds out because they don't make any noise.

One night, a beetle starts flying around the room. Yikes, I might have put a beetle grub in my insect cage without knowing it was a beetle. "Who brought the insect into my house?" Mother asks rhetorically. We all know who does that kind of thing. I have to move my collection to my Grandma's house. Grandma seems happy to accept my unwanted goods. "If you'd like to collect things, why don't we go clam gathering?" Grandma suggests. Grandma does not just accept my unwanted goods, but she always gives me new ideas and new experiences.

## - An Untamed Child -

The following Saturday morning, before sunrise, Grandma and I leave the house to get to the city of Abashiri, which faces the Pacific Ocean. Aunt Kazu is picking Grandma and me up at the Abashiri bus station, and taking us to Lake Notoro-ko. Grandma and I sleep on the bus. We got up too early. After a good nap, the sun hits my face and wakes me up. I look out at the window; I see the water in front of us. Aunt Kazu appears with wading pants for fishing, and she is waving from the bus stop. Grandma seems happy to see her only daughter.

The sun peeks over the mountain overlooking the lake, I get off the bus. The early morning wind quickly moves my yellow rain coat. It's chilly, yet the water is calm. Lake Notoro-ko is a salt lake connected to the ocean. The low tide seems to begin to affect the dark wet sand on the beach. Here, the moon dominates the ocean; the moon's gravity pulls the water of Lake Notoro-ko away from the beach. Pushed by the water, pulled by the moon, during summer, Lake Notoroko has been available for families to enjoy clam gathering.

Grandma walks on my right, wearing a mompe for clam gathering. The mompe is a women's pant that looks like baggy trousers. Ocean bathing is a fun activity for children, but in Hokkaido, the water is too cold after mid August. Grandma and I are all well equipped for clam digging on a muddy beach, with long rubber fisherman's boots.

"How was the bus ride?" Aunt Kazu asks and takes a freezer bag from Grandma's hand before we can answer.

The sun is finally above the mountain. The wet dark muddy sand starts to look clear in my eyes. As the sun gets a little higher, the water and air temperature at Lake Notoro-ko get more comfortable. The best time for gathering clams is two hours before and after low tide.

"Look for a pair of little holes, called 'asari's eyes,' " Aunt Kazu says as she pulls her right foot out of the muddy sands. Grandma and I look around without words.

"Don't hesitate to change your digging spot frequently if you don't find any clams," Aunt Kazu says when she sees Grandma and me stay in the same spot. Aunt Kazu continues, "The trick is to dig in a wide but shallow manner. Dig up the clams while staying on the move, don't only stay in one spot."

"We should leave clams that are smaller than 2 centimeters – they are young and still need to grow into proper clams," Grandma tells me quietly.

"I'm having a lot more fun collecting clams than collecting the cicada skins," I say to Grandma as I crouch down in the muddy sand. Grandma stops her small rake, and looks at me with a smile that indicates unending wisdom.

Before I turn my eyes to my yellow bucket, I look at Grandma again. There is a big black ship behind her in the distance. I blink. I blink again so I can see more clearly. It does not seem to be moving, but just floating on the surface of the water. The calm waves around the ship shine silver with the reflections of the sun. I was unaware of how far I had moved since early morning. My eyes were glued to the clams in the muddy sand, and had not looked up at the surroundings.

"There is a big ship in the ocean." I quickly stand up and point at the ship.

As Grandma's chin gently rises, she turns and says, "It's a cargo ship. It transport things to the other countries."

"What's behind the big ship? Beyond the ocean?" I ask with curious eyes.

"It's a country called America." Grandma replies, half sitting, half standing as she straightens her pants.

"What kind of county is America? What kind of people live there?"

"It's a big county and big people live there," Grandma mumbles as her eyes skim over the cargo ship in front of her.

"My mother always says I'm too tall for a girl, and no men would want a tall woman. Are people in America taller than me?"

"Your Great Grandfather once told me that I'm too short. Too tall, too short, never just right. Do you remember wabi-sabi? The beauty is imperfect, impermanent, incomplete, and irregular. Sometimes gods deliberately create imperfection." As I keep staring at the horizon, Grandma starts speaking to herself in a serious voice, "I wonder what America is like..." I see Grandma standing by the water and looking at the horizon.

Grandma has never seen a foreigner, and she has no way of knowing about American or what life in America is really like. America isn't an actual country to me. It's a vague fluctuating idea of unconventional and idiosyncrasy; it's a land of unknown. America is east of Japan, but people refer to America as part of the western world. I look at Grandma's wondering eyes. Then, I look at east. I keep gazing to the east, the location of a western country.

It is chilly even before the sunset during the summer in Hokkaido. Soon, summer will be over. Grandma fills the cooler with sea water to transport the clams home. My clam collecting trip with Grandma is coming to the end. Our time together always seems to pass too quickly. My eyes have been glued to the sand, for searching clams, all day. For the first time in hours, I look at the sky to stretch my neck. I see a white half moon above the mountain. I've learned in my class that the moon not only causes tides, but also slows the earth's rotation. If we didn't have the moon, a day on earth would last only 6-12 hour. Without the moon, my time together with Grandma would be even shorter. After saying goodbye to aunt Kazu, Grandma and I get into the bus and fall asleep.

Before we know it, we are back in the house where Grandpa and Mimi wait, surrounded by huge maple trees full of green leaves. Grandpa is waiting for fresh clam miso soup for dinner. The sun is sinking below the horizon, but its rays are scattered by the atmosphere, creating a large drape of orange across a region of the sky. There are short bamboo trees with large leaves all around the creek on the north side of the house. I can still see the creek clearly, but the water looks dark without sunlight. Grandma wants to make a sticky mochi dessert wrapped in bamboo leaves. Grandma and I go to the backyard, where we end up making boats out of bamboo leaves and making them compete. We always get off track. Whose ship goes straight without sinking? My cat, Mimi, watches the bamboo boats curiously. She chases the boats by running sideways. I run with her. The boats go faster, and I can't catch up with them.

"Don't run near the creek," Grandma says. Mimi keeps running, but I stop.

"Do you think my boat can get to America?" I ask Grandma from a distance. "We'll see." Grandma laughs out loud. As I watch Grandma's leaf boats moving away, I become anxious that I will never see them again. I come back to Grandma, who is carefully selecting the right size and color of bamboo leaves, and sit beside her.

"The boats will leave a creek, then reach a river and eventually the ocean, and they will have a new adventure," Grandma says with a smile that implies special acuity.

I imagine two bamboo leaf boats are floating in the Pacific Ocean. Grandma and I are picking the bamboo leaves for wrapping sticky mochi cakes for tonight. When I look at Grandma one more time, my fear fades away.

月

# Working Through

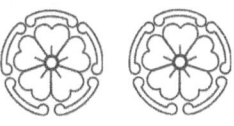

## PART II

## CHAPTER FOUR
## The Beginning

I'm dreaming I'm in an elevator made of glass, and it's going up. I cannot get out, I believe. I should not get out, I know. The elevator stops on the fifth floor, and strangers get in, strangers get out, but I have to stay. The glass elevator keeps going up. I look out at the glass. I see trees and buildings below. Above me, I notice the elevator has a single wire that is too thin, too fragile for an elevator of this size, but it continues up, it continues to stop at floor after floor, and people get out. I had repetitive glass elevator dreams when I lived in America as a young woman.

On a narrow street one block north of Pico Boulevard in West Los Angeles, surrounded by two-story apartment complexes, I'm parking my silver Mitsubishi next to a large ginkgo tree full of lively leaves. In March, the tree's fan-shaped leaves already cover all of its twisted branches. Over time, the roots expand horizontally, lifting and damaging the concrete. As the roots grow stronger, they can crack and open up concrete. The tree's

– The Beginning –

powerful roots make me aware of how rootless and powerless my life is. My trips to and from America didn't help my strong roots to grow in either land.

I arrive a half hour early. It's hot even after sundown. I take off my jean jacket and dry my sweaty palms on my black ankle-length pants. I still feel suffocated, but I hesitate to open the car window. I have an urge to cage myself in the car so that I can't run away. I'm too anxious to read or listen to music, so I'm mindlessly daydreaming about possible conversations with my first English-speaking therapist in America. What if this therapist does not understand me? My grammar, syntax, and pronunciation reflect my recent arrival in this country, especially when I'm confused and emotional.

Fifteen minutes pass too quickly. Looking in the rear view mirror, I use my sticky fingers to fix my long wavy hair so that it's not too frizzy. I grab my purse and jacket, and get out of the car. I squeeze my hands as I walk fast. It's not quite dark outside, so I can find the large street number on the building. A security officer in the building calls the therapist's office and escorts me to the elevator. As the elevator door opens, I get in. Quietly, the door closes and I'm transported to the 7th floor.

When the elevator door opens, I slowly walk down a hallway that has windows on one side and a series of doors on the other. Outside a window, I see apartments, candle trees, and cars that all look miniature. The scene seems familiar; I feel that I've been here before, then I realize it's my repetitive glass elevator dream. At the end of the long quiet hallway, I find a door with a silver plate that says Donna Rosenberg. I grab the brushed nickel door knob – it feels cool. I turn the doorknob and use my whole body to push the heavy wooden door. Inside, it's quiet. No one is in the waiting room. Cool air blows from the ceiling vent, and I feel the draft on my neck.

I sit on a wooden guest chair facing the receptionist's window, but there is no receptionist. I notice that there are eight chairs in the waiting room, and two pastel paintings side by side on the wall. Suddenly, the door from the hallway opens. A man who looks as if he is in his late twenties comes in and sits down. I look at him when he starts reading a book, and wonder what his problem is, and how long he's been in therapy. He does not look crazy.

I look at my watch. It's 6:29 pm. Before I take a breath, the door next to the receptionist's window opens, and a woman appears. When her eyes meet mine, she gently nods. I stand up and start walking. I reach the door, I stop, I look at her face. Her warm eyes sparkle, I feel as if I know that eyes, from the past, so I decide to enter. As we walk down the hallway together, my heart is pounding.

Her office is open, inviting me to walk in. There are two windows with closed blinds, but I can see the light between the blinds. I sit in the middle of the gray couch with matching pillows on either side, and notice a gold pendulum clock on the glass side table next to the couch – I have 48 minutes left. I am aware that the therapist is looking at me. I look into her eyes with my do-nothing-wrong face. She wears no makeup and no perfume, yet she has colors and fragrances within herself. She seems gentle and pure, secure and authentic, and then she looks straight through me. Through her eyes, I sense the solidity of

## - The Beginning -

her power. The eyes are the windows of the soul, Grandma told me when I was a little girl.

She is holding some papers in her lap. It must be my application.

"What brought you here?" Donna starts.

"My clinical supervisor recommended you," I lie.

I start my prepared speech. "Professionals who work intimately with others have a responsibility to be committed to the awareness of their own life issues. It would be difficult to take clients places where you have never been. You can't give something you have never gotten. Sometimes, self awareness will only assist the therapy work." I complete the speech that my mentor once told me. After taking a breath, I glance at Donna's straight, short and perfect hair. Then, I look at her wrinkles when she smiles. I sense that she does not buy my fake speech.

"Have you ever been in therapy before?" Donna asks as she leans forward.

"Only for 6 months," I respond with shame.

"How did it go?" Donna sits back.

My memory of my first personal therapy experience, in Los Angeles with Dr. K, comes back to my mind.

I am flipping through a phone book looking for a therapist on a Sunday afternoon in my apartment. Getting 40 hours of personal therapy sessions is one of the requirements for my Master's degree. There aren't many Japanese-speaking therapists even in the big city of Los Angeles. As I'm flipping through the phone book, I'm thinking about the conversation I had with a cognitive psychology professor who was Japanese. He mentioned that it would be difficult for a patient to undergo therapy and analysis in a second language because childhood memories are in your native language. I feel as if I must find a Japanese-speaking therapist. One ad in the phone book captures my eye because it contains a drawing of the therapist's face. Growing up in the 1970's in Japan, I read Manga books and watched animated TV shows every day. Cartoons were part of daily life, so I choose Dr. K, a cartoon therapist.

Making my appointment with Dr. K is easy. I leave a voice mail. He calls me back and we talk, it is easy to communicate in Japanese. I arrive at Dr. K's office fifteen minutes early. The two-story building is empty on this Saturday afternoon. I am alone in the waiting room. There are a few children's books on the side table in front of the window, those books are written in Japanese. I glance at the books, and then turn my eyes to the door. Five minutes after my appointment time, the door finally opens, and a man appears with a smile and says "Konichiwa." He is a middle-aged Japanese man, average height and weight. Speaking Japanese is still a natural thing for me even after years living and going to school in the U.S., but speaking Japanese in a therapy session is a new exercise. Although I am on time for every session to show my respect for the authority of the older man, I have nothing to say to this stranger. Talking and being with a Japanese man brought me back to the world of "Don't think, don't talk." As Dr. K asks me questions and I answer diplomatically, I sit on the couch with proper posture and pay attention to Dr. K. I act as if I were a good Japanese girl until

## - The Beginning -

one warm sunny afternoon, when Dr. K falls asleep during a Saturday session.

"Dr. K, why are you doing boke-boke?" I ask calmly. After a short silence, Dr. K responds, "How rude, what do you mean? Does it look like I'm doing boke-boke?" His expression makes me think of an animated character with smoke coming out of his ears. "Boke-boke" is a Japanese idiom, meaning something like losing your head or growing senile or being mentally slow or befuddled. I smile when he gets offended.

It seems as if I catch Dr. K completely by surprise. I can't help wondering if taking a nap during weekend sessions is his routine, but no Japanese clients ever confronted him. I'm insulted not only by his rudeness, but also by the fact that he is offended by my comment after he insulted me by falling asleep during a session. In Japanese culture, the way I, as a younger female, confronted Dr. K, who is an older male with an advanced degree, is considered impolite. I am not deliberately trying to offend him. I am just incapable of following cultural rules. Nonetheless, it would have been better if I had followed those rules.

Dr. K is not fond of me after all, which I can understand as a Japanese who shares the same cultural background. I experience rejection from my first therapist, but this is not my first rejection. I was rejected by my own mother, by most Japanese universities I applied to in Japan, by my Japanese husband, and now, by my Japanese therapist. It is not a big deal, I've done this before. I bury my feelings all deep in the ground, pick myself up and move on. I complete 40 hours of personal therapy sessions with Dr. K and graduate. Shorty after my graduation, my disappointment in therapy leads me to go back to Japan to get a job.

## - The Moon Home -

"Actually, I've decided to come here because I broke up with a minister a few weeks ago. I also divorced my second husband before that." I defensively cool down and change the subject to erase my shameful memories of failed therapy, but I understand deep down that my beliefs, decisions, and actions are no longer working. Donna continues to listen.

"I don't think it's normal to have a second divorce before age forty," I say as I look down at the beige carpet, "at least in my culture." I pause again.

"My first divorce was in my twenties, and my second was in my thirties. Statistically, I am getting divorced every ten years. I don't want to end up a woman with seven divorces when my hair gets all white. That would not be good." I look at Donna.

Donna is curious. "How did you meet your second husband? How long were you married to him?"

"My second husband and I both worked on the same street. Our marriage did not last long. It was very short." I look down. "He looked like Sponge Bob. When I called him Sponge Bob, he laughed. He was four years younger than me." The memory of my second husband and divorce comes back to me.

Randy and I see each other every morning at a coffee shop near our offices on Martin Luther Kind Boulevard. We start saying good morning to each other. One morning, he introduces himself and tells me that he is a school teacher. Randy started his job six months before he met me, and I started my new job

## - The Beginning -

a month before I met Randy. He came to Los Angeles from Pennsylvania, and I came to Los Angeles from Japan. We are both new to Los Angeles, we both haven't made many friends. His eyes sparkle when he sees me, his eyes twinkle when he looks at me. He asks If I would like to go to dinner with him on Saturday night, so I agree to go. He lives in Redondo Beach and I live in Torrance. He tells me that he will make a reservation at an Italian restaurant in Manhattan Beach.

I wake up early on Saturday morning and realize that I don't have any clothes to wear for the date. I came to Los Angeles with one suitcase when I got this new job. After digging into my closet, I decide to drive to the mall to get some clothes for my first date in America. The moment I park my car at the mall parking lot on Hawthorne Boulevard, my cell phone rings. An unknown number shows, but I answer. It's Mother. Her voice is weak, something is different. She says she has been diagnosed with thyroid cancer. "Mother, I can't go back now," I response with anger. "I know. Don't worry." Her voice becomes weaker, as if her shadow were speaking. "I just started this job, and I'm on probation," I tell her with an irritated voice. "I know. I will be fine. I'm going to have surgery next week," she whispers. "Ok, I'll call you in a few days," I say in a monotone and hang up, and I start thinking about getting a plane ticket to go back.

I sit for a while and think about the reason why I am so upset about her illness. When I left Japan to come to America for the first time in 1990, Mother was hospitalized for one month for kidney problems. I remember that I was thinking about canceling my flight to America, which would mean that I would have to cancel my first quarter in college. Now that I have a job I would probably lose it if I go back to Japan. Every time my new life is about to start, Mother announces that she is ill. Why does she get ill every time I decide to do something? Mother has mostly been a vegetarian, she never smokes or drinks, she never gets ill. I don't remember her even staying in bed for colds or flu. How does she get ill? Why is she doing this to me? Suddenly, the feeling of guilt comes. I'm thinking about my job over Mother's life. I don't need a new dress, instead, I start driving, and think about canceling my date tonight and about getting a ticket to go back to Japan.

After parking my car on the street, in front of my apartment, I call Randy. His answering machine picks up, so I hang up. I've never cancelled a date in English, I don't know what to say. I sit for a while thinking about what to do next. I have to eat dinner either by myself or with someone, so I decide to have dinner with someone who I don't know very well.

Randy comes to my apartment to pick me up at 5:30 pm – he is on time. He is wearing a well-ironed long sleeve shirt, but I'm wearing jeans – no makeup. Randy smiles at me with his sparkling eyes, and I look at him with a fake smile to mask my fear about Mother's illness. He opens the car door for me to get in, and I smile at him once more. He takes me to a small Italian restaurant in Manhattan Beach, and we sit at the table face to face. He talks about his job and family, he asks me about my job and family. He is from a small town in Pennsylvania, and he has never seen or talked to Asians from Asia. He is curious and asks me about the beliefs, customs, and history of Japan. He seems to be interested in getting to know me and my family, and I try so hard to avoid my feelings and forget about my

## - The Beginning -

family. The past keep rising up on the small wooden table. The yellow small flowers on the table are too bright. The more I try not to talk about Mother, the more I'm filled with fear. I start telling Randy about Mother and the phone call this morning. He suggests that we spend time together on the day Mother is to have surgery. He has no reason to come and spend time with me on Mother's surgery day, I feel. I am comfortable being alone when I'm sick or sad, so I'm reluctant to accept his offer, but Randy insists. He drops me off in front of my apartment and gets out. He pulls me toward him and kisses on my cheek, and says good bye.

Later the same week, Randy visits me in my apartment on the day of Mother's thyroid cancer surgery. He does not want me to be alone on the day of Mother's surgery; he wants to make sure I have someone to talk to. He brings a Neil Diamond video for us to watch while I'm waiting for my mother's surgery to be done. We watch the video while eating pizza. "Coming to America" and "Sweet Caroline" fill the silence between us — we keep watching without exchanging a word. After we finish watching the video, Randy asks me to call my father. I hesitate to make a call. Randy tells me that he will not leave until I call. His right hand reaches for the phone, and I take the phone from his hand. It's 9 pm in Los Angeles and 1 pm in Japan. I call Father's cell phone, he answers and tells me that Mother's surgery was successful. She is sleeping and will be able to go home in two weeks. After the tension dissipated, and Randy sees me smile, he starts sharing the story of his father dying of brain cancer years ago. He mentions how his father's death affected his faith for a while. As I listen to him, I feel he is releasing his

## The Moon Home

emotions that he has been holding onto. The time seems to pass very quickly, but we both have to work tomorrow. When Randy stands at the door to leave, I pull him toward me and tightly squeeze his broad shoulders. As I watch him leaving, I thank him for the video and pizza, instead of thanking him for spending time with me. That night, I don't have any dreams.

The following month, Randy invites me to his nephew's Bar Mitzvah at a hotel in Redondo Beach. All of his relatives are coming from the east coast. I have no idea what the Bar Mitzvah is about, but I put my hair up and put on a sleeveless knee length black dress for the evening party. That evening, before the music and dancing, Randy introduces me to his mother, brothers, and everybody else. Before I know it, I'm surrounded by Randy's family and their two hundred guests. When I notice that I'm the only Asian in the room, I feel a bit self-conscious, so I stay behind Randy, instead of socializing.

A month ago, Randy's nephew, David, turned 13. David wears a black suit – he looks confident. He finds me and says hi and keeps talking to his friends. In front of fine food and drinks on the table, people are dancing the Hora, which is dancing around in circles as they sing Havah Nagilah. In the Hebrew language, it means let us rejoice, Randy tells me. David is lifted on a chair in the middle of the circle. I've never seen a chair-lifted dance in person, but I don't question the meaning of the song or dance, I just dance with them. Once Grandpa told me, there is no "why" in life, just dance. The night is not over, the DJ announces the last dance. "Is it OK with you if I dance with my mom?" Randy asks with his eyebrows up. "Sure." I tilt my head slightly to the left and look at his face. I sit at the table by myself until the last dance is over.

That same winter, Randy proposes to me at Disneyland in front of Mickey, Goofy, and Donald Duck. His beautiful brown eyes crinkle and sparkle when he looks at me. His cheeks turn red when he says he is madly in love with me. I feel wanted, loved, and protected. I say "Yes!" to his proposal. Mickey, Goofy and Donald Duck are witnesses.

I'm dreaming I am in the forest. There's a large spruce, blue-green with flexible needles and little aroma. Its branches turn slightly upward, and its branches become extremely dense, creating a good nesting site for woodpeckers. I'm on the top of the tree. The spruce moves left and right. I move left and right. There are three small apes on the ground. They are all looking at me with big round eyes. Their eyes are like white eggs with brown yolks. They want something from me. I have to stay. They are little, seem harmless, and look innocent, yet I hesitate to come down from the tree. They keep staring at me with their eyes wide open. I'm on top of the tree. I have nowhere to escape. I don't see myself, but I feel I must look like them. It fills me with fear. What do they want from me?

Abruptly, my eyes open. I wonder what could have woken me. My neck muscles ache, I may have slept the wrong way. The blue light from the TV lightens the dark room. I think I must have fallen asleep as I was watching TV. The clock on the TV shows 8:55 pm. "Zip-A-Dee-Do-Dah," the Mickey Mouse parade song, is coming from the TV. The song plays endlessly. I'm imagining those three small apes on the ground in my dream; they could be advanced animals or pre-humans. It seems as if I have a lack of awareness of the other part of myself or I'm unable to make a distinction between myself and the natural world. Suddenly, Randy speaks softly, "Honey, do you remember that day? We were there." I realize he is lying down next to me. His eyes are stuck on the TV. "Yes," I say to him without turning my head from the TV. "It was a good day," he tries to sound optimistic but it comes out more hopeless. "Yes, it was," I respond with a soulless voice.

We continue watching TV so that we don't pay attention to the darkness of the room. The Mickey Mouse parade song never sounded so sad and empty. The dimly orange light next to the TV spotlights the dust on the wood floor. I feel an ache in my chest as if there is not enough air in the room. Having a strange tightening sensation, trying to grasp something so small that it can't be seen and held. I rouse myself from the bed without looking at him. Two pillows drop to the floor at the foot of the bed. My bare feet reach the wood floor – it's cold. When I stand in front of the bathroom mirror, the tile floor feels even colder. I stare at the mirror and am relieved that I am not an ape, then I realize that I don't remember the last time I saw my face in the mirror. Why am I choosing to stay in this marriage and helping him get healthy when I have no energy to take care of him? I have to end this before Mickey Mouse overtakes my life.

## - The Beginning -

I've been rejected by my parents, and I know rejection would hurt. In any case, I always wanted to believe people are able to change, grow, or get better if they receive love and care. That's what I do. It's called therapy. The phenomenon is seductive to people like me, a therapist, but he wasn't the person I'd hoped he would be. The question is; am I satisfied with the changes he made or am I afraid that he is going to back to the way he was?

Before I figure out what it is all about, I free myself by saying goodbye to the marriage. The divorce is a relief although I still have love for him. Randy calls me on Valentine's Day and my birthday even after we have divorced. Randy went back to Pennsylvania after our divorce. I'm feeling lonely. Is it because he left? Is it because my fantasy is gone? We still hang on to the memories of all the good times when we talk. Every couple has good times and bad times. The question is whether the ratios necessarily reflect reality. What percent of our time together was good and what percent was bad. The ratios might not be it. Even when 90% of the time spent together is wonderful, 10% of crucial damage would brake us apart. What is a happy marriage? I never knew what a happy marriage is.

"Randy, my second husband is still calling me and I'm still answering his calls," I say in an irritable voice.

"Do you miss him?" Donna asks.

"I don't miss our fights," I quickly reply to her.

"What do you miss?" Donna asks again.

"When his eyes would sparkle when he saw me," I slowly respond to her.

When I hear myself out loud, I realize that Randy's sparkling eyes were what I missed – they were flirtatious. As soon as I hear my own voice, my eyes open, I have to admit that is a missing piece. After all those years of dating numerous men, Japanese or American, I still can't get it right. I feel as if I am a failure again. From the moment I left Randy, feelings of rejection, loneliness, and emptiness return from childhood, when I needed love and care and didn't receive them from own mother. If my own mother didn't bother to love me, why should others possibly love me, I must be totally worthless.

"How's your parents' relationship?"

I say nothing.

"Were there any people around you that you think were happily married when you were growing up?"

I remain silent. My heart is empty at this important moment.

"Anybody in your family? Aunts or uncles?"

Donna looks in my eyes as if she knows why I stumble over the answers.

"My parents are still married. No one in my family is divorced, except me." I cannot think of any couple that is happily married, so I smile helplessly and look at Donna for guidance.

"Do you know about yourself? What kind of person you want to be?" Donna asks.

Nothing comes out from my mouth, but I wish to answer her question.

## - The Beginning -

"How do you feel now?" Donna does not give up.

I look down and avoid her eyes, but my mind tells me that I have to say something.

"I don't know how I feel," I say, thinking that it sounds peculiar, especially from people like me, a therapist.

"That's why you are here," Donna says placidly.

My gaze moves to her from the floor. My unspoken voice is heard for the first time in a long time. Donna's simple word brings me back to the base line, and my floating mind and heart are grounded. Her nature reminds me of someone, someone who I know very well. The feeling of nostalgic or being home returns without knowing why.

"I would like to work with you," Donna says as she looks directly at me. My eyes are wildly open, like an owl in a tree in a dark night. No one ever chose me. For the first time in my life, I am chosen by someone. Donna devotes her full attention to the conversation, nothing could make her hurried or distracted. As Donna's eyes light up and her eyes sparkle, my heartbeat slightly increases with feelings of anxiety and excitement. I feel as if I am just waking up from a long hibernation, I feel as if I am five years old again, I have found a home. After Donna and I set our next meeting, I leave her office. Outside, it's dark and chilly, so I put my jacket on. I get back into my car and sit for a while. As I look at the ginkgo trees lining the street, I realize that my roots aren't yet strong enough to crack and open the concrete, but I begin to see a little hope. I sit a little longer without turning the engine on. It feels so fragile that if I start to drive, it might be taken away from me. How can I hold on this feeling longer?

***SESSION: See In Your Eyes, Not Mine***
"Right after my divorce with Randy, I was dating many guys without processing what went wrong with our marriage. I guess it was a rebound." I sigh to express my tiredness. I keep looking at the carpet. Donna is listening.

"Recently I broke up with three men. I'm tired of dating, dating unsuccessfully. They were all in their late thirties, educated, tall, never been married, never had children. They were good on paper. They sounded like perfect catches. They said they were interested in me and ready to make commitments." I look at Donna and ask, "What's wrong with me?" I quickly look down to the floor and continue, "I make bad decisions. I can't trust my judgment." I keep looking down.

"What's happening? What happened with those guys?" Donna asks.

"I can't bring my ex boyfriends into my sessions and ask you what is wrong with them, so I brought some of their writings so that you can tell me what is wrong with them." I pull post cards and a letter from my bag, and hand them to Donna. I want Donna to see with her eyes, not mine.

"May I?" Donna reaches out her hand as she speaks. I nod my head. Donna starts reading the four post cards. The post cards are from Carl, who is a satellite engineer from New Jersey. He sent them from his trip to Asia. Carl had failed in his mission and found another mission in Asia, and upon returning to Los Angeles, he starts dating a woman who followed him on his Kyoto trip.

#1. Dear Yasuko – I am writing this after getting back from my trek. (I tried calling a few times-ob-

## - The Beginning -

viously unsuccessful.) It was a great – easily the best part of my trip so far. I went with a guide to villages tourists do no usually go to. Not an easy hike (high 80's, humid) but worth it. The villagers were almost as fascinated by me (my beard, my digital camera) as I was by them. As an engineer I found their huts interesting, but I also found the people very interesting. They were very friendly, but they were also shy – especially the women. I would have liked to talk to them more, but ....
And finally, the cuisine. I had a tribal delicacy – roasted bee larva. Yummy! Anyway, if I ever come back to Thailand I will have to spend more time in the hills.

Love, Carl

P.S. I really enjoy some Thai art – Hence this postcard.


#2. Hi Yasuko – I am in Korea now and so far I like it as much as Thailand (except for my stay at the Teibal village) although it is very different. First, the esthetic is much less ornate, much more like Japan, although the Koreans wouldn't like my saying that. I much prefer the simpler esthetic of Korea and Japan. Second, the Korean culture is very different from Thai. It is a relief not to be fighting off scams; to just be able to relax. Last night I wandered out to find kimbop (a cheap

*- The Moon Home -*

Korean version of Sushi) and was in a section of town where it was actually hard to walk there were so many other people. And they were almost all couples – either two women or a woman and a man and in both cases they were normally holding hands. Very endearing but very different. Very foreign. And I am also finding the Koreans very friendly. Every time I open my map someone comes to help me, sometimes walking a little way to point out the right road. Anyway, right now I am waiting to get into a traditional Korean dance, and it should be starting shortly. So, I hope things are going well with you. See you in about two weeks.

Love, Carl


#3. Dear Yasuko – Although we are not actually getting to see anything like this, I would love to be able to. Just the wrong time of year right now. Oh well. I imagine that the reality is nowhere as peaceful as this looks (huge crowds for cherry blossoms), but nonetheless spectacular. I like the Japanese esthetic even more than the Korean. The Japanese esthetic is a little more formal, a little more structured than Korean, but still very simple. I really enjoyed the war memorial in Tokyo (regardless of its social significance) and the garden in back. Anyway, on my way to Kyoto

## - The Beginning -

today.

Still miss you.

Those cards were intelligently written and full of information, and, yet not quite connected with my heart. I feel as if I am reading a travel book that was written for the general public, not for me personally. "Look forward to seeing you in a week," Carl signed off. In Kyoto, Carl became intimate with a woman who followed him to Kyoto from Los Angeles.

Donna finishes the postcards and opens a letter from Brent, the minister from Wisconsin. Brent was excited about possibility of a future together after he brought me to meet his parents in Wisconsin. I was sick during the trip and was even sicker after my return.

Yasuko,

I know and appreciate that this is a confusing time for you as you sort out your feelings about our relationship. I don't want to make that process more difficult for you but I wanted to take the time to state as clearly as I can my feelings toward you. I, too, need to sort some things out but there are some things I know to be true. First, I find myself very much attracted to you. You have a striking beauty and grace that has the power to take my breath away. I don't know if I have told you that enough and for that I am more sorry that words can express. You have a strength and maturity that moves me. Just knowing you – your judgment, courage, sense of

## - The Moon Home -

yourself – make me want to be a better person. I watch you with the people who are important to you; listen as you talk with friends on the phone; and how you intersect with my family and friends and I see a grace, close, and sense of yourself that makes me glad to have you in my life. You have a generosity, compassion, and gentleness that shows not only your strength of character but your soul as well. And what does this lead me to? It leads me to want even more. When we are together, I don't want it to end. When we are both silent, I find myself wanting to know what you are thinking and feeling. I want to know how work is and what you are happy about or struggling with. I want to hear about your talks with your friends and how you are moved by them. I want to know what you are proud of; angry at; happy with; sad about; frustrated with; excited about. My greatest joys are making you laugh and bringing you happiness. It tears me up to bring you tears and confusion. I don't know how and where our relationship is going. I guess we both have some work to do but I do know that I will never regret knowing you and loving you. I also know that I want and hope to know you and love you deeper and more fully. There is so much more that I could write about what causes me to feel the way that I do about you. Just know that I consider myself blessed to be as close to you as

## - The Beginning -

I am and I want to come closer if you want it too. I have never felt the way I do for anyone else and can't imagine ever doing so.

The letter was kindly, sincerely and beautifully written, yet not fully connected with my mind, as if I were reading a part of captivating novel that I wasn't in. The hidden part of him remains unknown, and our relationship puzzled me even more after the beautiful letter. "Please know I love you," Brent closed his letter. Two weeks later, we broke up.

Donna finishes reading the letter and puts it back in the envelope. She looks at the address on the upper left corner of the envelope. She quietly returns the post cards and letter to me.

"I received my ex's wedding invitation this week. My two exes got engaged shortly after we broke up. They got new lives. I should be happy for them. I'm still here, the same apartment, same job, and stuck in the same life." Am I nostalgic about my past relationships? Did I make mistakes? Did I miss the boat and I will just have to live with that? My head is down.

"I'm still alone. I should have married one of them," I mumble, still looking at the floor.

"Do you feel jealous when you think of your exes with other women?" Donna asks.

My face is blank.

"Do you wish to be with them?" Donna rephrases.

"No," I quickly reply to her.

"Then, that's not jealousy, it's envy," Donna confirms.

I sit, motionlessly.

"They have something you wish you have." Donna demonstrates her keen eye.

"I really don't want to envy anybody. It's an ugly feeling. But it's true, I don't envy Josh because he doesn't have anybody. He is still single, and most likely he will be alone for the rest of his life," I'm nodding as I speak, and I begin to whimper.

Josh, 42 years old, 6 feet tall, 200 pounds, is a former college hockey player in Minnesota. The day after Valentine's day, he comes to my office to pick me up for a hokey game date. I'm waiting for him in front of my office building. Is he going to bring flowers or chocolates? He gets out of his car, and has no flowers or chocolates in his hands. He wears a dark brown polo shirt and beige chino pants with brown leather shoes. He has a receding hairline, but it's less noticeable because of his light hair color. He smiles when he sees me, but he gives me no hug and no kiss. He opens the car door for me, and gently closes the door when I get in.

This is our third date. We don't talk much while we are in the car. Josh says he's never been married and has never had children. He doesn't say whether he wants to get married or not. He takes me to his office in downtown Los Angeles. He says he is the vice president of an insurance company. In front of his office, there are five desks for his assistants. Some people work even on Saturdays in this company, he says. He introduces me to his colleagues and assistants. As he is talking, he keeps one eye on me while his other eye is on his assistant. Does he think I might steal something? I get closer to the window and look out. There is nothing to look at but other high-rise buildings

## - The Beginning -

in downtown L.A. I look at the shiny floor and wonder why he takes me to his office and introduces me to his colleagues.

After Josh gives me a tour of the office, he takes me to a hockey game at the Staples Center in downtown L.A. Watching hockey games on the weekends later becomes our weekly routine. He gets us third-row seats that cost a few hundred dollars each. He says his company gave him his car and hockey tickets for free. I know the hockey rules, I grew up in the far north of Japan, and ski slopes and skating rinks were some of my childhood playgrounds. Between the first and second period, Josh leaves his seat to get a beer. I follow Josh, I try to not lose him. Hundreds of people are passing by, the crowd makes me swoon. I tell him that I have to go to the lady's room. He says he'll wait in front of the bar. When I come back from the lady's room, I see Josh talking to several women who look as if they are out of Vogue magazine. Josh introduces me to his 6 feet tall blonde friends. They look at me with confusion, and quickly back to focus on him. Josh never turns his eyes off of me while he is listening to his friends. I pretend looking at a pretzel store. Though they are not eyes of love, his eyes are continuously on me. Does he want to show off to me about his Swedish model friends? Does he want me to know that he could have those women instead of me? Is he waiting to see if I accuse him of talking to other women, so that he would know if I'm a crazy jealous bitch? What does he want from me? I have to figure it out.

Josh is always on time when he picks me up and takes me to nice restaurants near the beach, but he never holds my hand or touches me. After four weeks from our first date, he invites me to one of his houses, a one story house with a yard in Palos Verdes. There is an elementary school across the street. A dark brown suede sofa sits in front of a fireplace in the living room. His golf bag and hockey gear are in the hallway. Trophies and plaques from golf and hockey are on the shelf in the living room. I look around but there is nothing suspicious. In the kitchen, there is no toaster or blender on the counter. He probably eats out, or he does not live here. A bright white light shines on the simple wood dining table next to the white kitchen counter. He cooks steak in a frying pan, and while the steak cooks, he opens a bottle of Pinot. We have nothing to talk about – we just eat. After dinner, he invites me to sit on the sofa and watch a golf tournament on TV. I notice eight inches of space between us. Then, he falls asleep. When the golf tournament on TV is over, I remove myself from the sofa, and it wakes him up. He says he will take me home. On the way back to my place, he detours. He pulls over to the sidewalk and says, "This is my condo." I say nothing. He drives around the condo, and gets back to the road. Why is he showing me his property? What was the house that I just had dinner? Does he live in the house or the condo or somewhere else? I don't ask questions. Verbalizing thoughts and asking questions are considered to be demanding in my culture.

The following week, on Friday night, Josh takes me to a bistro in downtown Los Angeles. We are escorted to the table next to the window. We sit not next to each other, but face to face. Josh orders a bottle of red wine. "Your birthday is coming." He sips the red wine from a wine glass. "I'm thinking about getting tickets to Paris for your birthday." He smiles without blinking. The yellow candlelight on the table illuminates his face. We look

## The Beginning

at each other with an awkward silence. Something is not clear here, but I don't mention. Instead, "I've never been to Paris," I say with a calm voice to hide my confusion and anxiety. He still looks at me warmly. "How much money do you make a year?" He looks at me as he is cutting a piece of rib-eye. "32 K," I say honestly. "Why are you working? Why don't you quit your job and live with me and play golf every day?" His steak knife stops moving. I keep staring at the knife in my left hand and keep cutting a piece of filet mignon, pretending I did not understand his question. Then, he brings up a more appropriate question. "How's your work?" Josh asks. "I came back to LA a year ago. I'm learning new English at work." I look at him. "What kind of new English?" he asks curiously. "I provide group therapy sessions. People in my group are comfortable using the F word as an adjective. I have also learned the word for mother and father," I chuckle. Josh's green eyes become puzzling ones. He repeats the letters, "mother and father…" In three seconds, he is able to fill the blank in his head. He laughs out loud and keeps laughing. The tickets to Paris are no longer a significant topic for us. As he lost his focus, we lost the way to get to Paris. Thanks to mother and father.

The very next day, I drive to Josh's house at 5 a.m. I park my car in his garage and Josh drives us to the golf course. As usual, we don't talk much in the car. The 405 freeway is empty this early on a Saturday morning. Josh parks his car in a parking lot by the beautiful golf course. Josh finds a shiny black Porsche on the parking lot and says "Kris is here." There are not many people in the clubhouse, but there are golfers out on the course. Josh says, "I'll get a cup of coffee. Order anything you want." "Where is the menu?" I ask. "There is no menu. Just say what you'd like." Josh smiles and winks. A waiter comes, and I tell him "I'd like to have some fruit, please." Josh orders a cup of coffee and eggs. I notice his eyes keep looking at me, so I turn my head to the window, and pretend to look outside. Josh puts a half and a half into his coffee and says, "You'll meet my friends." I think of the shiny black Porsche in the parking lot. What kind of man drives that type of car? All my life, I've thought Porsches are not real cars. There is no Porsches in Hokkaido. I work in South Central L.A. and live in Torrance, and I don't see Porsches there, either. This whole thing makes me very uncomfortable. I've already met his colleagues. Why does he want me to keep meeting his people? When I finally look at Josh, the waiter brings me a whole pineapple that looks like a flower decorated with berries and grapes. Slices of mangos and watermelons are around the plate. It looks like a party plate for thirty people. "Enjoy." The waiter looks at me with a big smile. "I meant a cup of fruit." I look at Josh with the biggest Asian eyes ever. "That's a lot of fruit." He sips his coffee and smiles. The ostentatious fruit display overrides my thoughts about the Porsche. For a moment, I forget about searching for Josh's motives.

After Jose signs for breakfast, he and I walk to the golf course to catch up with his friend, Kris. Josh introduces me to Kris and some other friends. Kris looks as if he's in his late thirties, handsome and well mannered. Josh's friends are all friendly, but they are focusing on their game. Josh pulls me aside and whispers, "Kris just had a baby boy. The mother and baby are living in his condo. Kris lives in his own house. Kris pays for everything

## - The Beginning -

for the mother, so that the mother can stay home and raise his child. The mother goes shopping every day." Josh searches for reactions in my eyes. "Would you be interested in that kind of arrangement?" I finally figure it out. Josh is searching for something important in his life. It's a serious business investment, looking for some important property, a copy machine for offspring. He is looking for someone to have his baby without getting married and raise the child in his condo that is separated from his house. "Marriage is not a good investment in California. Smart men have children without marriage," he says with unassailable confidence.

It is such a release. I spend my time and energy wondering why a date did not go well, why I cannot understand his odd behavior, whether I am seeing the truth about him, and whether I am crazy to think that he is not good for me. What Josh has been doing for the past a few months is researching and assessing a potential mother of his child. For months, I'd tried to justify his odd behaviors and figure out his motives. I could not give up until I figured it out. Now, I can move on to the next question, which is what did Josh see in me that led him to think that I might deliver his baby and stay home without marriage? What made me keep seeing him? Why couldn't I just ask him a question? I cannot say no to him, especially for such a generous offer, so I ghost him instead. Saying no is inappropriate in Japanese culture. Saying no has a deeper meaning to me, as I find out later on in the therapy.

"I don't want to change my partner every two years. I get intimate with a man, and then I get bored. I didn't get bored with Josh because he's never touched me, and he acted mysterious and suspicious."

"You get bored or you think you will get hurt?" Donna asks and I don't respond, so she rephrases.

"What's the worst thing that could happen when you get intimate with a man?"

"The man might leave me," I say tentatively.

"Is that how you really feel or you got it from the textbook?" Donna challenges me.

I look at her intently.

"Are you afraid of getting to know the person, or are you afraid of the person leaving you after they get to know you?" Donna gives me a gentle push.

"Men never left me. Well, they left me, but I never put my whole self into the relationships. I was chasing a rainbow that does not exist, but it looks pretty from distance. I wanted to hold on to the beauty. I don't know what I'm looking for." I say as I look at Donna's perfect shiny shoes.

"What would happen if you got intimate with a person you respected?" Out of the corner of my eye, I see Donna watching me feeling anxious. How do I get away from her question? Then, the old clueless reflex takes over me. My mind tells me to run. I want to run towards the dark hallway. I push it all down. Am I giving myself away? Donna looks straight into my eyes.

"I would lose respect, I would lose interest," I say. At this time, I couldn't run, instead, my eyes are glued to the beige carpet.

## - The Beginning -

"You have sex when you don't know the person. You lose sexual interest when you get to know the person. When the relationship becomes sexual, you lose respect," Donna speaks gently.

I keep looking at the carpet, so Donna speaks again.

"It sounds as if you tend to date men who are boring or bad, so you can avoid intimacy. By doing so, you don't have to be exposed to overwhelming deep basic unmet needs still inside of you. You are afraid of intimacy, so you feel anxious," Donna continues, "You saw red flags in the men from the beginning, and you kept seeing them. You doubted your gut feeling," Donna says undoubtedly.

Donna pauses so that I can catch up my mind. Usually I start with intuition, and the reasons come later, but when it comes to men, my intuition becomes an illusion and cannot be trusted. I doubt myself when I start feeling untruthfulness from men. Donna encourages self reliance in times of self doubt; my eyes slowly move from the floor and look at Donna's eyes.

"Would you be able to hurt them if you were in a similar situation next time?"

I don't answer her question. I have difficulty rejecting people who have a negative influence on me, so I keep them. How do I change the habit? What are my deep unmet needs?

After I lost my beliefs, innocence, and existence as a child, I no longer trusted my intuition. Over the years, I built a wall to protect myself so that no one could ever get through me. Then I survived, not by feeling but by suppressing. Each time I deny my intuition, the wall gets taller and thicker. The more I date, the more I fail. For me to recover, I might have to tear down the wall that I've built over the years. There might be some doors that impede progress. Perhaps I need several keys to open the closed doors. A hammer or crowbar may be necessary to open the doors that are nailed shut. In therapy, we revisit childhood not because we are trying to fix it, but so that we can separate it from the adult who can make choices. Can I trust this woman to teach me how to use those tools and remove the wall that I've built so that I can put down my new roots? Is it possible for me to have powerful roots that can even crack and open the concrete?

## CHAPTER FIVE
## Death, Compulsion and Secret
### 五

I'm dreaming I'm in an elevator made of glass, and it's going up. I cannot get out, I believe. I should not get out, I know. The elevator stops on the fifth floor, and strangers get in. Strangers get out. But I have to stay. The glass elevator keeps going up until I can see trees and buildings below. Above me, I notice the elevator has a single wire that is too thin, too fragile for an elevator of this size, but it continues up, it continues to stop at floor after floor, and people get out.

And when they exit, the elevator sways left, and then right, fragile, sensitive to the weight change, but it continues up to the next stop. Men and women leave. Again, the elevator sways, and as it sways, I turn my eyes to the bottom where gray apartment buildings and houses are lined up in rows like ants in an ant colony — a few oak trees with knobby trunks bend as if they are following the sunlight. So many people are in the big city. I am alone. Everybody left.

**SESSION: Loss**

"Did you have anyone who was really close to you when you were growing up?" Donna asks.

"That would be my Grandma," I respond immediately. Donna keeps looking at me, so I decide to continue. "She died when I was 12." I gaze down at a wood table next to Donna.

"What happened?" Donna asks.

I pause. "She was..," suddenly, the blast from the past, I choke. Sudden tightness of the esophagus and blurry vision turn my mind empty. I try to fight back the horrible choking sensation. Now, I am afraid to see Donna, so I keep looking down at the carpet. Instead of focusing on my feelings, I focus on her office floor. If I look at her face, I might not hide my feelings. The simple words do not come out from my mouth. I try to take a deep breath, but I can't breathe in. I clear my throat and I try again. "She was…" Something is clogging up. The more I fight, the more I become stuck. I wait for 5 seconds so that I won't cry like a crazy person in front of a stranger, my therapist who I just met a few weeks ago. At the third attempt, which is filled with confusion, I say, "She was ill." The moment those words come out from my mouth, tears burst out from my eyes. I am not able to stop my tears from running down my cheek. I'm scared. Tears continuously overflow my eyes but I don't wipe my tears, hoping that Donna won't know that I'm crying. I'm still pretending.

For the first time in my life, I speak about my Grandma's death. Anger is still pouring over me, it's still under my skin and in my organs. After 25 years, my body remembers the profound and confusing disappointment and uncontrollable anger – my pain is real. "My father told me to stop crying, so I had to stop." Tears stream down my face. My runny nose becomes water, and it runs all over my face. Donna sits very still in front of me.

After a long moment of silence, I take 3 breaths followed by deep exhales. When I exhale, the air comes back into my lungs automatically. As my breathing become soft and tender, my shoulders drop down deep into the back of the couch. Donna reaches up to grasp a Kleenex and hand it to me to blow my nose so that I breathe more. All the water stored in my body from my childhood comes out from my eyes and nose. When I recuperate from the exhaustion of sobbing, Donna slowly sits back in her beige leather arm chair. She waits patiently for my mind to catch up.

After I re-lived the loss, all the fluids from my body rose up in the air and evaporated into the room. When shame and guilt are drained away, my anger and pain slowly fade away. Now I can see, I can remember, and I can talk. It was full of dark, perplexing pain that I could not comprehend when I was a child, so I buried the feelings.

There is still a large amount of snow in early March in Hokkaido. I'm preparing for a middle school entrance exam in my room on a Sunday afternoon. The heater makes the room too warm and dry. My desk faces the frosted window, so the landscape outside is blurry. The phone rings. Mother answers the phone in the living room. I can't hear her voice clearly. Mother hangs up the phone quickly, comes to my room, and says the phone call was from Grandpa. Grandma has not eaten for days. I drop my pencil and get up from my desk chair. Quickly, Mother and I get into the car and drive to visit Grandma. When the snow becomes more like a sorbet, spring is almost here. I enter from the main entrance, and walk behind Grandpa through the living room and the dining room. The meditation room is open. It's dark – it's very dark – it's cold – it's very cold. There is no flower arrangement on the tokonoma in the tatami room. There is no song, no dance, no bedtime story. My haiku and tanka disappeared.

In meditation room, Grandma is lying on the futon bed on a tatami mat. Her body is covered by a heavy futon, but her head, with its mop of white hair, is on the pillow. The white pillow cover has become yellow. Her chin touches her neck. When I see her gray skin and oval face, she seems to float up in the air. I'm standing in front of her, I'm scared to move, I'm losing my voice. "Yasuko is here to see you," Grandpa says to Grandma. Grandma opens her eyes with her last strength. She gazes, but she doesn't have enough strength to say a word. When I look at her colorless eyes, her face becomes blurry. Grandpa leaves and quickly returns with apple sauce he made. He asks me to feed Grandma, so I bring a spoonful of apple sauce to her mouth. Her jaw turns into a shell, the spoon won't go into her mouth, she doesn't have enough energy to sip. I close my eyes before Grandma closes hers so that I won't see her pain. I can't take care of a beloved woman who took such exquisite care of me. Unbearable shame and intolerable guilt are trapped in my gut. The next day, Grandma dies.

## Death, Compulsion and Secret

There is nothing I want to say and need to say. My face is down and it remains down. I keep my body hunching.

"When you were with your grandmother, you felt you were accepted, but it was such a short period of time. Every time you get that warm feeling, you believed the feeling soon would be gone," Donna looks at me.

"You've been angry. Your parents did not take care of the person who took care of you and loved you. Your father could not handle his own sadness and pain so he told you not to cry." Donna is solid.

I look at Donna without a word. Father's pain was too much to add to my own, Father told me not to cry, so I tried not to cry for most of my life. Then, I stopped feeling. Hearing my own words out loud in front of Donna leads me to recognize those feelings that I'd buried a long time ago.

Donna continues gently, yet certainly, "You don't need to feel. You don't need to be loved. You don't need to be connected with anyone. It worked well. It worked perfectly for a long time. That made you educated and gave you the strength to survive, but it is not working anymore." She pauses.

"The happiness you felt when you were with your grandmother lasted such a short period of time so that you believed happiness would not last long. Losing someone who connected deeply with you was painful, so you decided that you would rather not be connected with anyone. As soon as someone cared, you pushed them away. As long as no one cared about you, you'd be safe." Donna looks at the floor, then at me. Her expression has hardly changed since the beginning of the session. There is a long silence. Sometimes, not say anything is something to do. Nothing means something in zen.

"When you were a little girl, you couldn't handle the pain, but now you can," Donna speak slowly. I stay silent as I look down at my feet, my black jazz shoes, staring at them for a while. If I open my mouth, the truth would disappear.

For so many years, I believed nothing would bring back the excitement of daily conversation with Grandma into my life, and nothing could bring me the feeling of being connected to someone. I sit up and begin to realize my consuming desire for existing. When my wounds from detachment are starting to heal, my roots are beginning to grow.

### *SESSION: Death Energy*

Seppuku, sometimes referred to as harakiri, is a form of Japanese ritual suicide by disembowelment. In writing, seppuku and harakiri are the same Japanese character, but they are pronounced a different way. Harakiri was used by warriors to avoid falling into enemy hands, and to attenuate shame and avoid possible torture. Samurai could also be ordered by their Shogun to carry out harakiri. A samurai who performed harakiri was either doing so voluntarily, as a form of capital punishment for samurai who had committed serious offenses, or doing so because he had brought shame to himself. The ceremonial disembowelment, which is usually part of a more elaborate ritual and performed in front of spectators, consists of plunging a short blade, traditionally into the abdomen.

Why do Japanese commit harakiri? It's meant to show a willingness to sacrifice oneself for a greater cause. Obligatory harakiri was abolished in 1868, but its voluntary form has persisted. For others, suicide is the way of avoiding pain, a way to remove the negative side of one's self. For some, suicide is a punishment for significant others.

"According to bushi-do (way of the warriors), if you don't get revenge, you are nobody. If you don't die with honor, you are nobody," I say as I look at Donna.

Donna looks at me curiously. "What made you talk about that today?"

I'm surprised Donna does not seem to be disgusted by this information, so I continue, "When I left our session last week, I realized March is my deceased Grandma's anniversary." I try to answer her question without knowing why I said what I said. "It also occurred to me that March is the anniversary of many people's death in Japan."

Donna seems curious and asks, "What does that mean?"

"Spring suicide", is what they call that phenomenon in Japan. Toward the end of February each year, parents and teachers of junior high school and high school students become tense. How many of them would commit? In March, the suicide rate skyrockets among teenagers because they get the results of their entrance exams from high schools and colleges. High schools, colleges, and universities are ranked like a caste system. Who wants to be in an untouchable? They don't create enough colleges and universities moving along with growing population, so higher educations are not for everyone from the 1970's to about 2000. There is competition between the students, and they don't get many chances. It is usually a one-time shot. If you fail an entrance exam, you never move on to the next level of schooling. You will be a failure for the rest of your life. Who is going to commit harakiri this year?

The most popular place for students to commit suicide is to go to the Aokigahara forest, which sits along the edge of Mount Fuji, roughly a two-hour drive west of Tokyo. Many Japanese people say it's "the perfect place to die," and the forest has the unfortunate distinction of being the world's second most popular place to take one's life (the first is the Golden Gate Bridge). At the entrance to the forest, a sign reminds visitors that "life is a precious gift from your parents." Some Aokigahara survivors report that they picked the place because they wanted to share the same place with others and belong to the same group. Does the sign's message that "Life is a precious gift from your parents" mean anything to people who decided to die?

Some people throw their bodies into the path of a subway train, but this costs too much for the family members. My parents once told me that using the subway or any public transportation to commit suicide is a really bad idea because the family of the dead person would owe the government a lot of money. It would usually take three generations to pay the fine for making the government stop the train for a few hours and causing inconvenience to thousands of people.

Another way people commit suicide is to hang themselves in their house while family members are not present. Many teens avoid trying to commit suicide by cutting themselves or taking pills, because these methods often fail and thereby cause

## - Death, Compulsion and Secret -

humiliation, known as "losing face." They view suicide as "making a rational decision." Suicide is not a moral sin in this society.

Late one afternoon at the beginning of March, the sky is gray and it looks as if it will snow. It is the last day of the school year, and all the kids are gone. I'm waiting for Mother to pick me up in front of the school, but she has not come. I call her from the school pay phone. When she answers the phone, she tells me to take a bus because she can't pick me up. My cousin killed himself.

My cousin hanged himself. He failed the entrance exam to the high school he wanted to attend. Three days ago, he received the results of his February entrance exam. This morning, he hung himself in his parents' garage. The garage has no windows but has a high ceiling; there is a metal storage loft for ski equipment. He attached a rope to the loft, put it around his neck, and jumped. He was wearing a black school uniform. His black shoes were next to each other on the cold concrete garage floor. His glasses were on top of his shoes. He does not have to read or write anymore. At 6 am on Monday morning, aunt Sadako found him when she went to the garage to get pickled vegetables for their breakfast. His body was already cold – he was gone.

The following day, I wear my school uniform to the funeral. For junior high and high school students, school uniforms are formal outfits for celebrations or funerals. Families, relatives, and friends wear black suits and dresses. I smell death at the moment I enter Sadako's house. Sadako finds me before I find her. Her eyes meet mine from a distance. She looks at me in despair, then turns her eyes to the casket. I follow her eyes. She

## The Moon Home

gets close to me. "You came," she says as she looks into my eyes as if we were the only two in the entire room. No words. No tears. I stand in front of Sadako with my motionless body and paralyzed mind. She looks at the casket with her colorless eyes and says she found a letter on his desk. He wrote that he was sorry that he failed his parents. I wonder how Sadako is going to live the rest of her life without her oldest son. Then, I push the thought out of my mind. I push everything out of my mind. There is nothing to say or do to ease her pain.

People take turns cleaning his dead body with alcohol. It's a Japanese custom that relatives take turns cleaning the dead person's body before they put the corpse in the casket. We don't exchange a word. Uncles, aunts, and cousins take turns and rub his dead body gently with cotton balls dabbed in alcohol. Relatives seem to seek a mental state of non-being and nothingness. When it's Sadako's turn, she talks to his dead body. "We are here for you. You are not alone. You are cared for and loved by your family," Sadako says without crying or weeping. Then all of my cousins start to cry; their crying become sobbing. I find myself outside of it; there are still no tears in me.

Ancient Japanese believed that there is a river between this world and the world of the dead. Crossing the Sanzu River after our death is a Japanese Buddhist tradition and religious belief. In modern Japanese funerals, three coins are placed in the casket with the dead. When dead people pass the river to be at rest and peace, we have to pay a fee to get them to the world of the dead. There is a Japanese saying, "Even in hell, the extent of one's suffering is determined by money." I put 30 yen into the casket. I imagine my cousin crosses the river safely. His name was Hiroshi. He was fourteen years old.

I look at his dark face in the casket covered by a white gauze, and wonder if this could have been me. Several tall incense sticks in a large bronze cup next to the casket release smoke as they burn. The smoke from the incense moves all over in the small living room, making it so that I can't see his face clearly. I want this to be a non-dream because it means I didn't die. I would cross the Pacific Ocean instead of the Sanzu River. Grandma once told me about the other side of the world when we were at a lake for clam gathering. When my mind is crossing the Pacific Ocean, Sadako holds my hand and says "don't blow out the incense by mouth. Out of respect for the deceased person, use your hand to blow it out." In Buddhist beliefs, human mouths are not clean because sometimes we lie, or say things to hurt others. "We are going to keep the incense burning for 49 days. It takes 49 days for a deceased person to go to the pure land of perfect bliss."

In Japan, they cremate corpses, leaving only the bones. For them, cremation means to keep the deceased as bone, not ashes. After the funeral, a hearse takes us to a crematorium. A slow-burning fire burns and smoke comes from the chimney; I see it from a distance. Someone else is also dead, and they are cremating that body. Gray smoke in the air makes it look as if the spirit has been removed from the body.

I find myself on the second floor, where there are caskets for cremation. I'm standing in a dark hallway with dimmed light. When I feel the power of darkness, I get the urge to explore the whole building. My interest is now intense. I go down the stairs,

I reach one floor, and then another floor. On the walls, there is neither painting nor decoration. I touch and tap the white wall. I keep tapping until it sounds hollow. I see a stairway of narrow stone steps leading down into the depths. Thick gray dust covers the floor. It looks as if there are scattered bones on the floor. Does anyone leave the bone on the floor? Then, I realize that they are just dusty broken pottery.

The funeral is over. I leave the mortuary. I step out and stand up under the gray sky until Mother calls me into the car. Later in the evening, the dust turns into snow. Who had killed Hiroshi? Did he find his enemy?

Nobody told me anything about my cousin's death. He wanted to enter high school, not just any high school, but a particular high school. Having expectations can lead to death but so can setting life goals. Wanting something only makes things worse. But that is not all. The belief that there is no future for him, and the shame he felt, made him feel that he had no choice but to not exist. His shame and hopelessness did not allow him to live. Death is honorable and is preferred to being humiliated. It is hard to live with shame. Ending life is easier than living. As for me, I keep living life as a failed student. I could deal with failure, I could deal with humiliation, I could deal with unhappiness. I sit in the car going back home, and I can't help wonder how many of us are going to fail again in our lifetime, and how many of us would live after failed lives. His body as bone and my mind as ashes are flowing around the mortuary with the last snow of the year in Hokkaido.

## - Death, Compulsion and Secret -

My shoulders hunch as I say to Donna, "Everything had failed me. I failed schools and marriages. I failed as a woman. I'm nothing, but I didn't die." Donna listens, her body leaning towards me.

"I don't know why my parents had me. I should never been born. They should not be together. I wish none of my family existed. They should not exist. I wish they would disappear, including me. I don't want to exist." My lifeless eyes are looking far, far from Donna.

"That's exactly what you have been doing," Donna says sternly as she looks directly at me. I look at her without blinking. I'm shocked by her boldness and strength. I hear her strong voice come from her petite body. When I look up at her face, I slowly lean back on the couch. I take a deep breath as my back touches the couch.

"Do you hate them?" Donna asks calmly.

My chin gently rises without words.

"Would you miss them if they were gone?" Donna's voice has softened.

"I hate my country, I hate my people, I hate myself." My voice hits crescendo.

"I don't miss them, I don't love them, but I worry about them." I begin to whimper, and I feel pain in my neck as I speak.

"My parents never missed me but they always worried about me, that's how they felt about me, and now I am feeling the same about them. I'm sick just like them," I say with an intense tone of voice.

"They didn't understand you as a child, and it is hard for you to think that your parents were cruel to you when you were good." Donna looks at me and continues.

"As therapy moves forward, feelings of sadness or anger may come to clients, because they may feel frustrated about their own feelings that come up in the therapy. For us to explore the reasons for your reactions to particular situations, or the reasons for certain words and situations, might make you angry or anxious. You can tell me when my words make you angry or sad, so that we can discover what caused you to get angry or sad."

I realize that the reason I never talk or think about my parents is that it makes me angry. When I take a deep breath, I feel the air fills into my lungs. I still don't know why I did not kill myself. Perhaps, I've always believed on some level that there is a rabbit on the moon. I am from the moon. There might be a real parents on the moon. I could cross the Pacific Ocean instead of the Sanzu River. There is a place for me to live freely. Hanging on hope and not giving up my life no matter what. Grandma told me that in her bedtime stories.

### *SESSION: Psychosomatic*

"I've been very sick for the past three weeks, and I missed work and sessions." I pause. "As long as I'm with my clients and listening to their problems, I don't have to face my own problems. For a long time, it worked very well, but it doesn't seem to be working anymore." I say numbly and look at the air in the room.

## - Death, Compulsion and Secret -

"Why do you think you couldn't tell yourself that you needed to take time off until your doctor ordered you to take time off?" Donna asks.

"I didn't want my supervisor to be disappointed in me as my parents are disappointed in me," I say with paled face.

"I think you are disappointed in your parents," Donna prompts.

The truth is I've never looked at my own feelings. I look at Donna's face and start wondering why I wasn't aware of this simple thought. Why did I need to come to another country to remind me of that?

Donna continues, "In your past relationships, you felt it when people value you, but you didn't feel it from you. You feel valued only when other people value you. You feel through them."

The moment I hear Donna, my life before America comes back to my mind. "I'm doing the same thing. I'm repeating. Nothing has changed."

"Talk to me," Donna says in a strong voice. I start telling Donna how I have been trying to prove my competency, so I work compulsively until I become physically ill. My mind is quickly teleported to 1980's.

In the 1980's, real estate and other parts of the economy are booming in Japan. People are referring to women like me as "bubble women." Corporations buy buildings in other countries and ostentatiously display their wealth. The 1980's bubble economy skew my perception of money and the economy, creating a mirage of happiness. Bubble men and women drink daily, and spend money thoughtlessly. With my $5000 summer bonus, I purchase designer clothes and purses, and $380 shoes. With my $7000 winter bonus, I spend $10,000 for a five-day trip to Hawaii, and buy more and more stuff there. This seems to be a good enough life for a 21 year old woman. In the bubble economy society, Confucianism oddly underlies beliefs and actions in business settings: respect elders and authorities, give up material possessions, and control emotions until you get drunk after work.

I finish a glass of beer and then a glass of cold sake. The cool clear liquor goes through my empty stomach. My office mates and I drink with cheerfulness and to good work at our bank, Sapporo. Salarymen and women bow to the boss. If I can drink like men, that means I can work like men. I bow low in the direction of my boss, Mr. Suzuki, who is sitting on the other side of the bar. His glass is half empty. I come up to Mr. Suzuki and pour sake into his glass, letting him know that I am aware of his half-empty glass even when I'm drunk. I look at the other side of the bar. A boss who from another unit is getting more sake from his subordinates. Mr. Suzuki becomes paralyzed and speaks nonsense words. His tongue becomes a slice of rotten tuna sashimi. Unable to sit on the chair, he falls. His subordinates put him back on the chair. He falls again. One of the subordinates is hitting his bald head. Animated discussions between the subordinates begin. Nobody is contradicted. This is called "bureikou," which means to put aside rank. Let's forget all the formalities and enjoy our drinks. This is the unspoken

## - Death, Compulsion and Secret -

rule established for the purpose of stress reduction. Salarymen and women perform this as a part of our work.

After we drink, we move to karaoke bar. I swallow more sake to empty the glass and empty my mind. My boss tells me to sing. I stand up quickly and move to the karaoke stage to prove that drinks won't interfere with my abilities. I pick a song quickly to prove that I am efficient. I sing to prove I'm brave. Many people sing "My Way," a popular karaoke song in Japan. Though there is never "My Way" – it's always "Our Way" in their society. Nobody listens to anybody else's song. I am drunk and careless. The singing is getting louder and out of tune as we drink more. New employees are here to perform as geisha girls and boys. My drunk colleague is telling everyone how stupid he is, and making his boss laugh. Self-denigration is beauty in Japanese society. During the day at work, people put up a front. At night, while drinking at the karaoke bar, people can show their real selves as if they are Draculas. They call this phenomenon "tatemae" which means front and back. It is taboo to talk about what happens at the karaoke bar when we are in the office the next day. What happens in the karaoke bar stays in the karaoke bar. I drink nightly and sleep 3 hours year round.

No matter how drunk and how late I get home, I have to get up early in the morning and get to the office on time to prove that I am mentally strong. Physical exhaustion does not affect my work. I work tirelessly and perform consistently. The next morning, Mr. Suzuki is already in his office working. He wears a well-ironed white shirt. He must have gone back home and slept a few hours. He seems like a typical salaryman again. Some people sleep at their desks or in a capsule hotel to save commuting time. Convenience stores such as 7/11 sell shirts for workers who have no time to go home and change. Salarymen and women work over 100 hours per week. Daily happy hours, which run until midnight, are considered a part of work that is not included in the 100 hours of official work. I hesitate to leave the office before my peers, and certainly before my boss.

Companies offer to look after employees for life in return for a willingness to dedicate that life to the company, including working unpaid overtime. Many employees move to new houses in another city when the company tells them to. Some salarymen leave their wives and children at home, and move to another city or country for their works. There is no "No" in their dictionary.

The word "karoshi" (death by overwork) originated in the post-war economic boom and continues to exist during the bubble economy. Sudden death without any specific causes, bodies just shutting down –it's karoshi. Is this not harakiri? As a country and society, the Japanese have never done anything about karoshi or spring suicides. They talk about it, but no action, no changes. If you are lucky, you don't kill yourself, and instead pick yourself up and move forward with feelings of humiliation and worthlessness. I realize I can't get rid of the name "failure for life," but I am still living. Don't they want to save failures?

I tried to fit in with the cultural norm in order to survive in that culture. Therefore, distortion of character was necessary. It is important for the Japanese to fly low, not make waves especially at work. This society keeps me in a cave and prevents me from knowing the truth and speaking the truth. Now, as an adult, I'm much less vocal. I've lost my voice.

## Death, Compulsion and Secret

The bubble economy was a mirage in the distance, and it masked all of my pain, suffering, and grief. For years, I acted as if I were a happy bubble woman, full of energy. Until I collapsed.

"What do you think about saying no to other people?" Donna asks. I glance over at Donna as if I don't understand her question.

Donna looks at my puzzling paled face and says, "Can you say, I'm so sorry, I have lots of things to do, not this time?" I keep looking at her without blinking.

"I understand that you believed saying no marks the end of the relationship and saying yes, means to keep the relationship. Your parents said no to you when you wanted something. Your parents shut you down as soon as you asked for something. But you can separate those two things. One relationship you ended because of dishonesty. The other you ended because things didn't go well. You put yourself in a little box and find a person that you can be satisfied with." Donna pauses.

"I've been trying so hard to be like others and trying so hard not disappoint them," I say with a wounded voice. Donna looks down and thinks for a moment. She herself is conscious of it, but I, as a client, am not.

So, I ask, "Would you associate with people like that?"

"It's not about whether you associate with people like that or not, it's about asking yourself if you would feel OK with people who are different from you, if you would still feel OK about yourself?" Donna tries to simplify her comments and ask, "Do you believe you have the right to say things that you want to do in any relationship?"

"I've never done that," I answer without a moment's hesitation.

"I know that," Donna immediately says.

Donna slowly speaks, "In a relationship, people do things because they want to do, or people do things because they get something in return." Donna looks at me as if she is begging me to see her points.

In my culture, people do things because they are told to do so, they get punished if they don't; but I don't say anything to Donna, I think she knows.

"I don't know how and when to say no to people and still keep the relationships," I tell Donna.

"Your parents didn't want you to say or do things they didn't like. If you did, they didn't approve or support, they didn't even love. You've been rejected by your parents. You know how it hurt, so you don't want to do that to people, but you wish them to give up. You can't say what you want and you can't express how you feel. You have to be a little girl so that you are safe and even loved. By doing so, you are not taking care of your needs and wants." Donna pauses, then she asks, "What is the worst thing that would happen if you say no or reject them?"

After a long pause, I tell Donna, "I would become a bad mother."

For the first time in my life, I'm aware of the reason for my anger, I don't say no to people because I am fearful of becoming my mother. With Donna's gentle push, I get real pushes from deep inside my mind and gut. Then, my memory of the bubble economy has begin to seem like a distant illusion.

For a long time, I chose sickness rather than verbal communication. I refused to acknowledge my physical tiredness and mental pain. When my mind is unable to contain, manage, and express feelings, my body takes over and expresses itself. The blind spot is the shame aspects of myself. When I feel shame, I attack myself until I'm completely broken and unable to move. Over the months of being in sessions with Donna, I begin to realize that I might be able to say no before I collapse, despite feeling discomfort, if I put down roots in Donna's office. Then, I would really be leaving Japan behind. That is the progress I've made.

### *SESSION: Failure as a Woman*

"Tell me," Donna starts the session when she looks at my face.

"I have a mess, I am a mess, I am a failure. I am a failure with a mess. I'm screwed," I speak with restless and powerless voice. For the first time in my life, I'm not afraid to express my anger. I've made progress, but the progress itself does not help me. I'm completely lost. I believed that people would get angry simply because someone did something terrible to us, but this might not be the case.

"This week, I've been angry, about everything and everybody." I keep staring at the floor.

"When you are working on your feelings that you've held in for a long time, you get confused, angry, sometimes even hurt. But the more you feel these emotions, and the longer you work on them, the easier it will be for you to tell yourself that you are OK and that you will be OK because you have survived. It might be easier to think nothing happened and that therefore you're OK, rather than feeling your pain and working on it."

"I've been angry for most of my life, but I've never attached to my anger and much less expressed it. Now, I can say I'm angry, but anger takes my energy away from me. I'm tired."

"Anger is usually covering for something. Something that we don't want to talk about, something that we don't want to see because it's painful." Donna looks at my face and continues, "Many years ago, you buried your feelings in order to protect yourself from getting hurt and disappointed again. You needed to do that in order to survive."

My suppressed feelings and denied anger are still in me, and they are coming back. My established old brick wall no longer exists so that the strong frozen wind pokes my nerves.

After a long pause, Donna asks, "Do you think that anger is the only emotion in you?"

Apparently, I'm not ready to discuss my other emotions, so I change the subject. "I started dating again."

Donna listens as she keeps looking into my eyes.

"I keep seeing a high school boxing coach and a guy who was in special forces although we have nothing in common. They don't know how to get to know me."

"Why do you think you keep seeing them? There must be a reason for that."

I'm trying to give Donna the right answer, but no answer seems to be right. I don't say anything.

"Can you leave men after you have sex?" Donna asks.

"It's not easy," I say in muted tone.

## - Death, Compulsion and Secret -

"Because you don't want to hurt them or you don't want to get hurt?"

I think back to past mistakes and say, "I sleep with someone and minimize all of his faults."

"It's OK to date someone and find out whether they're right for you. It's a problem if you keep seeing them after you know it's not fun or they are bad for you."

"What are you afraid of?" Donna pushes.

"I'm not getting wiser, but just getting older, I'm stuck."

Donna tries a different angle. "What does intimacy mean to you?"

The word intimacy was never in my vocabulary, so I don't say anything.

"Couples who have intimacy, what do they have? What don't they have?"

I remain silent because I feel stuck.

"It doesn't have to be the same way that you've been doing. If we can talk about it, maybe you can get unstuck."

"I haven't had an intimate relationship, even with my mother. I don't know what intimate means. The only time my mother and I had a intimate moment was the time she told me her stories."

Donna is listening, so I start telling her my mother's story.

Over the years, Mother told me the same story over and over again. It's not the story of Cinderella, It's not the story of Princess Kaguya from the moon, It's a story of Mother's deceased mother, my grandmother whom I've never met. It's about the childhood

## The Moon Home

sorrow, suffering, miseries, and poverty that Mother grew up in. I am taken to a deep dark place without a filter to the story. Then the story of the dark clouds implanted that fear and hopelessness in me. When no one is around, Mother starts telling me the story of death.

Mother's mother was brought to the hospital for complications of childbirth. Then her mother was away over a period of time. It seemed as if it was beyond a certain limit measured in minutes, hours, or days for a little girl. Her mother never returned home, but instead, the girl was taken to the hospital. When her father opened the door to the room, her mother's dead body was lying down on a metal hospital bed. A nurse placed a white handkerchief on the dead mother's face. The girl ran into her mother. She ran, she grabbed, she pushed her head on the blanket covering her dead mother. The girl's short arms were around the dead body. When she squeezed the dead body, the white handkerchief on the dead mother's face slid off. The girl reached for her dead mother, but her mother's body was already cold. The girl howled, she sank her face into the dead body like a newborn baby looking for the mother's breasts. Her dead mother's face was white like snow, her skin was as cold as ice. It was December 29 and starting to snow heavily outside. The girl begged her father to let her be placed into the casket with her dead mother. For the reason, the girl was not allowed to be in her own mother's funeral. Then, her mother was gone forever. After the funeral, the girl never visited her mother's grave, so her tiny memory faded away quickly. Her mother no longer existed in her mind, she was 5 years old.

## Death, Compulsion and Secret

Ever since the death of my grandmother who I'd never gotten to know, Mother's life had changed. Mother never visited her mother's grave. That's the way she kept her life moving forward. By the time she got older, she no longer remembered much about her mother. Mother had no idea that this death was a prelude to denial, fear, madness, and despair. Her preoccupation with fear and anxiety about her daughter, replaced her need to grief her dead mother. Then, trying to capture maternal affection that I was never given became my bereavement. All her life, she was haunted by the fear of losing everything. Mother's subconscious, fearful, fractured dark energy made me feel as if I was being violently pulled into opposite directions in a senseless black hall. It destroyed my existence by causing me to live with fear. And this problem continues to haunt me even in my womanhood.

I'm not going to lie, I'm curious about Donna's life. Who Donna really is. But I understand that most of the time, therapist self-disclosure is unnecessary, and often harmful to the therapeutic process. I see Donna's wedding band, there is no need for me to ask whether she is married.

So I ask, "Do you have any children?"

"I have daughters," Donna replies without hesitation.

"Thank you for telling me," I say.

"It must be important for you to know," Donna says.

I pause and fantasize about the relationship between Donna and her daughters, what her daughters think of her as a mother. Rationally, I understand that no perfect mother exists, but

I realize that I need to keep believing that Donna is the perfect mother I never had. I appreciate that Donna keeps her life private, despite my curiosity.

I realize that Donna keeps looking at me, so I start talking.

"My mother worries about everything and especially worries about me. I then constantly worry about what I do." My voice becomes weak.

"Your mother sees danger in everything. Being fearful was a quality that you inherited from her."

"I have another inheritance story from my mother, do you want to hear it?"

"I'm here," Donna smiles.

I must feel my dating patterns have something to do with my mother. I start telling Donna another story that Mother told me.

Every time I go back to Japan, I run into Sadako, who is Mother's aunt. Everywhere I go, I see her, whether it's at the doctor's office, the hot spring, or the grocery store, and over the years, I wondered about these coincidences. When she happens to see me, she says "Oh my dear, you are so tall." I am 5'7 and she is 4'1. Asian women often look young until they hit seventy, and after that they look 100 years old. Sadako still does not look 100 years old. Every time I bump into Sadako, Mother starts talking about her story after she leaves.

The story of Sadako starts when Mother was younger than I am now, and I was not yet born, and she still lived in her family house with her father, her stepmother, her five siblings,

## Death, Compulsion and Secret

her grandmother, and her grandmother's youngest daughter, Sadako. Sadako was quite an obedient daughter, and she never expressed her opinions to her mother until matchmakers tried to fix Sadako up with men for an arranged marriage.

One night, a snow storm makes wheezing sounds as cold air and snow blow in through the clay-and-mud wall. The old house is cheaply built, and the cold air and the powder snow are entering through the gaps around the window. Everyone is asleep except Sadako, who starts weeping in her futon in the tatami room next to Mother. It is so cold even inside the house that Sadako's weeping breath becomes white.

Mother wakes up and whispers to Sadako's mother, "Grandmother, Sadako is crying again."

"Leave her alone," Sadako's mother says without looking at Sadako.

Sadako cries even harder, and her weeping turns into sobbing that lasts for hours. There is no private conversation in the house of nine family members sharing two bedrooms with thin paper walls.

Earlier in the winter, a matchmaker and Sadako's mother decide Sadako's arranged marriage. A matchmaker had introduced two men to Sadako when she was 23. One man is tall, handsome, and owns some businesses in town. The other man is short, introverted, and farms in the countryside. Sadako's mother tells her to marry the farmer, but Sadako likes the businessman. Mother asks Sadako's mother why Sadako can't marry the guy she likes. "It's because Sadako does not have the beauty to match the handsome man who has money, and she is also short and has no education. The handsome man would be unfaithful to Sadako, which would make her life miserable and the family disgraced. It would be dishonorable to ancestors."

Sadako's night sobbing remains until she gets married. Sadako's tears are mixed with the powder snow that comes through the cracked window. When she wakes up in the morning, her tears-soaked futon is frozen. Sadako cries for three more months, and the following spring, Sadako gets married to the farmer and leaves her family house.

One night, three years after the wedding, Sadako and her husband come to visit her family house. For most farmers on the island, the harvest is over, and there is no more field work for the rest of the year. Outside, it smells of wet straw after the heavy September rain. When Sadako and her husband arrive, the thunder gets louder and shakes the old cheaply built house. Sadako's mother gives Sadako's husband a towel to dry his wet jacket. Sadako is looking down on the tatami floor as she enters the house. Her sweater is wet. Her mother greets Sadako's husband and starts preparing green tea for him. Sadako's husband bows to his mother in law, and noisily sips his hot tea. Sadako's mother anticipates something is wrong when she looks at her daughter's emotionless face. Sadako's anger, revenge and cursing linger all in her gut.

"Sadako has been cooking, cleaning, and helping to farm all day long," Sadako's husband says as Sadako looks down emotionlessly and sits next to him. The rain starts pouring. Sadako's mother listens as she sits on the zafu cushion in the tatami room. She says nothing, but pays attention to Sadako's husband.

"Sadako has not let me touch her during the three years of our marriage, not even once. We have not slept together,"

## - Death, Compulsion and Secret -

he says as he looks down at the tea cup shamefully. When the loudest thunder hits and shakes the old house, Sadako's mother quickly stands up and slaps Sadako's left cheek. Sadako's body falls off from the cushion, her palm reaches the tatami mat, and she quickly pulls her body back to the cushion. She does not look at her mother, she does not cry, her three months of crying before she was to be married to her husband made her tears run out.

The slap did it. Six months later, Sadako was pregnant with a baby boy. A year after that, without a slap, she had another boy. Mother was also pregnant the same year that Sadako had her second son. Sadako's second son and I were in the same class. Sadako's husband was not bad after all, and she stayed with him until he died of old age.

When Mother finishes Sadako's story, she starts telling the story of her own arranged marriage. A man who was short and wore thick glasses came to see Mother day after day at the bank where she worked. Apparently, there was no reason for him to withdraw money that often. Every day, he sent Mother gifts. One day, he and his mother came to Mother's parents' house and asked for their permission to marry Mother, and they gave their permission, so he took Mother to a dinner and a movie. When he held Mother's hand at the movie theater, Mother felt it was creepy. That was their last date. Mother never wanted to see him again.

Because Mother refused to see the man, her grandmother and a matchmaker arranged her marriage. Mother married a different man who became my father. According to Mother, Father picked the cheapest noodle restaurant for their first date.

They didn't talk while they ate. When he finished, he pretended to look for his wallet. Since Mother was willing to contribute, Father said, "Oh, that is very kind of you." He left the restaurant while Mother was paying the bill. Father never holds Mother's hand on their dates. There was no gift from him. Mother chose a man who did not want to touch her and spend money on her.

"Apparently, this relationship dynamic seems to have passed down to me. I made relationships choice similar to my mother's. I chose men who didn't satisfy me." Donna sits still and listens.

"I don't seem to be able to escape from multigenerational relationship choices." The distant past comes to my mind. I decide to tell Donna about my first husband, how we met and how we got divorced.

So, I start: Working at a financial company is painfully boring, so I find myself focusing on other interests. I work like a dog and drink like a hippopotamus, and I also look for a man like a female chimp. During the 1980's bubble economy, there is a Japanese saying "Women are like a Christmas cake." It means that if you are not sold by the 24th, Christmas Eve, you would have to drastically reduce your price because men consider 25 year old women to be no longer young. Many women try to leave work before they turn 24. Hiring a babysitter and a house keeper is frowned upon in Japanese society, so they become full time wives and mothers.

## *Death, Compulsion and Secret*

Falling in love at first sight is something you either believe in or don't, and I didn't. Until I met a man who works in my office building when I was about leaving the building for the company's tennis tournament. He is a 27 year old single educated man and looks like Ken Watanabe, with sparkling brown eyes and a beautiful smile with perfect white teeth. He smiles us and says "Good luck to you guys." Many women in my office have a crush on him. Who is this guy? Why haven't I seen him for the past two years I've been working?

Later the week, as I'm waiting for the elevator, Ken Watanabe man comes up to me and asks, "Do you have anything scheduled for this evening? Would you like to get a coffee or something?" I quickly reply, "No, thanks." He seems shocked, but he turns around and uses the stairs to get to his first floor office. Did he just ask me out? Why? Men who would be attracted me wouldn't be smart or sophisticated because they would be unable to see my ugly side. Is this thought coming from my subconscious?

I continue waiting for the elevator. This time of day, the elevator is very busy because people are going home for the day. A single, 28 year old, depressed looking man who makes no eye contact comes to the hall. No women in my office are interested in him, and they laugh about him because he seems weird. He does not look at me, but he nods his head to acknowledge my presence. "Are you done for today?" I ask without looking at him. "Yes," he says as he looks down at the floor. "Would you like to go to dinner or something?" I ask him. "No, thanks," he immediately responds. After the silence, the elevator door opens, he gets in, the elevator door closes. I'm still standing in front of the elevator and forgetting to press the button. My girlfriend from the office comes and asks me what I am doing by standing here without pushing the elevator button. "The weirdo just said no to my invitation for dinner," I say to her. The weird guy later becomes my first husband.

My first husband looks serious most of the time. The time he is not so serious, he has a twitchy demeanor with a piercing laugh that sounds like a squeaking old bicycle. His character fit myself, he seems right for me. When I see men who are not interested in me, some part of me awakes with chemistry and sexuality. I feel alive with some excitement. I'm confident that it is love – he is the one.

I refer to my first husband and his family as the weasels of wizard family. They have magical powers that suck my mind and heart so that I can't make rational decisions. They do not reveal much to each other. This is even more attractive to me. His mother looks down, and never makes eye contact. She never smiles, and she whispers as she talks. His sister always has one eye on me. I feel as if I fit right in. I get a sense, something is familiar – deceptive, distorted, deceitful, and disingenuous. I can do this because I know this.

Why am I doing this? I seek out partners who remind me of my childhood wounds, so that I can fix my family of origin issues. If I can make this weasels of wizard family into a wonderful lovely family, then I can prove to myself that I am a lovable worthwhile human being?

## - Death, Compulsion and Secret -

"He was not into me. He continued looking for someone else," I say to Donna.

Donna looks at me and says, "You said you chose men who didn't satisfy you. So, you could easily dump them. You were not in love in the relationships from the beginning so that the end would not be so painful." Donna pauses and continues, "You felt that with your both husbands; your first husband did not choose you, and your second husband chose his mother over you. It reminded you of how your mother didn't choose you, but she chose your sister over you."

"I couldn't make my own mother love me, so I found a man who didn't love me and hoped that he would change into someone who loves me deeply. But I haven't been successful."

"We need to understand the little girl and let the little girl to explore. Your needs and wants…"

I sit still. It's not easy to recognize and feel my needs and wants, which I buried as a child. I'm fearful of finding out my needs and wants – they must be bad and ugly. I'm not ready to look at the big picture of my life. I'm stuck.

"I got divorced when I was 23, and my family and friends thought my miscarriage caused the divorce. When I had the miscarriage, I had to have a curettage procedure, and the funniest part was that my husband was at work and my mother went shopping the day I was in the hospital. I had to catch a cab to get home." I begin to withdraw, turning away from Donna.

"Are you angry at him, or your mother, or yourself?" Donna asks.

I don't say anything. The emptiness comes back from the past.

"Are you disappointed?"

I remain silent because I don't want to deal with my feelings.

"Are you sad?"

"I don't want to feel sad, I'm just mad. I feel bad and sad for other people, but not for myself. I don't want to be depressed."

"I'm not into the word 'depressed', but can you think of it as 'I did not have lot of good things in my life?' Can you think like a woman in the movies, who wanted to have things but it didn't happen because something went wrong?"

"I made a bad decision because I'm stupid," I insist.

"In most twenty three years old, it is pretty healthy to be pregnant, it would be OK what you eat or do. I believe that neither your and your husband's negative thoughts caused it. You are blaming yourself and afraid of falling in love again. When you made the decisions to get divorced twice, you had good reasons. You could have stayed in the marriages and relationships, but if you did, you would have become smaller and smaller." Donna understands the ache I'm feeling.

Silence. I don't know what to do except blame myself and feel shame.

"When you feel shame, where do your other feelings go?" Donna asks.

"The doctor explained that 30% of pregnancies end up like me during the first trimester, but among all of his words, I only remember three words: 'It's not growing,' 'I'm sorry,' and 'Don't cry.'" I pause, "The miscarriage itself didn't lead us to the divorce, but the feelings of worthlessness and loneliness that I had after my miscarriage were intolerable."

Donna slowly nods twice. She already knows. Her face gently rises. I look up too, then my confusion clears on my face. Talking about my shame no longer frightens me. I sit in the chair and embrace my feeling of sadness. Then I realize, this time, I am not alone.

When I was disappointed about a relationship, I was dealing not only with that relationship, but also with my grief over all my past relationships. Mother often said that she did not have a choice. For her, escape was not an option, the option was not available. I wanted to have choices. Somehow, I found a way to escape my husband and remove my roots from married life, but I could not quite escape my fears.

### SESSION: Dirty Secret

"I just came back from clinical supervision. I have to meet with Ralph, my clinical supervisor for another 2500 hours in order to get a state license." I take a deep breath and continue, "Today, in a case conference, I read my notes on a session with a client that I presented. When I needed to give a few words of explanation about client's sexual issues, I could not talk about it because I kept laughing. Ralph probably thought I was crazy. He told me that it seemed as if certain issues were affecting my ability to discuss my cases in the supervision."

"What part of you don't want him to know?" Donna asks.

After a long pause, I whisper, "I'm not pure or innocent. I'm dirty. I'm damaged."

"Do you think a pure and innocent therapist exists?"

It sounds as if the question is rhetorical, but it makes me question my beliefs.

"You've never had an equal relationship, having both love and respect. I can imagine it would be terrifying to give yourself away." Donna's eyes meet mine.

"I don't want to lose Ralph," I say.

"I know," Donna says softy.

"I'm afraid that I might lose him if one of us crosses the line."

"Who would cross the line? You or him?"

"I don't know," I say, with obvious reluctance.

"Do you want him to cross the line?"

"I don't know. It's terrible."

"He has been your mother and father. He protects you and provides a safe environment for you. He is good at taking care of you. You haven't had those feelings for a long time." Donna looks at me transparently.

"Your needs and wants are not met. It's like an infant's needs. As an adult, sexual feelings are connected to that. You don't answer to yourself or to anyone tomorrow or in two days. You have a lot of time to think and talk about."

"I'm a damaged good. I'm a dirty secret," I whisper shamefully, "my mother hid me from neighbors and relatives when I lived at my parents' house after my first divorce."

"How did she hide you?"

"I'm a demodori. Japanese call returned divorced daughters demodori, which means returned after going out. Parents would lose face if people found out that they have demodori in their house." I start telling Donna about Mother's dirty secret – me.

## - Death, Compulsion and Secret -

My relationship with my first husband quickly deteriorated. Although I stayed with him for 6 months, our relationship was over before we got married. I left my job when we married, so I didn't have any income to support myself. I had no place to go other than my parents' house.

My parents pick me up at the airport. People are usually happy to see each other at the airport, but I'm terrified about seeing my parents' faces, so I keep looking down. My parents do not look at my face, and we keep walking toward the parking structure without talking. The silence in the car with my parents evokes my childhood feelings of being rejected, and it makes me feel disgusted. Getting into my parents' house reminds me of the feeling of being isolated and abandoned. Seeing my sister, who is now a college student, brings back a feeling of failure. At home is silence; nobody says anything. My parents and sister look disappointed, but they are scared to say anything. They are terrified that their neighbors and friends might find out about me. My parents would lose face if people found out about me. There is a desperate need to keep me hidden because I'm a shameful member of the family. My family is too afraid to lie so they omit, they pretend that I don't exist. This phenomenon makes the entire house seem fake, and the silence of the cold air in the house does not help me to heal.

The doorbell rings in the middle of the day – I have to hide. I grab everything around me, as if I'm a bank robber trying to grab every dollar before the police arrive. Mother stands in front of the door and becomes extremely nervous. "Hurry" she says with a strong whisper. I run into my room without making a sound. Mother closes the door to my room and opens the front door at the same time. She welcomes a sudden visit by a neighbor with her high pitched voice to prove that nothing is wrong in the house. The neighbor comes in and sits on the couch in the small living room. Mother is entertaining the neighbor with her laugh. She is preparing hot green tea to cover her dirty secret in the next room. I can't make noise, so I sit on top of the bed without moving. Silently, I inhale. I realize I'm holding the coffee cup tight. I must have grabbed it when the doorbell rang. I slowly remove my fingers from the coffee cup and put it on the side table without making noise. Suddenly, the story of the day I was born comes to mind, the story that Mother told me repeatedly when I was growing up.

Mother delivered me, her first baby, in the hospital. The baby didn't want to come out, so Mother suffered, she was miserable. After 24 hours of suffering, the baby was finally pushed out into the world. Mother was lying down on a hospital bed with exhaustion. The nurse brought a baby girl to her. Before she saw her baby's face, she checked the baby's hands. She had been obsessed with the fear that her baby would be born imperfect, so she counted the baby's fingers before anybody sees the baby. There were six fingers on the baby's left hand. She became more intense and anxious. She counted again, but still, there was an extra digit. She was disparate, she couldn't let anybody know about the baby's flaw, so she hid the baby deeper in her hospital bed. She felt urgency to cut off the baby's extra finger before anybody saw it. Mother became more anxious as though she had encountered an abnormal baby's hands. The baby cried

## - Death, Compulsion and Secret -

in rage and fought against being held by her mother. Then the tone of baby's cry became clear and trembled. She took a deep breath and counted again. Finally, she saw five fingers on each hand. She made sure again and again. Does it matter if I have extra fingers or no fingers at all? Before she got to know me, she hid me. Mother hid me the day I was born, then again, twenty-three years later.

Fall quickly ended, though I was never able to see lines of gingko and maple trees turn yellow, red, and then brown. Recently, Christmas came and went, though I was never able to touch snowflakes. I survive by hiding. Now it's New Year's Eve. In Japan, instead of a countdown to midnight and fireworks, temples ring their bells 108 times. Most Buddhist temples start ringing their bells late on New Year's Eve and continue into the early hours of New Year's Day. In Buddhist belief, the 108 tolls of the bell symbolize the casting away of 108 earthly desires. Each ring of the bell erases one of your earthly desires so that you can begin the New Year feeling refreshed. The sound is a deep bass; the initial rise is soft, then the afterglow echoes. With each ring of the bell, I think of my days in hiding. The echoes of the bell sound so lonely to my ears. I'm getting used to living my hidden life.

It's 11:30 pm on New Year's Eve. I'm watching TV in my bedroom and listening to the bell from the temple. Mother comes in and asks if I want to go to the Shrine for New Year prayers. Many people visit a Shinto shrine during the first three days of January in order to make traditional New Year's wishes for health and happiness. The shrine is open specially on the night of New Year's Eve, and some people arrive right after they hear the 108 bells. Does Mother want to start anew and leave old misery behind?

I put on my black down jacket and get into Mother's car, hoping that the 108 bells will cast away all my memories. There's silence in the car. I can see my white breath – it's snowing outside. The shrine is surrounded by trees, and it's night time, so I hope that no one will see me. After midnight, many people are already there for their prayers. Through the deep snow in front of the shrine is a path created by people's feet. We all follow the path to get to the inner temple alter. I hear no talking, only squeaky sounds as the snow from peoples' shoes rubs against the frozen snow on the ground. Mother and I step forward to the alter. We throw coins into a large heavy wood donation box. We bow twice, and clap our hands twice. Then, bow once to pray. As I join my hands in prayer, I see Mother putting her hands together and I wonder what she's praying for.

It's still dark when we start walking back to the path, but I pull a hood over my head to hide my face. I can't see people's faces, so they should not be able to see me. Suddenly, from behind me, a woman starts calling my name. No one can hide forever, but I must not reveal myself while I still have nothing in my life. I don't turn around but keep walking. I keep walking until she does not call me anymore. What I have so far are: no job, no apartment, no friends, no family, and no love. There seems no way forward when I don't exist; but Mother and whole family would lose face if I exist.

## - Death, Compulsion and Secret -

"My family felt shame having me in their house. My own mother believed I was imperfect from the day I was born. I don't know why Ralph believes I could be a good therapist.".

"You don't want to be criticized or get hurt," Donna pauses and asks. "How do you feel if you think you're a good person?"

"I don't feel right because I'm not."

"You don't trust people who thinks you're good or worthwhile."

I say nothing because it's true.

"Do you trust Ralph?" Donna asks.

"I trust what he does for clients, but I don't trust his opinions and decisions about me."

"Sometimes, people want to believe they are bad because their parents didn't treat them well. People want to believe that they have been punished because they are bad. If parents treat children badly even though the children are good, then those parents are cruel."

"Ralph will be disappointed in me. I'm not his perfect baby."

"He is not your parent. You're not 5 years old," Donna says sharply, then pauses to think whether I can digest her words.

I remain silent. As Donna and I occasionally discuss the internship supervision sessions I had with Ralph, it becomes clear to me that my feelings for Ralph are still ambivalent. I fear that one day I will be disappointed in him as I was disappointed in my parents.

This time, Donna is looking down at the floor. I keep looking at the shadow of the desk lamp on the side table next to me. It seems like long time since I start coming here, yet I feel that my therapy has just begun.

## CHAPTER SIX
## New Home

## 六

I'm dreaming I'm in an elevator made of glass, and it's going up. I cannot get out, I believe. I should not get out, I know. The elevator stops on the fifth floor, and strangers get in. Strangers get out. But I have to stay. The glass elevator keeps going up until I can see trees and buildings below. Above me, I notice the elevator has a single wire that is too thin, too fragile for an elevator of this size, but it continues up, it continues to stop at floor after floor, and people get out.

And when they exit, the elevator sways left, and then right, fragile, sensitive to the weight change, but it continues up to the next stop. Men and women leave. Again, the elevator sways, and as it sways, I turn my eyes to the bottom where gray apartment buildings and houses are lined up in rows like ants in an ant colony — a few oak trees with knobby trunks bend as if they are following the sunlight. So many people are in the big city. I am alone. Everybody has left.

I feel overwhelming fear and I imagine this glass box falling, crashing to the concrete in the middle of the big city, and then I have a sensation of falling. I wake up in terror. Terror turns to loneliness. Loneliness turns to sadness. Sadness turns to sorrow.

## - New Home -

My neck is stiff. My throat is tight and feels as if I've swallowed a little slimy goldfish, and it's stuck in my esophagus and cannot be digested.

### SESSION: All or Nothing

"What?" At the moment I sit down on the sofa, Donna asks.

"Everything goes wrong. I can't do anything right," I touch both of my temples as I sit on the chair in Donna's office.

Donna looks at me and waits instead of asking me a question.

"I had to role play in front of Ralph, my supervisor in the case conference. I played a therapist and my co-worker played a client. I'm a terrible therapist. Ralph looked so disappointed in me." The veins on my left temple stand out.

"You have things that are going well even though one thing is not. Where did the good parts go?" Donna asks.

"I don't know," my favorite response comes out as usual. I can't think when I feel shame.

"You've accomplished many things in your life. You came to the US and learned the language, earned degrees, made many good friends who admire you and trust you."

I stare at Donna, my face blank.

"Tell me how you learned a new language and finished graduate school."

I start telling Donna about how I got tired of being hidden in my parents' house, so I decided to cross the Pacific Ocean.

# - The Moon Home -

I'm tired of doing nothing but hiding in my parents' house after my first divorce, so I decide to get a job. I move to a studio apartment in Sapporo and work for a financial company with no goals or purpose. One night, when I am drinking beer with my girlfriend, she invites me to come to her English class. She says she is taking the class because she likes traveling. Apparently, the first session is free of charge. My girlfriend tells me to try it because we have nothing to lose. Doing something other than drinking would be a new thing to do, so I decide to go to the school after work.

A brand new building in downtown Sapporo has a brand new private English school for adults. When the elevator opens, I see a wall of clear glass on the bottom and frosted glass on top, with an open space through which we enter the class. I see people's legs and feet through the clear glass, but I can't see their faces because of the frosted glass on the upper wall. After my girlfriend introduces me to a lady in the front, she leaves to attend the beginner's class. The lady at the front desk tells me to try speaking English with a native speaker. The lady escorts me to a table. A red haired guy in his early twenties shows up. The lady introduces him and tells me in Japanese that he is a college student from New York traveling around Japan during his summer vacation. The lady and the guy talk briefly in English. I don't understand a word they say. The lady smiles at me and leaves. I stare at the guy's eyes without saying anything. After a awkward moment, he begins.

"Do . . . you . . . speak . . . English?"

## - New Home -

I understand the sentence, so I shake my head.

"Not one word?" the guy asks very slowly.

I've never been that close to a foreigner before. I'm nervous.

"Just one word, please," he is looking at me with his big round eyes wide open.

I search for some English words from a high school textbook, but I don't remember anything. I got Fs in most of my English classes. The guy's round eyes are getting bigger. I become more anxious to respond to his request. There is still some bubble woman sprit left in me after I've been hidden for six months. I should not say no to his request. I search for any English words from a movie, a video that I just saw on the weekend. My empty mind says, any word, say something.

"Fuck you," I finally articulate my first words.

The red hair guy starts laughing loud and hard while bending over his body – American people laugh loud. He gets up, and runs towards the hallway, still laughing – American people over-react. I sit up straight in the chair and wait for him to come back, but he is not coming back to the table. I sit on the chair as I look blank and absent-minded with an innocent look. I'm confused and shocked at the same time by his reaction. "Fuck you" is not funny, at least not in the movie I watched. When the guy sees the serious look on my face, he runs into the office and tells people about my first words. I still sit on the chair without moving. In my culture, students don't get up until the teacher dismisses us. Finally, the guy comes back to the table, and asks me one more question. This time, he does not slow down his words.

"Do you know any other words?" He looks at me curiously. I can see his enlarged black pupils in his eyes.

"Go ahead, make my day." This time, it isn't that hard.

"Dirty Harry!" He understood.

My daily routine changed from the day I had my first English lesson. I am not scolded for saying anything that comes to mind. I'm free, I feel alive, I exist.

Last night, I fell asleep without finishing chapter 1 of the "Basic English" educational tape, and the tape played repeatedly all night long. A mean and loud alarm clock on my bedside table starts making noise, and I wake up with an American woman's voice in my ear. As I get up, I pull the earphone out of my left ear. I shower, and then leave my apartment before my hair is dry, holding a coffee mug in my left hand. I go down the elevator and run toward to the subway station. I keep listening to the unfinished chapter 1 on the subway train. I have a place to live and the school to attend, but everything else would be unpredictable. I could never possibly know what would happen next. I'm now a 24 year old divorced woman who does not speak English.

Perhaps getting away from all the Japanese who rejected me would help my life get better. I hate my life here – it's broken. This country and my family can't give me what I need and want. In 1990, during the peak of the bubble economy, I decide to leave Japan and go to America, hoping to turn myself into a different person. I don't have any family or friends in America. I have not spoken to American people since I was 21 when I visited Hawaii. English class is the only preparation for my trip to America. However, when I determined to do something, I usually make it happen. It's a combination of my work ethic and bubble economy optimism. Even before I leave Japan, I start to feel that my life would soon be changing.

People say they go to America to have bigger houses, to feed their children better, and to achieve the American dreams. For me, after living in the extravagant bubble economy, ostentatious houses and plenty of wasted food are not attractive, and there is no American dream. I just want to escape from the rejection by my own people and society. I am not pursuing anything in particular other than change of location.

I've already left my job. I sold my furniture and almost everything else I owned. I say sayonara to my past and to the bubble effect. I purchase international health insurance for one year and a non-refundable plane ticket. I pack five t-shirts, two pair of jeans, a pair of walking shoes, two pair of socks, a pair of sandals, an English and Japanese dictionary, three pens, an eraser, and souvenirs for a host family in America.

When everything is ready for my trip to America, Mother is hospitalized after her kidney starts bleeding. Physicians don't know the cause, but Mother might need to have surgery. During my daily hospital visits, I debate whether I should postpone my trip to America. My school in California starts at the end of September, and if I don't arrive in time, I'll have to wait for the next quarter. I have a student visa, but it limits the time I can be in the U.S. If I stay in Japan, I'll stay a jobless, homeless demodori.

## - The Moon Home -

In the hospital, I follow Mother's physician and surgeon. After they've explained everything to me, I still follow them daily. When Mother's physician sees me in the hallway, he turns around and runs. He is tired of my questions, and I'm tired of asking questions. Father is busy working, and Sister is busy with her work and her new boyfriend, I have no one to talk to. One day, when I see Father and Sister at home, I burst into tears without any words. Father and Sister see my tears and think that this means Mother is dying. Sister cries all the way to the hospital, regretting that she hasn't been visiting her mother. Mother asks me why Sister is crying and why Father seems so kind. Mother asks if she is dying. I can't tell Mother that I want to shift the blame onto my family rather than blaming the illness. The next day, Father crashes his car, and tells the ambulance men that his wife is dying. Rational discussions do not occur in my family, and they opt to ignore reality and truth.

In the same month, Mother had two surgeries and the last one was successful. Mother's surgeon tells me that she can return home in a week. I wait for Mother to wake up from the anesthesia, and tell her that she will be home soon. When I'm leaving the hospital, I look at the sky. For the first time in a month, I am able to see something other than Mother. There is no way of knowing whether a storm is coming or if there will be a rainbow in the blue sky. I look to the east. It is the direction to America.

The last week of September in 1990, I fly from Sapporo to Tokyo Narita airport, then Tokyo to the Los Angeles airport. I'm wearing a white T-shirt and light color blue jeans, and carrying a

## New Home

heavy, silver 32 inch Samsonite suitcase. I'm sweating, Tokyo is still hot in September. Now, I'm alone in the airport knowing there is no turning back. I have not been sleeping well for months – I am exhausted. I can't explain rationally why I'm going to America, why this trip is a good idea, or how this will benefit me in the future. When I sit in the airport waiting for boarding, I begin having a flashback about a conversation I had with Mother a month ago. "Perhaps you should try a shorter trip first," Mother speaks from the kitchen. "Why?" I immediately respond. "You have never been to America." Mother is washing dishes. "I went to Hawaii twice," I respond. "Hawaii is not America. You know what I mean. Many people speak Japanese in Hawaii. People speak English in America. Remember, you got an F in English." Mother looks at me.

Could it be that I would've never thought about going to America if I had not failed college or marriage? Am I running away from something? Why is it so bad to run away? The reality of failing is inviting me to address some significant aspects of myself that I had kept in my safety box for a long time. I'm eager to disconnect myself from the past, a past of failure that includes left handed, failures in piano lessons, my high school entrance exam, my college entrance exam, marriages, being a female in Japan, and being a good daughter to my parents.

I am on my way to America with a one way ticket. I promise myself that I won't return until I finish school. I have never been to an airport alone or traveled by myself. I thought about all the different ways I could say goodbye to my family and friends, but I chose to be by myself. I pick up a pay phone and call Mother from the airport. She cries. I tell her that I

— *The Moon Home* —

will be OK, without knowing if I will be. People are waiving hands good-bye and leaving others on the other side of the gate knowing they will see each other again. When the plane starts to move, I see lights in the Tokyo bay. I wonder if I will see this land again. The airplane takes off. Everything is getting smaller in the blink of a moment. The city of Tokyo is fading away very quickly. And then, I forget the reason I'm leaving this land and what I'm leaving behind.

I arrive in Los Angles. I'm passing through customs and looking for a sign of the school I'm supposed to attend. The bus from the school is supposed to pick me up at the airport. I carefully listen to the airport announcements, but I don't understand a word of the announcements. I look for an information counter. I ask a lady at the information desk to make an announcement of my arrival so that the school pick up can find me. She looks at me and makes an annoyed face. She does not understand the English I've learned from the NHK radio station. I wait in front of the information counter but no one comes. After 30 minutes, the lady says something to me. I'm guessing she is saying that people from my school have left already. She probably just wants to get rid of me, but I can't be bothered by her annoyed look and uncharitable gesture. I have to get some transportation to get to my host family's house in Loma Linda, but I don't know how. English here does not sound like the English I have been listing to on NHK radio station for the past year. People speak so fast and with slang. I have no idea what the people around me are saying. I find some Asians, they look

- *New Home* -

like Japanese but they don't speak Japanese. People walk fast and try to get out of the annoying airport. I struggle for one hour dragging my heavy suitcase and trying to figure out how to get transportation at the noisy arrival area. The outdoor air quality at the airport is horrible, so I try not to inhale. Not many shuttle buses to go to Loma Linda, but I find one shuttle bus that goes to Loma Linda after it stops in downtown Los Angeles.

I get into the bus and sit in the back. A foreign shuttle bus driver is dropping off people at downtown LA. It is just like my repetitive dream of the glass elevator, where people leave one by one. In one hour, they are all gone. Now, it's just two of us, a foreign driver and a foreign exchange student. We are driving east on the 10 freeway. The sun is hitting the driver's dark short hair from the west. His wide shoulders extend beyond the back of the driver's seat. He looks at me through the rear mirror, I pretend to look outside. He makes gestures to come up and sit next to him, I ignore his gestures. He takes a piece of gum from his green polo shirt pocket and shows it to me. I move to the front of the shuttle to get the gum from his hand as if I were a puppy trying to get treats. I have no one to depend on but him. He looks at the address on the paper I gave him at the airport. "Are you a model?" he asks me with his accent and sarcastic eyes. "No," I say. Does he mean I look underdeveloped? Is he making jokes to break the ice? I can't read social cues in this culture.

Outside, it's getting dark. The foreign driver and the foreign student are not interacting anymore. As we get to Ritchie Canyon, San Bernardino county, it is completely dark. It seems as if the driver is lost. In 1990, there is no GPS or cell phones for ordinary people. The driver stops at an Albertsons near Loma Linda University, and steps out without telling me anything. He calls someone from the payphone. Multiple scenarios are going through my mind, like when one scrolls down computer screens as quickly as possible. I'm 25 years old, but I look a lot younger in this country. He might think I'm a teen. He might be thinking about selling me into the child pornography industry, or into human trafficking. What if he is calling his dealers to sell me to be shipped to another country for child sex slavery? I can't hear what he is saying. Is he talking to his associates to negotiate how much I could be worth in the black market? I don't want to be sold. I would rather be dead here than be shipped to another country for human trafficking. In this country, how many women and children are tortured, raped, and left for dead in the dark desert? If I die here, my dead body would be eaten by wild coyotes or mountain lions, and no one would ever know I made it this far. I start regretting leaving my old home.

The driver comes back to the shuttle without a word. He does not look happy, but he starts driving on the road with no lights or houses. Maybe his negotiation with the mafia didn't go well, maybe Asian girls are not popular in their industry. The moment that I feel that it is all over, the shuttle starts slowing down, I see something in the dark, a woman. Her blond hair and white dress stand out sharply against the dark. Her tanned skin makes her hair and the casual white summer dress look bold in the dark night of Ritchie Canyon. The driver gets out from the bus and approaches the woman. She looks petite next to the driver. While they are talking and laughing, I still sit in

## - New Home -

the shuttle, not moving. When they look at me through the windshield, I realize I should open the shuttle door and get out. I hand a $20 tip to the driver with the $90 ride fee. He says goodbye and leaves without counting the money. I stand in the dark driveway after he drives away. I could not thank him for his kindness. Somehow, I had made my way from Sapporo to a new home in Ritchie Canyon.

The recognition of my previous life and the stance of my identity are start to change. I had taken risks, left my old home behind. I come to America. I have a new home, with a new family and possible new friends. No one questions my failed past – I am reborn. I now have to grow new arms and legs and learn to crawl before walking a new way, hoping that this will be enough for a lifetime of happiness.

Tonight, I am greeted by a new family: Joy, her husband Kevin, their only daughter Melody, and a number of animals. Joy introduces Melody, who has blonde hair and green eyes, a petite 12 year old who seems shy. Kevin shakes my hand and takes my suitcase into their house. Joy takes me to the kitchen and opens the pantry, and she tells me to have anything I want. The unrecognizable boxes on the pantry shelves look like boxes of mysterious equipment. Ziggy, a German shepherd comes from the back yard and sniffs me and then the foods in the pantry. Puff, a white cat, runs under the sofa to hide when she sees me. Beauty, a black long-fur cat with golden yellow eyes, comes up to me and says hi. Her paws are damaged. Joy tells me that Beauty's paws got infected when her nails were removed. Every step she takes, she shakes her damaged paws before she lands a paw on to the carpet. But she keeps taking steps to get her destination. Joy takes me to the garage. Samantha, a long fur dachshund, lives in the garage because she is old and incontinent. Cinnamon and Angie, two other street cats, live in the garage with Samantha and keep her company.

I hear a loud screaming noise from the back of their house. A parrot is in a cage that is covered with a green and yellow gingham plaid linen cover. Her name is Georgia, but they call her George. Joy tells me that her neighbor abandoned George when they moved, so Joy took George home. I can hear her screaming voice along with pecking on the metal cage. The sounds of her hard beak pecking the metal cage are like construction noises. She sounds ferocious and infuriated. I sense her unending pecking sounds more than her frustration. Hidden anger can manifest itself in many ways, she is hidden under the cover, but her anger is not hidden. Somehow, this phenomenon becomes familiar to me.

Kevin seems embarrassed about George's outrageous behavior. He tries to move my attention to something else by saying, "We've received a letter from the school and it's said you are from Sapporo. What are the tourist attractions in Sapporo?"

I stare at him.

"What is the best sightseeing spot in Sapporo?" Kevin rephrases.

I understand his question this time, and say, "Hitsujikgaoka."

"What do they have there?" Kevin tries to have a conversation.

"Shiipu," I reply.

"What is Shiipu?" Kevin asks.

"Shiipu," I say little lauder.

## New Home

Kevin looks at Joy, but Joy shrugs.

"You know Shiipu." I insist.

Kevin looks at Joy for help. Joy shrugs with both palms open. It's hard to believe they don't know what Shiipu is.

"Cow?" I ask myself and them. "No," I quickly answer my own question, and shake my head. "Horse?" I ask myself and them. "No," I quickly answer my own question and shake my head harder. "Shiipu?" I ask myself and them. "Yes, shiipu!" I raise my index finger with my eyes wide open.

"Oh, it's sheep. She is saying sheep," Kevin looks at Joy with joyful sparkling eyes.

They finally understand. While they are figuring it out, I come to recognize that shiipu is Japanglish; Japanese pronounce the English word sheep "shiipu." It would have been easier for me to write what I wanted to say to them, because I can spell sheep. Then, I remember that one reason for me to stay with a host family is to learn the culture and improve my listening and speaking skills.

What I wanted to say is that there is a grassy hill called Hitsujigaoka (Hill of Sheep) in the middle of Sapporo near the Sapporo beer factory. We can eat fresh barbequed lamb and drink cold Sapporo beers at the restaurant on the hill. By the time I get them to understand what shiipu means, I'm too exhausted to try to explain the rest of the story. My English ability barely allows me to communicate about basic daily life and prevents me from sharing complicated thoughts.

I think I met the whole family, so I take a deep breath. The moment I try to sit on the couch, I hear a noise from the white fireplace next to the sliding door to the backyard. Two white mice in a plastic cage are running on their wheels. When Melody sees that I've noticed her mice, she pulls ET, a Texas desert turtle, out from under the white sofa in the living room. Joy tells Melody not to bother me with ET, then Joy escorts me through a wide hallway to see the rest of the house. Past the guest bathroom and Melody's bedroom, Joy takes me to my room. The bedroom looks three times the size of my studio apartment in Sapporo. A green glass antique lamp softly shines on a wooden desk. Next to it is a white metal antique bed in the middle of the room, against a window. I see something old that leads me into the new life. From the window, I see a pond with many orange-gold fish, and an orange backyard light makes their color even brighter. Melody opens the window, and she starts telling me the names of all 30 goldfish. Joy then takes Melody out of my bedroom so that I can rest.

After Joy closes my bedroom door, I lie down on my antique bed, I hear the sounds of sheep and crickets outside. The next door neighbor has several pet sheep and rabbits. The sounds of sheep and crickets are exactly the same as those in Japan. I feel relief knowing that something is the same in both lands. The moment I turn the side lamp off, sprinklers start in the back yard. The ceiling fan circles slowly above me and gently brings cool air. When the cool air brushes my skin, I smell wet grass. I sniff the breeze from the window, and sense what lays ahead in my new life in that new home.

The cool breeze from the open window wakes me up the next morning. It takes a moment to remember where I am, and I

## New Home

realize I forgot to close the window last night. How many times in my life have I woken up with a sense of excitement, excitement of the unknown? The clicking sound of a woodpecker echoes in the large silent backyard. Then, I hear some noise in the bush under the window. I get up from the bed and peek outside to see who is visiting the backyard in this early morning. I can't see the visitor. The wild desert covers Ritchie Canyon, and the temperature can still rise over 100 during September. The Canyon is home to many species of wild animals, including deer, coyotes, and mountain lions. Deer and squirrels are not inhibited about entering the yard in the early morning, when the air is still cool and people are still asleep.

Something is burning. There is a smell from the other side of the house. I wrinkle my nose, and follow the smell. Joy had lit incense in the living room. I hear noise and smell food cooking in the kitchen. The moment Joy sees me, she starts talking to me in English as she cooks bacon and eggs. I pay attention to Joy's mouth and try to figure out what she says. Joy figures out that I have no idea what she is talking about, yet she keeps talking to me the way a mother talks to her baby knowing that the baby does not understand a word. "Do you like this?" Joy points at the sizzling bacon on the pan. "Yes," I nod. I am not a fussy eater, so I eat everything that Joy provides. The food is not a problem, but the language is.

Meanwhile, Melody brings things from her bedroom and puts them on the floor for me to see. She speaks really fast, and I have no idea what she is saying. When she is showing me her Sanrio goods, I notice that she and I have something in common. I understand the words and the characters called Hello

## - The Moon Home -

Kitty and Kero Kero Keroppi. I can guess that Melody is telling me that there are Sanrio stores here in the state. Hello Kitty came to America before me. The idea of a cat with no mouth is like little Japanese girls with no voice. Hello Kitty sits in front of me. I look at Hello Kitty with my peripheral vision while Melody is telling me about her other Sanrio things.

The first thing I had to learn is to leave the door open when leaving the bathroom or bedroom. The opposite is true, in Japan, where they close the door when leaving the bathroom or bedroom. The second thing I had to learn is to walk and drive on the opposite side of the road. Everything I learn comes from my new family. Not many English words come out of my mouth, so I communicate with gestures and facial expressions, and my new family seems to understand me very well. I use my left hand to use the fork and spoon in my new home. I get no criticism for it. America brings my old self back into my life and removes my trauma and old bad memories. Joy and Kevin treated me with nothing but kindness during my time in their house. A few weeks after my arrival, Joy wrote to my parents telling them how they enjoy having me in their house, enclosing of her family photos and a box of American cookies and candies. Within a few weeks, my mother wrote back to Joy expressing her appreciation of Joy's kindness with more Sanrio goods for Melody.

I begin to babysit Melody on Wednesday nights because Joy and Kevin are gone for a few hours to attend couple therapy. For dinner, Melody and I find Dr. Peppers and Twinkies in the pantry. When we sit on the couch, Melody closes her eyes and prays, "Thank you for this food, thank you for these drinks,

## - New Home -

Amen." She then opens her eyes and looks at me. "Amen." I quickly catch up with her. Melody plays with Puff, the white cat, while she is eating her Twinkies. Melody figured out that I don't understand English. After our dinner, we bring beef jerky and popcorn into the living room and watch "I Love Lucy." Melody loves black and white movies and TV shows. Ziggy, the German shepherd, comes to me and steals my beef jerky. His eyes follows the beef jerky every time I bring it into my mouth. I throw a tiny piece of beef jerky in the air for Ziggy to catch. The tiny piece goes into his mouth and disappears before he chews. I throw a piece of popcorn into the air for Ziggy to catch. This time, I hear a popcorn smash between his teeth. We have the whole house to ourselves. We eat on the couch without using utensils and while watching TV.

Joy never asks me if I'm a Christian or I'm interested in going to church. She takes Melody and me to church on Sundays just like she has been introducing me the other daily activities such as going to school or to the grocery store. Joy shows me her ordinary daily life, and I learn how she lives. At first, I cannot understand the Minister's sermons. One day, however, I find myself able to understand some sentences. "Keep doing the right thing when you are in wrong situation. God closes one door because it's too small for you. His way is not our way, so be ready for the new way." The church music is sometimes a cappella and other times instrumental. It sounds clean, and seems to sink deep into my soul. I realize that I have not been drinking since I moved here. There is no alcohol in the house, and perhaps there is no reason to drink. The more I spend time with my new family the more I question why I had to drink so much in Japan, where I kept doing the wrong things when I was in the wrong situation. For many years, I thought I was so unfortunate failing in every aspect of my life, but If I hadn't failed at schools and marriage, I never would have left Japan. My spiritual healing starts with my new family. While most college exchange students are showing signs of homesickness, I don't experience homesickness. I find myself in much better hands. I sense that my roots can grow in the land of positive spirits.

"For a moment, it looked as if my hope that I would turn into a different person and have a totally new life ahead of me was coming true," I tell Donna, "but it was something much deeper than changing locations. I was hoping that I would become a little different when I kept staying away from Japan."

"When you have one bad thing, your mind become chaos, then you forget what you've accomplished in your life which is understandable. When you wanted to do something, your parents put you down. Your idea couldn't be supported."

"I still feel empty, especially when things don't go well. I feel alone."

"When you have broad ideas, you might feel empty, but maybe you can specify what it is you are looking for. For instance, what do you want from your mother? What are you looking for?"

"I don't know." My favorite word comes from my mouth when I don't want to think.

"Try not to find an answer. It could be X, could be Y, could be Z…"

## - New Home -

"I guess, fundamental things, like maybe awareness? Or affection? No, that's not it. I didn't get affection from my mother, why do I miss not having affection?" I'm looking at Donna's face as if for guidance.

"You believe everyone has answers except Yasuko. People don't give you the answer to you, they are hiding from you."

Seeking answers without my parents was all I did when growing up, and now I feel lonely when I try to find an answer by myself. Donna's giving me the answers has deep meaning to me. "Do I need my mother?" I ask myself.

"Can you say, I want this, instead of thinking I need this?" Donna pauses, looking at me.

My needs and wants haven't been satisfied. I become aware of the power of my aggression and disappointment, which occasionally turn inward to self-sabotage when things get chaotic.

### SESSION: Panic

"Disorganized, chaos..." I mutter to myself.

"What about being disorganized?" Donna asks.

"I easily spiral into chaos and panic when someone asks me to do things. For example, today, when my supervisor asked me for the first time to lead the case conference, I stuttered and couldn't respond. I now understand that my supervisor asked me because she believed I could do the job, but I didn't believe I could do it."

"How did it go? The case conference?"

"It went ok, but I hate my feelings. I hate that I panic."

"How did you do in school when you were growing up?"

"Nobody helped me."

"So you did everything by yourself?"

"I didn't do well."

"What things didn't you do well?"

"School, piano lessons, almost everything. I went to a stupid school and did stupid things." I keep looking at the floor.

"Last week, we talked about how you accomplished things in the US."

"I was able to do that because many people helped me."

Donna is waiting for me to speak. I think back to my first achievement in class when I was new to this country.

When I come to America, I start feeling like a 25 year old divorced infant. My life is consumed with learning a new language, experiencing new culture, and connecting with a new family. I don't have time to consume alcohol. I go everywhere with Joy and Melody, including to Melody's parent-teacher conferences, Melody's doctor appointments, the bank, grocery stores, movies, and vacations. I absorb the American way of living through my new family. Even before I learn much English, I have to learn some things quickly from Joy, such as how to prepare American foods, and how to drive on the other side of the road. I am like a rootless circular plant abruptly transplanted to the desert in Loma Linda. How long would it take to get accustomed to the new soil I was planted in? Would I be able to survive? At this time, my focus is on life in this house, not on school.

On the weekends, Melody's grandpa, grandma, uncle John, and aunt Mary visit Joy, Kevin and Melody. Physical touch is taboo in Japan, but not here. Hugs and kisses are daily accustom in the new family. I had read a book and watched movies about American people, so that I would not be surprised by their gestures and actions, yet it takes a while to get used to be touched. Nonetheless, despite my feelings of awkwardness, I start to feel loved and cared for, and even belonging, in this warm, caring, and loving environment in the new home.

During the first Christmas with my new family, Joy places a new white Christmas tree next to a pastel colored flowery fabric sofa in the living room and a green old Christmas tree in another room. Grandpa, grandma, aunts, uncles, and their siblings and cousins, come and visit us from Arizona and New York. I add more family members into my new life. Grandpa makes a wooden name plate and paints self-portraits, and gives them as Christmas gifts. Grandma bakes banana bread and wraps them in silver and green paper. Grandma's sister makes a doll with small plastic crystals. I have twelve presents under the Christmas tree for me to open. I've never had so many presents to open. I don't want Christmas to end.

On Christmas day, Grandma and Joy get up early to prepare the Christmas feast. Grandma makes turkey with gravy, green bean casserole, and apple pie. I have never seen or eaten turkey before. Joy bakes honey ham and some cranberry sauce, and Melody and I make mashed potatoes. Joy's dining room is large enough to hold everyone. Turkey, ham, corn, mashed potatoes, and macaroni salad are on my place. "We love Yasuko," grandmother tells the family members from other states. Though this is unfamiliar, I don't feel awkwardness anymore. I've found a new home and family, but I still haven't found goals or dreams.

My new family never asks me to go to school or do well in class, but as an exchange student, I must attend college full time in order to stay with my new family.

My mind was so preoccupied with Christmas and my new family that I forgot to register for the classes that I was supposed to take in the coming quarter. There are only a few classes that are still open, so I have to take computer science, psychology 101, philosophy/logic, and drawing. I am particularly worried about taking psychology 101, because the professor is supposed to be a very tough grader. I hesitate to register for these classes even though I have no choice. The lady at the registration desk is aware of my anxiety, so she tells me that I won't be at much of a disadvantage in psychology, because even for Americans, reading psychology books is like reading a foreign language – so many of the words are new.

Professor Thrasher, a behaviorist, teaches psychology 101. He does not smile while he lectures. At the end of the first class, he asks us if we have any questions. A young girl raises her hand and asks him a question about her romantic relationship. He replies, "If you want your boyfriend to keep coming back to you, you'd better not kiss him every time you see him, but only occasionally. It would be hard for him to stop coming back to you because he won't know when he'll get a kiss." The key to keeping a boyfriend is to give him intermittent reinforcement. The girl is not satisfied by the professor's answer to her question, so she keeps talking about her relationship problems. Was he referring to staying in the relationship or leaving the relationship? Unpredictability is the key to human behavior? Professor Thrasher then compares romantic relationships to slot

– New Home –

machines. Addictions and obsessions become conditions when people are waiting for a big payoff. People keep trying if they don't know when they'll get a reward.

"If you want to change your boyfriend's behavior, you should instead find someone who already meets your criteria, because that would be faster than trying to change your boyfriend." The professor gives us an important lesson: the key to human behavior. Rationally, it makes total sense, but most of us try to fix our significant others, and don't give up easily. I know I try really hard to change people's behavior around me.

Based on many human conditions that the professor talked about in his class, I start to see answers. The intellectual ones, so I keep taking psychology classes one after another. The missing pieces are starting to fall into place as my mind's work is shifting around me. My curiosity about human behavior takes me forward, even when my life goal is far from clear.

Although I find myself interested in psychology, the days of listening to lectures in English without comprehension or clear goals leave me melancholic. Psychological survival in the face of academic and language barriers, on top of financial challenges, make me feel distressed and isolated. Taking psychology classes brings back my memories of childhood, and makes me question my identity. My struggles between internal and external conflicts of longing continue, and sometimes I feel that I should just go back to Japan.

Before the mid-term exam, I go to an art gallery for a drawing class assignment. I stand up in front of an oil painting. A man sitting on a wooden rocking chair is looking through a window. Outside, a naked woman with long, brown hair is

## The Moon Home

facing the other way and looking at a beach. The man in the chair is holding a book and looking outside. He is looking far, farther than the landscape in the painting. My eyes are glued to the painting on the wall. Suddenly, I hear the voice of a guy. The guy is talking to himself as if I were not there.

"He looks familiar. I think I know him." He keeps looking straight at the painting.

I return my eyes back to the painting, and say, "The man in the painting looks like professor Thrasher."

"That's it," the guy says loudly.

He looks at me, I look at him, and say to each other, "You are in Dr. Thrasher's class." I've met Victor.

Victor and I study together at the library after class. Most of the time we are silent and read textbooks, but I feel less anxious knowing that I'm not alone and that I'm with someone who has the same interests and is doing things that I am also doing. I've made a friend outside of my new home, my first Mexican-American friend in America.

I've been reading the textbook for weeks with and without Victor. Tomorrow is the mid-term exam. Today, I read in the library for three hours and also read as I eat dinner. It's 10 pm, I'm not even close to the end, but my glasses break. I don't have money or time to fix them, so I tape the broken frame as a temporary fix. As time passes, I begin to sweat. The temporary scotch tape falls off my glasses. The letters in the textbook don't look horizontal. Is this my eyesight or is the book not written straight? Am I becoming crazy? Or stupid?

Though a 12 year old school girl should sleep more, Melody usually does not sleep long hours, she stays up late. She comes

## New Home

to my room to check if I'm still up as usual. She looks at my face and laughs. My glasses are crooked, and my messed up hair makes me look like a wild porcupine. Melody appears curious and energetic, her confident eyes seems lit from within. She looks at my notes for the psychology exam, she seems unsatisfied with my writing. I hear the garage door opens. Kevin gets home – he often works overtime. The moment Kevin gets into the house, Melody runs into her dad's arms and asks him to correct my writing.

"No, it's too much to trouble Kevin with. He just got home," I say to Melody.

"Melody, she is not comfortable," Kevin says as he tries to leave.

Melody begins begging her dad, "No, she will get a bad grade if she writes like this."

The difference between English and Japanese writing is not just grammar, it's also the structure of the writing. Since I haven't even taken English 101, the exam consisted of essay questions will be very difficult for me. I start thinking about the F I got in my high school English class in Japan.

Kevin takes his jacket off and removes his tie, and starts looking at my psychology notes. As he reads, he decides to correct grammatical mistakes. After he finishes correcting my grammar, Melody and I eat Twinkies to celebrate my finishing studying for the mid-term exam.

The following week, Kevin congratulates me for getting an A on the exam and takes Melody and me to a movie and for ice cream. From this experience, I've learned that seeking help when I need it is a key to success; at the same time, I am impressed with Melody's maturity. Despite my limited comprehension of English, despite the inhibition of my Japanese cultural norms, I am connecting with people in this country. If I stay in the new home with my new family, and keep attending school, will my future be brighter? Soon, the days of my dependence on the Windchack family are coming to the end.

After two years, I moved away from my American family and moved into a dorm. My purpose in coming to America had been educational, but living with this warm and loving family changed me emotionally and spiritually. I separated myself from Japanese customs by distancing myself from the rest of the Japanese. During my college years, part of me has changed and become Americanized, but the rest of me remains very Japanese. My dichotomized identity makes me continue to feel ambivalent toward both lands.

"All my life, I believed that people destroyed my goals and dreams, but many people helped me here in this country."

Donna nods. "Your parents didn't support your opinions. Your own ideas couldn't be supported. The feelings you had as a child came back when you faced similar situations and experiences, but you are not a little child anymore. Now, you have supervisors, colleagues and friends who support you."

For a long time, childhood passion and determination seemed to fade away, because I forgot the excitement of learning and living. My own people didn't teach me how to love myself; Ironically, I had to come to another country to learn. As I begin

## New Home

learning about myself, the excitement seems to be coming back to me. Now, the retrospectively, the time I spent in college to learn and eager to challenge my limitations seems to be purposeful. Donna's reflections target my feelings, my existence, and my recognition of accomplishments. When I feel my roots are growing in the soil of my new land, I start to feel alive again.

## CHAPTER SEVEN
## Therapist

I'm dreaming I'm in an elevator made of glass, and it's going up. I cannot get out, I believe. I should not get out, I know. The elevator stops on the fifth floor, and strangers get in. Strangers get out. But I have to stay. The glass elevator keeps going up until I can see trees and building below. Above me, I notice the elevator has a single rusty wire that is too thin, too fragile to for an elevator of this size, but it continues up, it continues to stop at floor after floor, and people get out.

And when they exit, the elevator sways left, and then right, fragile, sensitive to the weight change, but it continues up to the next stop. Men and women leave. Again, the elevator sways, and as it sways, I turn my eyes to the elevator's glass floor, where gray apartment buildings and houses are lined up in rows like ants in an ant colony. A few oak trees with knobby trunks bend as if they are following the sunlight. So many people are in the big city. I am alone. Everybody left.

My emptiness is filled with overwhelming fear and I imagine this glass box falling, crashing to the concrete in the middle of the big city, and then I have a sensation of falling. I wake up in fearful terror. Terror turns to loneliness. Loneliness turns to sadness. Sadness turns to sorrow. My neck is stiff. My throat is tight and feels as if I've swallowed a little slimy goldfish, and it's stuck in my esophagus and cannot be digested.

Suddenly, the glass elevator moves quickly. A sudden rush of coldness in my spine. My body elevates in the air with the quick motion. I look up through the glass ceiling. The rusty thin wire is no longer able to hold the weight. The elevator drops with accelerating speed. It crashes on the ground and breaks into small pieces. My soul lifts off while my body is still on the ground. I stand up. I look at a woman who died on the ground. I look at her face. She is not me. I didn't die. I wake up with a relief.

### SESSION: *Failure as a Therapist*

Clients learn much about themselves talking to therapists; I know I did. But today, I can't help asking Donna how she feels about listening my complains for many years. "Are you tired of listening to my blah, blah, blah stories for years and years?"

"Working as a therapist puts me in a such privileged position, people share with me their life events that they've never shared with anyone before, and I feel honored to be part of their lives," Donna says. As a therapist, I feel that is true, and even if it's not, Donna's response makes me feel less guilty about telling her one more blah today. I must start to feel my stories cannot be completely worthless.

"My day didn't go well. I had an disagreement with one of my colleagues. It wasn't a big deal. It shouldn't bother me, but I can't shake my feelings. My colleagues are studying for the licensing exam, but I'm not motivated. I'm irritated. I don't know if I even want this."

"You said that you came back from Tokyo to get a license." Donna demurs.

"It's not as if I wanted to go back to Japan, but I was rejected from the all agencies I applied to at the time of my graduation. Because I didn't get a working visa, I had to leave the country."

"You said you did some internships in California."

"I did a one-year internship at Lutheran Social Services."

Donna's questions make me revisit my past. The internship memory comes back to my mind.

I'm sending my resume to Asian-related non-profit organizations in the Los Angeles area, applying for the required practicum internship experience during my graduate program. No organization has contacted me. I'm getting nervous and thinking that I might not be able to graduate this year. Then two week later, Dr. Blair at Lutheran Social Services contacts me. I don't remember if I had sent my resume, but I arranged an interview. On the phone, Dr. Blair says it will be a group interview.

As I enter the office, I see seven therapist interviewers in the room. Each of them asks me questions. Dr. Blair observes how the interviewers ask questions, and how I interact with each of them. Surprisingly, I am accepted by the team. Sue,

## Therapist

a therapist at Lutheran Social Services, is also a volunteer at a homeless shelter in Riverside County. Riverside County has created a new program that helps homeless people get housing, jobs, and mental health services. Sue takes me to the Riverside County homeless shelter so that I can volunteer there and get more experience.

My first client at the program is David, a homeless retired Vietnam veteran with a Master's degree in education. He is under psychiatric care and is looking for someone for weekly supportive therapy sessions.

At our first meeting, David walks into the session room slowly and carefully. He bends his head to go through the door so that he won't hit his head. He glances at me and sits on the chair without speaking. He wears clean jeans and tennis shoes – he does not look homeless. He starts talking without looking at me. I listen carefully. David does not stop talking for one hour, and I try hard to make sense out of his talk. After an hour, I feel guilty about not asking any questions, so I ask one question that has nothing to do with his talk. David answers my question, and continues to talk for another 30 minutes. Since I do not have another client after David, no one interrupt us. The more I listen to him, the more I get confused, and I start losing confidence in my ability to comprehend English. I can't leave the room – I can't abandon him.

Outside, it's getting dark. My butt is sweaty and glued onto a black plastic chair. My white eyes are turning red. I'm blinking faster so that I can get water in my eyes. After three hours, David asks me if it's OK for him to leave. With my permission, he leaves. All of my colleagues have left except a security guard.

After I get into my car and begin to drive on the 10 freeway, my tears starts running down. I am incapable of comprehending clients' English. I won't be able to be a therapist. I may be moving down the wrong path.

The next day, in a group supervision, a meeting where our supervisor meets with the therapists, Sue, my colleague asks me about my opinion of David. With little embarrassment, I tell her honestly that I did not understand what he was talking about. His speech did not make any sense. Sue smiles and tells me that he was diagnosed with schizophrenia, and often he shows up without taking his medications. When he doesn't take his medications, his talk becomes incomprehensible. I realize that that my tendency to doubt myself affects my professional work as well as my romantic relationships.

David continues to come and see me when he is on medication. He brings his Master's degree and his grade transcripts to our sessions. Maybe he feels that I don't believe his story; maybe many people around him had not believed him. After several weeks, he starts to bring his charger and charges his phone during our sessions. In 1997, many people did not have cell phones. Within a month, he starts to leave his gold card and his bank check book in my office. He gets a monthly pension from the US army and pays his cell phone and credit card bills by using the card. It is hard to believe his diagnosis of paranoid schizophrenia under these circumstances. After seeing and experiencing terrifying events in combat, people can develop serious mental conditions. I know that many returned veterans suffer from PTSD, but I also learned that war-zone trauma creates risk for developing other mental illness as well. I'm uncertain of David's hallucinations are organic or triggered by a traumatic-events.

David remains homeless. He does not want to find a permanent place to live because he is afraid that "the government" might find him and terminate him. There is a stunned silence when he has nothing to say. Some days, he just sleeps during the session and then wakes up, thanks me, and leaves. His speech and mannerism have been quite polite throughout the sessions.

At the weekly group supervision, I get a chance to present David's case. Other interns ask Dr. Blair about the reason for David's behavior, sounding as if they doubt what they are hearing from me. I feel that my colleagues do not believe my case presentation. I have an urge to show them proof of David's degree and gold credit card. I feel that I am experiencing something similar to what David is experiencing, helping me to understand what he has been experiencing such as the feeling of not being believed. The only way to truly understand David's world is to actually be in his world. David invites me to be in his world so that I can feel what he feels. "Perhaps David feels that Yasuko is harmless to him," Dr. Blair says to the therapist interns. Maybe that's what David needs, a place where he can feel safe and sleep. I decide to focus on David's symptoms rather than his diagnosis, and try to provide what he needs.

Two months later, Dr. Blair recommends that I see a five year old girl who is living with her unemployed single mother in the Lutheran Social Services' housing program. L.S.S. Counseling Center has a play room for children on the first floor. The play room becomes a therapy room when we have play therapy with children. A beige couch that looks as if it came from a second hand store sits in front of a window. Near a wooden bookshelf filled with colorful children's books and toys.

Ashley walks into the room with her mother. After several sessions, she does not hide behind her mom anymore. Her long brown hair is loose on her shoulders today. She seems a lot taller than the last time I saw her, which was a week ago. Her mother leaves the room as she waves to Ashley. Ashley is not interested in reading books today. She is not playing with her favorite stuffed bear either. She lies down on the carpet and touches my beige leather loafers. She tells me that she really likes my shoes. I keep looking at her face. She says she likes the color and shape of my shoes. I smile at her. Ashley moves close to a square plastic sand box filled with sand.

Ashley does not want to play with dolls or animals in the sand box. She grabs as much sand as she can with both hands and throws the sand in the air. I look at Ashley without saying a word. She looks at me and gives me a huge smile. I smile back at her, but my cheeks are twitching. Ashley shrieks with laughter as she grabs more sand and throws it over and over again, adding more and more sand on the carpet. I feel as if I'm sitting in the eye of a tornado in the Kalahari Desert. I can't breathe. Should I tell her to stop? Ashley gets into the sand box and jumps, then throws herself onto the couch with both arms open. She enjoys being dirty. She is free, she is alive, she exists.

After I vacuum the play therapy room, I sit on the couch for a while. I'm still paralyzed. Therapy textbooks don't say that children are going to throw sand. Aren't they supposed to play with dolls, animals, and soldiers in the sand box? I look around the play room. It's a mess. I'm a mess. Everything looks as dry as sand. The sand box is as empty as my mind. The next day, I purchase a plane ticket back to Tokyo.

I realize that I couldn't completely leave my old life when I left Japan the first time. I was afraid of Ashley's free sprit as my mother was afraid of me. I abandoned Ashley as my mother abandoned me. I felt guilty about rejecting the little girl, and I felt shameful for doing so as a therapist. I didn't know how to deal with Ashley's free sprit. She brought up emotions that I didn't want to deal with, I saw myself in her, so I rejected myself. Then, I felt terrifyingly lonely and empty. Eager to disconnect from my failed past, I created the same situations that I had experienced as a child. Does 6 years of studying psychology and getting a master's degree means anything to me at all?

"I wasn't a good therapist intern. I don't know if I should pursue this profession. I guess I'm feeling nervous because my internship hours are nearly complete."

"What makes you feel nervous?" Donna asks.

"I understand that I have a supervisor, a mentor, and colleagues, all of whom support me and guide me, but it is hard to believe that I'm capable of doing a good job in this field. Sometimes, I doubt if I even want this."

"Is that realistic?" Donna speaks, "As soon as you wanted something, you got hurt. As long as you don't want anything, you are safe. Now, you have knowledge, you are trained, you have colleagues and supervisors who support you and believe in you. All those goodies, you can give it to clients, but it's up to clients if they want to take it and make changes." Donna looks at me and continues, "You put all positive, good things on me and clients, except on you. That would be hard."

I close my eyes slowly. If I picture Ashley's sand box through my Grandma's eyes, the sand tornado would be rainbow sprinkles and stars in the Milky Way. Ashley reminds me of the feeling of being alive; running toward something that is fascinating, exciting, something that I'm in love with, and dreamed of. She was just exploring her world and telling me how to live.

When I get out from Donna's office building and look up at the sky, I notice that there are stars even above the city of Los Angeles.

### SESSION: Running Away?

"One of my colleagues said that she's been in personal therapy for nine years." I look at Donna as I'm crossing my arms. "I'm running back and forth between two countries for the past ten years, but I'm not sure if I'm getting anything from those moves. I've been coming to therapy for three years. Am I even getting anything from my sessions? Do I ever get better? Am I moving forward or stuck in the same spot?"

"In therapy, we experience our feelings and various systems of thought, through present relationships or events. Having feelings in the session by remembering and talking about the past event brings our various feelings from the past into the present." Donna takes a breath. "Understanding causes of emotion intellectually and experiencing feelings of the emotions are diffident. Experiencing emotions from the past and understanding them on an emotional level, not on an intellectual level, takes time." Donna looks at me.

## - Therapist -

In the past a few years of therapy sessions, memories of events and feelings have come back to me as if I were waking from a vivid dream. During the bad weeks, I express my miserable feelings of fearfulness. During the good weeks, I express my uncontainable feelings of loneliness. In therapy, I understand that people move forward at their own speed. Although I am eager to move as fast as I can, I also know that therapy does not work that way. I'm frustrated about the licensing exam and my therapy progress.

"Am I running away again?" From the licensing exam, therapy, and everything I've been doing? I've learned that the answers that I'm looking for are within me, but I can't help asking Donna.

Instead of answering my question, Donna asks, "A few years ago, you returned to the US to get a license. How were you able to do that? I believe not many people could come back to the US after they finish school here and then return to their own countries." My forgotten memory of living in Tokyo comes back quickly to my mind.

In March, 1999 in Tokyo, cherry blossoms are all around the Tokyo Narita Airport, as they were when I left in 1990. Returning to Japan is, for me, much more of a culture shock than coming to America from Japan. The Japanese people seem very different now compared to the time I left Japan during the bubble economy, they have lost powerful energy and money. People and the city look all gray. During the bubble economy, the Japanese were fascinated by everything foreign, but

- *The Moon Home* -

now they don't appreciate anything that is from overseas. My American degrees seem to have little value in Tokyo.

I take a subway and surface train straight to my aunt Kazu in Ginza, Tokyo to stay with her for a few weeks, because there are more job opportunities here than in Hokkaido. Aunt Kazu and I have not seen each other for decades. She moved to Tokyo from Hokkaido to be closer to her only son after her husband died. After we catch up on family matters, I find a news paper ad for a college teaching position in Tokyo. The college is looking for people who have a psychology degree. Even though this is not the path I want to take, I call and set up an interview for a non therapist position. Since the US did not permit me to work for pay during my student stay in America, I have no money. After the interview, the interviewer gives me 5000 yen ($50) for transportation before offering me the position. I have never earned that much for less than one hour's work. I take the money and the teaching position, and start looking for part-time therapist work that I can do during the hours I'm not teaching.

Those who can, do. Those who can't, teach. The first class I teach in college is psychology 101. I walk into the classroom, students are talking to each other and laughing. The moment I stand up in front of the blackboard, all 50 students stop talking. Their heads are all down, and no one looks at me or responds to my greetings. No one will volunteer to answer my questions unless I point to a particular student. Suddenly, one of students walks toward me from the back. He's 19, tall, and slender man. I stop lecturing and keep my eyes on him. He comes close to me, I step back. He gets closer to me again and whispers, "Can I go to the bathroom?" I look at him and the rest of the class,

## - Therapist -

"Of course." I find his question very odd, but then I realize I've forgotten the Japanese cultural norm after many years living in America. Japanese students are not allowed to leave the class without permission.

My lectures are in Japanese, which should be a comfortable language even for a returnee like me. I realize, however, that eight and a half years in America not speaking Japanese made my Japanese a little rusty, and two weeks in Tokyo is not enough time for me to get back up to speed. The students are sensitive, spoiled, and depressed city kids. Some complain to their advisor that they don't understand my Japanese. Because I did not learn psychology in Japanese, all of my psychology vocabulary is in English. Teachers and students confuse when I combine English words with Japanese. Sentences that start with "I" are very common in English, but very rare in Japanese. My Japanese co-workers and friends tell me that I use "I" way too often. I look like a typical Japanese, but I don't speak correct Japanese and don't have the proper mannerisms, and this is not acceptable in Japanese society.

I have nearly 500 students total in my classes. Each time I start a new class, I start by saying, "I came back from America a few weeks ago after eight and a half years of studying America.". As soon as I say this, students' heads come up and they pay attention. In the classes where I start with this explanation, the students don't complain about my rusty Japanese. After a few months, my Japanese gets much better, but I begin forgetting how to speak English.

My students are surprised by the discussions in my class. Instead of expecting students to just listen during the class and memorize things for the exam, I ask them to express their own opinions and to disagree with me or other students if their opinions differ. Also, despite the usual rules, I tell my students that they don't need permission to go to the restroom. At first, students are confused by these changes, and then they complain and become hesitant to comply, but I am determined not to change my position. If students like the normal Japanese class rules, they can find plenty of Japanese teachers in Tokyo who follow those rules. By the end of the first semester, the students seem to enjoy learning a new way in the classes, and become very good at it. When my students begin to use another way to identify themselves and connect with others, I become hopeful that this society might change so that kids can express themselves more freely. It has been my wish for many years that kids in this country can express their ideas and thoughts openly without any fear.

The same semester, one of my students comes up to me after class, smiles, and says, "Sensei, you have a good life. Don't you think you have a good life? You were able to go to America and get degrees." This simple thought never occurred to me until I hear from my student. I needed to come back to Tokyo and hear it from a 19 year old girl.

Teaching at a college in Tokyo might be attractive to many new graduates. Though I enjoy connecting with young students, I can't imagine devoting the rest of my life to teaching. Unfortunately, there are no full time therapist positions in Japan even in the stressful obsessed city of Tokyo. After sending 32 job applications to all over the country, I have not received any replies.

## *Therapist*

After my students become comfortable with classroom debate, they start to try it with other professors. The students are ready, but the professors are not. The professors don't want to acknowledge that students can have opinions and can express them, and the professors also feel that students are becoming disrespectful and rebellious. Students should not disagree with teachers and professors! Students must be obedient! Professors want to make sure that students grow up and fit in the society in which they should never question anything. Expressing one's ideas and opinions in Japan is self-centered and destroys harmony. Debating in class is disrespectful and rebellious. I'm hoping to give my students a taste of my school experiences in America, but the reality of their beliefs and school systems are far away from hopeful.

In my second year teaching, I struggle with my feeling of being disconnected from other professors. My ideas and style confuse them when I speak my mind in the American way. I try hard to replace my American thinking with Japanese thinking. I have to re-learn how to be obedient and quiet. The more I try to be a good Japanese woman, the more I become mute and mindless. Meanwhile, my 32 applications for therapist positions had been rejected. All my life I had yearned to be accepted by my own culture and people, but everything in Japan again becomes my place to fail. What was the point of going to America if I ended up feeling the same? Day by day, associating with people in Tokyo brings me back the familiar feeling: if I stay quiet, don't think, and don't talk, the feeling will soon be all gone and everything will be OK. I separate myself from others and stay in my own world of darkness.

## The Moon Home

Shortly after my second year started, I went back to Hokkaido for a funeral. My uncle's death from Alzheimer's disease had me in low spirits. I spent most of my time alone and stopped talking to my colleagues. After eight and a half years of my absence from Japan, I'd hoped that opportunities for people who earned degrees overseas would be more plentiful. Now, the reality is, people in Tokyo seem to be interested in themselves and comfortable with customary domestic affairs, and that keeps them from expanding their horizons. Their world had become smaller than it was before I left.

Even under my depressed state of mind, I have to learn a new way of living in Tokyo, just like I learned a new way of living in America. I must get used to using public transportation because of the constant traffic congestion on the street. People in the subway stations look down at the ground, standing silently and politely. I push my way toward the train by moving through the crowd. The best way to save your energy is to move as the others do and not push anyone. People keep quiet, usually close their eyes in the subway whether they are seated or not. They are all wearing dark, business attire, usually black, dark blue, or gray. Pale salarymen and office ladies with expensive brand name purses and watches stand up patiently in the packed train. A middle-aged salaryman folds his newspaper as small as possible to save space, as if he were doing origami. All one's body parts touch other bodies. You can even smell the breakfast they ate. Once you get off one train, people usually have another train to catch. My feet and legs move themselves to get to the next destination. The people seem always polite,

# - Therapist -

but indifferent. Everybody is in a hurry, everybody is silent. By the time I arrive in the office, I am already exhausted.

I have no idea how people have the energy to drink alcohol after work every night. They need to do this to smooth interpersonal relations at work. Happy hour lasts for several hours. Male-dominated workforces are expected to put in long hours, often without overtime pay, and then stay drinking with the boss in smoky bars until the last train departs. Night trains are full of drunks, mostly middle-aged salarymen, but some elementary school kids who just finished tutoring classes after their regular school are also in the last train which runs before midnight. The drunken salarymen with red faces are almost unconscious, with eyes closed and their bodies moving back and forth as the train moves. Some drunks fall down as they are unable to balance their bodies. Elementary school kids are used to those drunk salarymen and ignore them as they read their textbooks. This strange mismatched scene represents how safe Tokyo is.

At the end of the last semester, I'm sitting in the last train going back to my rented house in the city of Kamakura, which is an hour and a half by train from Tokyo. Being among many other Japanese, I get the same feeling that I had ten years ago. I look at a drunken salaryman who sits next to me. His head is touching my shoulder, I smell cigarettes from his ruffled sticky hair. Suddenly, I'm back in the late 1980's. I thought I left this society to be a different person. Here I am, after ten years, after spending tons of money and energy in American schools, and yet I am the same person I was ten years ago. Without moving my head, I look at the drunken man's head on my shoulder. I push his head off my shoulder – he doesn't even notice.

## - The Moon Home -

A young woman sitting opposite me pretends not to see my action. When I look at her emotionless face and the drunken salaryman's motionless body, I realize what I need. I need to get out of this society before I become careless and indifferent.

My desperation to leave Tokyo is caused by my rejection by the Japanese people and my disappointment in Japan. The same year, the summer of the year 2000, I decide to visit Los Angeles and stay with a college friend for three weeks. One benefit for working at a college is that there is a long summer vacation.

In Los Angeles, all of my friends are working during the day. I rent a car and go shopping. When I'm at a grocery store in Torrance, I find an ad on the board that is seeking a Japanese speaking volunteer counselor at a church in Van Nuys.

The next day, I drive on the congested 405 freeway to the church. I park my Honda rental car in the parking lot. As soon as I walk into the church, Reverend Haruko quickly finds a new face and smiles at me. I tell her that I'm only here for two more weeks, but that I want to volunteer for the church. Some part of me misses being a therapist, though the experience was a such a short period of time. I also miss having a great mentor and supervisor who provides and shares his knowledge. After we discuss my experience, Reverend Haruko asks a parishioner who works at a bookstore to help me to find a non-Christian counseling center in Los Angeles because I don't have training in Christian counseling. Reverend Haruko hands me the book she wrote, and tells me to keep in touch.

Two days later, the parishioner from the bookstore takes me to the medical clinic next to his bookstore. I bring my resume and a letter confirming that I did practicum intern hours at

## - Therapist -

Lutheran Social Services. The medical clinic is operated by a surgeon who works at Cedars Sinai Hospital. The clinic has several physicians including a therapist, but the therapist only works on Tuesdays and Thursdays. The lady at the front desk tells me that the therapist might have ten minutes between his sessions and that she would try talking to the therapist if I come back on Thursday.

My original plan is volunteering for the church for a few weeks as a counselor. Now, my direction seems to be changing. Like my first trip to America, this one didn't have a specific purpose or goal. The purpose and goal come to me later. I always thought I ran away, that's what I do, but every time, in this country, things work ironically and differently. That is why I've chosen this country, which is full of opportunities and people who help me to shape my life. And I hope I can do the same for others. This is where I belong.

The very next day, around 2 pm, I come back to the medical clinic hoping to see the therapist. I arrive a half hour early so that I won't miss his ten-minutes break. The therapist does not know that I am coming to see him today. He is still in session. I sit and wait in the cool waiting room. A 4x4 photo on the wall catches my eye. The photo is of two white origami cranes on a black background, in a silver photo frame. I get up from the chair and stand up in front of the photo for a while. The two white cranes sit together, but their beaks are pointed in the different directions. The photo is simple, clean, and serene. Mindlessly, I look at the piece on the wall. The office door opens. I hear my name, but my eyes are glued to the crane photo. I again hear my name, so I turn my head toward the door and look annoyed. When

## The Moon Home

I look at the man in the doorway, my shoes are still pointed at the photo. The man looks confused. "I'm sorry, I was so into the photo, I couldn't hear you," I say to him before I introduce myself. His face looks distinguished and serious. "I took the photo," he says in a deep tone without smiling.

Even though I don't have an appointment, Ralph says that he has 10 minutes between clients, so he escorts me into his office. He wears khaki chino pants and a dark green short sleeve polo shirt. He has the body of a gymnast. When I sit on the couch, I notice that the dim orange light next to his chair reflects off his bald head and shadows his thick dark beard. I know I have only 10 minutes, so I tell him that I want to volunteer while I'm in LA because I miss working with clients, and explain my passion and commitment for this work. Ralph listens to me skeptically and asks, "Would you be planning to get licensed in California? If you are, let's talk more on another day." He looks at his watch. I nod anxiously.

That's how I met Ralph, my mentor and father figure who would later become the most important sensei of my life. Two years of struggling to prove myself in my own country has brought me exhaustion, yet 10 minutes of meeting with Ralph seems to bring me hope, and I sense the direction of my life begins to change.

At the airport, on my way back to Tokyo, I'm thinking of the conversation with Ralph, a therapist who is also a photographer, competitive shooter, and martial arts practitioner. At our second meeting, he said that photography, competitive shooting, Aikido, and therapy have a common theme. We have to become one to be good at it. Understanding the concept might

## Therapist

take some time, but as I think about the next chapter of my life, having mutual trust and deep understanding between a mentor and me begin to seem important for my profession. I still have to complete the semester at the college in Tokyo, and if I decide to leave the college, there will be no turning back.

By the time I get back to Tokyo, I am determined that nobody can stop me from returning to America. My second trip to America will be different from my first, when I had no goals or plans, and was just running away. This time, I'd be running toward my goal to get licensed. The last semester of teaching at the college in Tokyo goes very quickly. My mind and heart are already in my other homeland. This time, I know how to prepare for the trip.

At the airport, I am anxious to leave. I had woken up too early. I had wanted to go quietly but Mother insist on coming to the airport with me. When I leave her on the other side of the gate, I stop and turn, stand and still, hoping that I will see her again. She smiles with sadness. She looks so old and small. I wave goodbye one more time, and I leave the gate. Her small body and sad smile make me feel scared. Part of me wonders, what if I change my mind? Should I go back to her? Should I stay with her? I then hear a departure announcement. No, that's not me. I am me. I won't be afraid.

I look at her face one more time. It is serene. Now, I can look at her. Now, I can remember her face. I run. I run toward my new home without any hesitation. In ten hours, I will be in a totally different land. The plane takes off. I close my eyes so that I won't see the lights of the city in Hokkaido.

"On my second trip to America, I thought I was running forward, not running away." I look at Donna for assurance.

"Your desires are driving yourself forward. That's what you always wanted," Donna says undoubtedly.

### SESSION: *Failed License Exam*

"It's good to see you," Donna starts the session, months after our last meeting.

"It's been a while." I pause. "I failed the exam."

"I know, I got your message."

"I'm here to talk about it, but I don't know where to start."

"Your roommate Brenda left for Georgia, your mentor Ralph left for Santa Fe, your friends Jan and Rick left California, and two ex boyfriends got married. You didn't have a lot of good things happen in the past a few years."

"I haven't been to therapy for months because I couldn't talk about it. I feel slow."

"That's because you were vulnerable. Under stress, people regress. Now you can talk about it."

After a long silence, I look at Donna. I realize that I talked about many shameful memories in past sessions, so I can do it one more time. I start telling Donna about my failed exam.

I'm sitting in my car in the parking lot while I gaze at the steering wheel without tears, feeling depleted. When I roll down the window to breath, the Santa Ana warm, dusty wind hits me in the face. Still no tears. I'm barely holding both hands on the

# - Therapist -

black steering wheel. I'm not ready to leave, so I keep holding the wheel until my mind is ready to process the exam. I am hoping for an explanation of my emptiness. I begin reflecting on the past four long hours of the state licensing exam.

The test room is uncomfortably cool. The air conditioning keeps blowing from the vent into the glass-walled room. My fingers are numb, my neck is chilled, my feet are freezing, and my mind is already frozen. I need to go outside and get some warm air, but I can't. I'm staring intently at the computer. I have to click on the "result" button if I want to leave the room. Do I want to know the result? I take a deep breath. Before I exhale, my right index finger move slightly. I click. I see the word FAIL. I failed the first part of state licensing exam.

I get up from the chair that I've been sitting in for four hours. I open the glass door, and get out of the cold glass room. "Sorry," the lady who printed out the result looks at my photo on the paper, and then looks at me. I take the paper from the lady and leave the room. The word FAIL looks so small, yet it's enormous in my mind. It is official. The one word, FAIL, is all it takes to crack open all my old stories of failing the high school entrance exam, the college entrance exam, and marriages.

After I failed the first part of the exam, I work harder to prove myself. As I treat drug abuse clients for overdoing behaviors, I struggle with being a workaholic and with compulsion. I have been working six days a week, Friday nights until 8 pm, Saturdays until 2 pm. Nothing is enough. The more I work, the more I become small. I feel as if I am disappearing. No tears or words. If I stay quiet, don't think, and don't talk, the feeling will soon be all gone and everything will be OK. These familiar feelings of comfort make me uncomfortable. Am I trying to compensate for my failure by working too hard?

Suddenly, my eyes are wide open at 2 am. I don't know what woke me up, but I'm thinking about my work. It happens again the following night, and the next, night after night with no dreams. I cannot have dreams. My conscious mind has been taking over. Soon, my voice twitches, my shoulders become crusty rocks, and my lungs lack oxygen, then my old self comes back and haunts my mind. My feeling of disappointment takes me back to old wounds that I had received in my childhood, and the damaged parts become alive again. I've forgotten that when I am determined to prove myself, I'm easily tempted to disappear, to feel despair, to dispute, discount, and destroy myself.

For me to get out of the state of mind, I physically have to remove myself from the current condition. This time, I decide to go back to Grandma's old house in Hokkaido. I don't even pack. I have no energy to pack. I take my passport and credit card, and fly from Los Angeles Airport to Tokyo, and from Tokyo to Hokkaido.

The ten long hours of flight seem like a short time for a mindless body. When I arrive at the airport in Hokkaido, I gaze at the winter view of the island. Flowers and green on the hills of the Kitoushi mountains are far below the snow line. The mute white land and the pale sky including the landscape has become all white. The gardens of gifts are all under snow. They all look dead.

I sleep, and eat a little, and then sleep more. Day after day I do nothing but sleep. After I lie in bed all day for one week,

## - Therapist -

I wake up in the afternoon, and lie on the couch for rest of the day. My eyes are open, but I am seeing nothing but air. I lay down and do nothing for two more weeks.

One afternoon, after three weeks of sleeping days and nights, I wake up. I'm scratching my head and body. My body is itchy; I start smelling myself; my pajamas are filthy; I don't remember the last time I changed my underwear; but it doesn't matter. I scratch more and use the blanket to cover my head. I scratch my neck, underarms, and legs. After I keep scratching my body like a monkey, I realize I can't sleep if I keep scratching. I need to take a bath so that I can sleep more. I have no energy to clean the tub or start the hot water, so I decide to go the neighbor's hot spring. Not because I want to, but it's because of physical necessity.

I get into my father's 4 wheel drive truck on the snow. The windows are foggy and frosty. When I start the engine, cold air comes out from the heater. I see my white breath coming out from my mouth. I haven't driven in snow for decades. Surprisingly, my body still remembers how to drive on the snow. The connection of thoughts and movement happen as I drive. There is no sidewalk on the narrow country roads, no cars on the road as I drive further. The flakes are coming down, then the snow starts falling thick and fast.

I stop in the middle of the road, which is stretches along the bottom of the Kitoushi Mountain. The slope is gentle. The monochrome white birch and failing snow on the hillside makes the landscape seem barren. Hundreds of white birch are on the left side of the hill, the dark trunks contrasting with the white snow. On the right side, there is a town below, but snow blocks the view. I look at the far end of the hillside, where the trees are so far away that I can't see the end. The white birch have been on this land for hundreds of years. There is no doubting what they are. Nature cannot be moved – they never get lost. Ancient trees are still here to pass down wisdom. Everything is surrounded, and everything except me seems certain of itself.

The drift of falling snow, the perfect whiteness lies on the miles of white birch on the slope. I get out of the truck. No jacket on. The snow is ankle deep. The pores on my skin close quickly. The temperature is much lower outside the truck. No wind, yet the air comes alive. No tracks, no snowplow has come, and no car has passed on the road. I start feeling the rest of my body become invisible. I don't feel cold anymore. Tiny flakes are swirling around. Snowflakes fall onto my eyelashes. I blink, and blink again so that I can see more. Snowflakes are melting on my eyelashes, and it tells me that I'm still alive.

I stand and gaze at the white birch. Time stops with the endless silence of snow. The falling snow sucks the noise from the atmosphere. The snow sucks the noise of thoughts out of my head as well. No more noise. No more thoughts. I am just standing. The whole world is silent, and the world is perfect except for my failed exam, failed past.

In the really cold days in Hokkaido, there is no snow, but the sun is bright, and the air and sky are crystal clear. Snow days are actually not cold, but a sign of warmness. I look at up the sky. Even the gray sky looks warm on this snowy day. I get back into the truck and start driving. When I empty my mind, I don't feel emptiness in my gut.

## *Therapist*

In front of the thousands of birch on the hill, from out of nowhere I see a three story brick and wood structure sheltering hot springs. The building has a peaked roof so that heavy snow can easily fall off. There is no fence or gate. The hot spring is part of nature. I hear a dog barking, but there is no dog. I turn the engine off, pull up the hood of my jacket, and open the door. When my right boot sinks into the fresh powdery snow, it creates a high pitch squeak. There is a white dog with a black nose in front of the building. I can see him now. The dog has blended into the snow, he is part of nature.

I walk across the parking lot to a glass door at the far end of the hillside, and I enter the building. I take my boots off and place them on a shoe rack attached to the wall. The inside of the building is wood and has a high ceiling. As I take the wood stairs to the second floor, the ceiling fan spreads an aroma of sulfur in all directions. There is a step from the fraying second-floor lobby into the tiled and glass room enclosing the hot spring.

I open the frosted sliding glass door and walk inside. I scan the area. I see no one yet. There is also silence, which is interrupted by the tinkle of the spring water and the odd groan of pleasure from one of the elderly customers sinking into a tub. In the tiled wall area by the entrance, there is a shower area. Inside are high, medium, and low temperature tubs of various sizes, the biggest being the size of a residential swimming pool. Wearing bathing suits is prohibited in the hot springs. I take off my clothes. People clean their body before they get into the tubs. I follow their rules.

## The Moon Home

My bare feet feel the rough engineered stone flooring. I dip my toes and feet first, then soak my naked body in two-foot-deep hot water in a rectangular stone tub. The hot water slowly overflows, then the warmness of water takes my entire body. My body starts to melt. I realize my neck and back are as hard as stone as my body sinks into the hot water. I focus on each part of my body. When I rub my toenails, I become aware that toes are alive. Every part of my body starts to become aware of the pain that I have ignored for a long time. The hot natural mountain water brings mindfulness to each joint, muscle, and tendon to improve body alignment. I breathe in the moist steam, which clears the congestion from my nose. I breathe in more steam to clear my lungs.

I move slowly into the calm and clear water, and place my elbows on the edge of the hot tub to see outside. Through the glass wall of the room, I see the white birches and pine trees. Snow covers their leaves and braches, and the sharp edges of the tops of pine trees. They look like cotton candy on sticks. During the winter, the snow protects plants from the cold mountain air. Nature knows how to protect itself. I've been forgetting to protect myself from the cold winter. My soaked body starts to recover from the winter of my life.

I start going to the hot spring every afternoon. All the treasures of the mountain and the garden of gifts underneath didn't die. They are just hibernating. In the spring, they will all be alive. After I peel off old skin tissue that I created by neglecting myself for a long time, my forgotten self starts coming back to me. My separated body and mind are finally integrated, and recharged energy begins to move everything toward my soul.

That night, Donna's words play themselves in my mind. I feel as if I'm sitting in her office and talking to her. I transport myself into her office from my parents' house. For the first time in three months, I open the study guide for the licensing exam. Now, I can see the letters and embrace the words. After a while, my anxiety and disbelief just fade away. It took so long for me to realize the process of forgiving myself. I had to take a side trip. So many detours, but I couldn't have gotten here any other way. It was a necessary trip.

"Somehow you found the place for yourself in Japan." Donna looks at me.

I raise my chin and slowly nod. "I felt chaos as usual, you know. But one night, I was able to remember your voice. I was able to retrace my feelings in the room with you. Then, I felt OK. It wasn't Grandma's voice, it was yours. I think I've heard Grandma's voice through your voice."

"Your former roommate, mother figure, Brenda, left for Georgia. During the same year, your mentor and father figure, Ralph, moved to Santa Fe. You lost your important people who had loved and protected you for a long time. Many years ago, you told me that you had failed many times in your life. Somehow, you always rose after a fall. You accomplished many things in your life. You have friends and a mentor who helped and supported you when you needed it." Donna furtively embraced my life.

"I miss Brenda and Ralph. I don't want to lose them."

"You can take all of their wisdoms, strengths, and knowledge, and make them your own. You can hold on to the goodness in yourself. You never lose them because they live in you."

Learning is painful and practicing a new pattern of life is difficult. There was a great polarity between good and bad in my mind, and I could rapidly reverse myself based on my own or others' criticisms. I easily became small, so small that I couldn't even see myself. When I fell on the bad side of those dichotomies, my whole being became bad. My therapy did not just change behavior or thought patterns, it helped me to grow. Donna picked up from my prematurely ended childhood where I left off, and re-raised me and guided me to adulthood and womanhood. Understanding rejections, disappointments, and hurts, and letting go of shame-based wounds, led me to increase my self-awareness, self-acceptance, and self-confidence so that I could feel free and exist again.

The following spring, I passed the first part of the state license exam. In 6 months from the first exam, I passed the second part of the state license exam and became a licensed therapist. The only person I called when I got out of the exam room was Donna. Today, I thought about Donna, what if I'd never met her. I would never have become civilized without her. Years of Donna's undivided attention and consistent recognition of my accomplishments helped me to reconstruct myself and to gain the ability to reconnect with others. Not only by superior

## − Therapist −

intellectual endowment, but by her capacity to embrace basic human trust, Donna guided me to become who I truly want to be. I was damaged by relationships, yet I was saved through this relationship. The frozen thick brick wall has been removed from my spirit in the safe and peaceful room. Donna was with me for six years, during my internship time and some post-licensed time, and then, she still lives within me.

月

# Free Association

## PART III

## CHAPTER EIGHT
## Trouble to be Loved

八

I'm dreaming I'm a baby in a crib waking up from a nap. I start crying for my needs and wants but nobody comes to see me. I cry louder but still nobody comes. Furiously, I'm screaming and kicking my feet. My anger is intense, so I become blind. Now, I can't see my scar. I wake up, and it's the morning of my 50th birthday. This far, is not far enough. Therapy won't reverse this regression?

A deep sigh quickly comes out from my mouth at the moment I park my white SUV between the white lines on the side of San Vicente Boulevard in Brentwood, Los Angeles. I made it through the constantly congested traffic in west Los Angeles. I look back through the window to make sure no car is coming before I open the door. I place eight quarters into the parking meter to give me enough time for a fifty minute appointment. A warm wind blowing between the buildings quickly swings my salt and pepper ponytail. As I reach the glass double entrance doors, I see a reflection of the abstract black and white patterns

*- Trouble to be Loved -*

on my dress, which look like a monochrome ink painting. This reflection brings up a memory of an elementary school calligraphy class, where the exercise entailed creating distinctive symbols or words to live by. Hope, dream, and ambition... This memory gives rise to strong sensations and the smell of carbon India Ink. Childhood memories have a such strong impact on our minds.

At a crossroads in my life, I feel trapped in a therapist's body. While I'm thinking about what to do next, I feel nothing inside. My mentor once said that being a therapist is not just an occupation. Even if you quit being a therapist, you will continue to have the mind of a therapist because it's an identity. It sounds as if there is no option for me to get rid of my therapist existence.

The elevator door opens. A middle aged man in a dark blue suit and yellow tie comes out. I get in. I press the button for the 7th floor, where I have an appointment with Jay Russo, the analyst from New York. Deja vu. It's the 7th floor, the elevator, and I all over again. Thirteen years ago, I was in an elevator in a building on Pico Boulevard, L.A. where I pressed the button for the 7th floor to meet Donna, the therapist from New York. The silver elevator stops on the 7th floor. I get out. There are so many rooms on this floor. I squint my eyes to look for room 710; the room numbers are too small for me to see at this age. When I find the room 710, I make sure it has Jay's name on the door. I touch the brass doorknob and I lean against the door. As I remove my left hand from the doorknob, the heavy wooden door slowly closes itself. Inside, all is quiet. There isn't anyone in the waiting room on this Monday afternoon. I press the button next to Jay's name on the white wall in the waiting room, and a small light turns red next to his name.

I have arrived fifteen minutes early. I sit on a white leather arm chair in the corner of the waiting room and grab a Time magazine from the side table. Under the Time magazine, I see another magazine, People. I change my mind and take the People magazine instead. I open the first page. Both Prince William and Prince Harry, who were 15 and 12 when their mother passed away, spoke to children who recently lost a parent. As adults who are getting closer to the age their mother was when she died, they have become the royal patrons of a child bereavement charity. At the Child Grieving Center, Harry shared his memory of feeling anger when his mother died. William spoke with a child who lost her father, saying, "I lost my mummy when I was very young too. I was 15, and my brother was 12. Do you speak to your daddy about it? It's very important to talk about it, very, very important."

How did they mourn their mother? I start wondering if they had received therapy as children after their mother's sudden death. As I'm looking at the air, thinking about the princes' words, the door next to the red light opens. It's 1:55 according to my watch. A man who has the right amount of silky brown hair, just like Prince William in People magazine, appears. He does not quite look at me, but gazes at me with subtlety, and without any expression in his eyes. He is wearing a blue and black checkered short sleeve shirt with dark chino pants, and brown leather loafers with black and brown striped socks. He pronounces my first name. The sound of my name is so foreign when Americans pronounce it. I nod and smile. As I get up

*- Trouble to be Loved -*

from the white leather chair and put the magazine back on the side table, Jay gently hands me forms. I take the papers from him, making sure our hands don't touch. He asks me to read and sign. It's a consent. After he leaves, I complete the form, sit back on the chair, and wait.

After five minutes, Jay returns to take the forms back. Now, he can take me to his office. Jay, who is nearly an inch taller than me, holds the first and second doors so that I can get in, then he closes the two doors. The two doors help to keep confidential conversations in the room. I enter the room, I stop, I stand for a moment. Then, I glance at the room; there is a dark blue fabric couch in front of a window. The blinds are closed so the afternoon sunlight won't get into the room. A black arm chair in front of a contemporary style narrow desk faces the white wall. There's a tall bookshelf next to the desk. I quickly scan the psychology and analysis books on the bookshelf. A light brown leather arm chair sits to the side of the couch. I ask Jay where I should sit. From behind me he tells me to sit anywhere I want. I can't see his facial expression. I try to figure out which seat is his, so that I won't take it. I sit on the couch; it seems like the right thing to do as a client.

Meanwhile, Jay explains that he wants to spend three to five sessions on assessment, and at the end of the assessment, we'll discuss if we are a good fit. Consciously, I understand the process of finding out whether this therapeutic relationship will be beneficial for me, and in doing so we can both enjoy the work and relationship. Subconsciously, I feel as if I have to impress him in order be able to be seen by him. The old feeling of insecurity comes back, I can't fail again, I can't be rejected again, I want him to like me. I feel desperate to be chosen by Jay because if he doesn't want to work with me, then I am unlovable. At the same time, some part of me wishes or expects that he will reject me. Nonetheless, at the moment of being with him, I was unaware of that.

Jay has a yellow note pad in his lap and asks me questions about my family, development, marriage/divorce history, and education and employment background. He makes sure there's a chronological timeline of those events. Calmly and seriously, he asks me for a little more detail on my current marriage, about Matt, my third husband. He writes down my answers quickly and noiselessly. I understand that he takes notes only at the time of assessments and at the beginning of the analysis process. He asks me the reason for seeking analysis. I tell him that my mentor has been recommending for years that I experience analysis, and I recently left a full-time government job so I have more available time. I also tell him that I suffer from insomnia. Then, I mention the most significant reason for seeking analysis is that my father was recently diagnosed with liver cancer, and I have been having strange dreams since.

After about 30 questions and answers, he gives me another day for continuing our assessment. At the end of my first session, I thank Jay for his time. I get up from the couch and give him a smile. Halfway to the exit, I stop. I turn around and say, "I know I'm not a standard American, and I am not sure if that's what you are looking for." I smile with my mouth closed. It sounds so preposterous, even to someone who speaks English as a second language. "I don't know what that means," Jay says in a solid whisper. I hesitate to open the door to leave. "You know exactly what I meant," the voice inside of my head says. I turn around and smile at him one more time. I reach the doorknob to exit. As I push the exit door, I realize that I'm not strong enough to open it. Jay stands up and comes next to me. He pushes the door open and I thank him again. When I get out of the building, the daylight sun is too bright so I pull my sunglasses from my purse. I've learned that the first and last words in a session are significant in therapy. I couldn't help wonder what made me say that to Jay before I left the session. Am I preparing for possible rejection? I might be rejected because I'm a foreigner, that would be less painful than being rejected by own culture, I tell myself as I sit in my car turning the engine on. The parking meter is blinking red, so I start driving.

### *The First Couch: Existence*

The first week, we have four face-to-face assessments cautiously weaving between my current concerns and my tangled past. Jay makes sure nothing is left for him to ask. After he completes the assessment form, he asks me if I want to work with him. I hesitate to answer his question; what do I want? I have no idea how analysis works, but I don't ask questions.

"Analysis is understanding how the mind works. All you need is to show up and talk about what comes to your mind," Jay kindly says as he looks at me.

"We only have a half hour left today, but would you like to start?" Jay asks.

"Yes," I have no hesitation.

Some believe that analysis has a significant focus on working through hidden guilt conflicts. Others refer to analysis as development. Do my father's liver cancer diagnosis and my strange dream have something to do with my guilt or development?

A paper napkin on the pillow and a cloth for my feet at the end of the couch are ready for me to lie down on. I feel awkward lying down in front of someone who does not know me well. He can see me, but I can't see him; and this makes me feel extremely vulnerable. The idea of opening my mind to him, of exposing my body and lying down in front of him, truly frightens me. I cross my legs, then I cross my arms on my chest. I gaze at my feet, then I stare at the clock on the wood side table next the couch. I have 30 minutes to talk about what's on my mind. Jay sits on the light brown leather reclining swivel chair, and puts both legs on the foot rest behind my head. I see no squint, frown, rolling eyes, or raised eyebrow. No facial expression, no body language. All I hear is the occasional sound of Jay's cough or my sigh. The sounds magnify between us in the silent room. I'm staring at nothing. There's a long silence after my deep breath, neither of us saying a word. I'm supposed to say whatever comes to mind, but my mind is blank. There is no space for thought. I don't exist when I can't see his face?

I can't find anything to talk about, so I look around the room without moving my head. The goal is to articulate what's on my mind. It would be embarrassing if Jay discovers that I have nothing on my mind. I don't want him to know that I'm a mindless stupid woman. I'm lying down on the couch with my legs crossed, confused but with nothing on my mind. Before the session, I fantasized about having one thought lead to another without forming connections in my mind, and then the analyst would put all the puzzle pieces together for me; but my fantasy of analysis is destroyed in the first two minutes of being on the couch. I've never felt so invisible in my entire life.

I glance at a framed water color painting on the wall. I look at the panting again and quickly turn my face away. The picture does not appeal to me, but my eyes keep going back to the painting. Dark brown trees, a gray sky, and a cloudy lake. I used that kind of colors when I painted as a child. I'm supposed to talk about whatever comes to mind. I have to say something, but I am not accustomed to say things that come to my mind. Jay and I have not said a word since I lay down on the couch 15 minutes ago.

"Nice painting," I say in order to be polite.

Silence.

"Hello," my voice echoes by itself. No response, no answer. I'm facing nobody, but myself. Then I feel lost and alone.

"I can't believe I mentioned the stupid picture my first time on the couch."

I hear Jay is writing something on his note pad, but I can't see his face. Having a blank mind, I wonder whether all my thoughts were just reflections of other people's thoughts.

"A decade ago, I told my therapist that I did not want to exist. She then told me that not existing is what I've been doing," I whisper.

"What does that mean to you? Not existing," Jay asks.

"I don't have to feel pain. I'm hoping that my father has no pain." I pause. "I want to bring my own pillow. I hope that's OK with you." There's hesitation in my voice.

"Tell me your thoughts about that."

"You are an analyst. You are here to analyze, not to change my diaper. I feel disgusted leaving a dirty napkin on your pillow. I don't want to bother you." I curl up on the couch.

"How do you think it would bother me?" Jay says in a strong whisper.

"My mother was bothered by taking care of me when I was a child. I don't want to trouble you," I say motionlessly.

"Tell me about trouble."

"I was trouble back then and I now have a trouble being a troubled person. Preparing a pillow is nurturing and it's like being taken care of. A pillow represents dependency or intimacy, such as taking care of others when they are sick, or old, or a baby." I answer uncertainly.

Jay listens but doesn't say anything.

"I was surprised that you wanted to work with me. I did not see any reason that would make you want to work with me," I say.

"Huh." Jay makes a sound.

"Nobody ever wanted me."

"Is it true that you want to prove that you are right?" Jay asks calmly.

It's true that being rejected and alone feels familiar, even comfortable to me.

"Last week, I was thrilled by the possibility that I could be chosen by you. Now, the excitement is gone and I'm left with a feeling of numbness." I uncross my arms. "I feel guilt and shame from not being able to take care of my father."

"When you feel shame, you stop working on your issue of existence?" Jay's voice is serene.

As I am thinking, my thoughts fly all the way to when I was 5, 11, and then 13. I start to realize two different things: one is of the feeling of my emotions, and the other is understanding the cause of my emotions. For me, the feeling of shame and of not existing are intertwined. There was a time that I felt nothing. Other times when I felt like not existing. Everything was in retrospect, yet so present. There is no nothing about it.

"We have to end," Jay says in a whisper.

I sit up and begin to want something, something unknown.

"Thank you, see you tomorrow," I say as I look at Jay.

I get out from the building and drag myself into my SUV while I imagine Jay seeing another client.

### Week 2: Protect Me

"What are your thoughts about being late today?" Jay asks.

"I don't know. You tell me, you know me better than I know myself." I reply bluntly after my feelings are evoked by Jay's implicit question.

"What does it mean to you when I ask why you were late?" Jay pushes.

"You are blaming me for a little thing. It was just ten minutes. It is not big deal." My reply is just simply a reflex.

Jay says nothing. I roll my head to the side, and I sink my face into the pillow on the back of the couch.

"My mother was very critical, so I react when I feel I'm being criticized, but I don't want to go there."

"I became your mother." I hear him from a distance.

I'm not admitting my shame and my guilt for punishing Jay, instead, I start talking.

"Since my father was diagnosed with cancer, my mother and I talk on the phone more than usual. I feel we are both anxious and stressed out. Years ago, I left Japan believing that my parents wouldn't be able to hurt me so much with all the distance," I tell Jay angrily, "I had to put the Pacific Ocean between us, but it seems that 3000 miles is not enough, now I have to go to another planet."

I hear Jay sniff. I make a conscious effort to figure out what has been happening in my mind.

"My mother called yesterday. She talked about my nephew's piano rehearsal instead of talking about my father's illness. She said that neither of her children is talented." I clear my throat several time as I speak lying on the couch, until I get my voice back.

"Yesterday, after I left here, I felt a little better. Actually, felt happy, but that feeling didn't last even 24 hours, so what's the point of coming here? Good feelings will be gone regardless of what we do here."

Jay says nothing.

"I'm punishing you because you failed to protect me from my mother, the Joker, who keeps coming back to me. You could not destroy the Joker. My happiness does not last for 24 hours because you are a weak Batman. If you are weak, the Joker, my crazy mother, will win. If you are weak, you won't be able to handle my craziness just as my mother could not handle me. She never wanted me. You will eventually get rid of me." My voice has gotten weak.

"Is it true that at some level, you wish to be gotten rid of and prove that you are right?"

I stay silent and think about his question, which sounds ridiculous, but nonetheless feels to be true.

"Is there anyone who protected you in the past?" Jay asks.

"Everyone failed to protect me after Grandma was gone." I pause. "But there was one person who protected me." My memory comes alive. "My first job in America was a being drug counselor in south Los Angeles. I was completely clueless about drug use, had no idea what even marijuana smelled or looked like, but I worked with all kinds of addictions."

My former clients' faces come back to me, an attorney with cocaine and sex addictions, a teacher with alcohol and gambling addictions, a truck driver with meth and pornography addictions, a prostitute with OxyContin and relationship addictions, a homeless man with a crack addiction. I myself struggled with eating and working addictions, but I'm not planning to mention that to Jay at this time.

I tell Jay that the non-profit substance abuse program hired me because they needed Japanese, Korean, and Chinese speaking counselors after proposition 36 passed. I agreed to take the position because they said they would provide supervision for state therapist licensing hours and support me in getting a work visa. I also tell Jay that getting a work visa took longer than expected because US immigration was extra cautious about approving visas after the 9/11 terrorist attack. I then hesitate to talk about 9/11 because Jay is from New York and I don't know anything about him. However, I find it fascinating that memories from decades ago come back to me very quickly, so I begin to talk about my first job in America.

As I walk through the hallway of the outpatient unit at the substance abuse program in South Los Angeles, I waive to Roy, a janitor. He is tall and slender; he has extremely long legs, and his skinny ankles are showing from the bottom of his pants. He wears black sweat pants and a wrinkled white T-shirt every day. He holds a mop in both hands and cleans the gray vinyl floor. I feel a bit self-conscious walking through the hall since I'm the only Asian foreigner in the unit. I pull down the hem of my white cotton sweater to smooth out the wrinkles. The other drug counselors and administrators are poking at one another and laughing in their office, offering each other a cup of coffee or donuts. Nobody talks to me since I started work, but Roy.

"What's up sexy mama?" Roy says loudly from a distance.

I look behind and whisper, "Nothing."

"I'll teach you English, you gotta respond like this, everything is everything." Roy shrugs his shoulders and looks at me with mischievous eyes.

"Everything is everything," I repeat his words.

"Then, you gotta ask me how my old lady is." Roy looks at me with a big smile.

"How is your old lady? Wait; do you mean your grandmother?"

"I call my lady an old lady." Roy laughs out loud, and leaves.

## - Trouble to be Loved -

Passing all the other offices on both sides of the hallway, I keep walking. Those offices have the lights on because they don't have windows. I feel vibrations through the floor and the wall. The vibrations are getting stronger as I get closer to the end of the hallway. The second to last office in the long hallway, right before the meeting room, is an office that has no ceiling lights, only a small dim lamp on the desk; it's my office. The room is dark and its walls are shaking with loud rap music. Aaron, my office mate, is a rapper, drug counselor, and ex-con who has been drug free for 15 years. Some female workers complain about the noise, but I have no complaints. I grew up in a household and society with a bunch of alcoholics who were singing karaoke all night, so this is nothing. Most people have three to four office mates, but here, it's just Aaron and I. Aaron let me share his office because none of the other staff wanted me to be in their offices. I walk into my dark, vibrating office. I stop for a while so that my eyes can adjust to the darkness. I start to see that Aaron is not there.

I turn on an iMac G3 and a desk lamp the moment I sit at my desk near the door. The blue translucent plastic cover flashes while the iMac starts making noise and warming up. I hear squeaky footsteps from the hallway. I tuck my chin in, pull my spine, and sit up straight as Aaron walks into our office. He says nothing, I say nothing. I don't make eye contact with him, I just pretend that I don't exist. I believe that he does not see me if I don't look at him.

When Aaron gets into the dark office, I pretend to check my emails on the iMac. Occasionally, I peek at him without moving my head. I smell fresh shaving cream that Aaron uses to shave his head, which always leaves it shiny. Today, he is wearing a well ironed dark blue dungaree jacket, matching pants, and clean running shoes. There's a large shiny gold cross pendant hidden under his jacket. Aaron obsessively cleans our office, which leaves it smelling fresh throughout the day. After he completes his morning ritual dusting, he sits at his desk and sips strong coffee as he strokes his neatly trimmed goatee.

Aaron and I are the same height, but his arms are the size of my thighs. He looks buff, and I look like a chopstick. As much as I try to avoid seeing him in the hall, it's impossible to avoid him the entire day. Every time Aaron and I pass each other in the hall, Aaron says "Wassup?" His deep voice echoes through the entire hall. I quickly look away, do a fake laugh and run away. The more I run, the more he feels comfortable with me.

One day, after three months of not existing in front of Aaron, I happen to pass him in the hall again. "Hey, 'Sup?" I feel obligated to respond when he emphasizes hey, so I say, "Nothing," without making eye contact. This how I answer Aaron's greeting for another three months. People in the office start asking me what it's like to share an office with Aaron. The administrative staff tells me that Aaron never had office mates because he likes to keep his office for himself. Since Aaron has not kicked me out of his office, other people start talking to me. I feel as if I'm getting a protection from a mafia boss. I start feeling safe at work in South Los Angeles.

Aaron acts as security in the building because he does not trust the security guard. He obsessively patrols the floor. People in the office say that he is obsessed and overreacting. But I'm somewhat amused by his protection role. He spends more time patrolling the building than counseling clients. He knows exactly what everyone is doing and what is going on in the building.

Though Aaron has ten years of counseling experience and 15 years of sobriety, he attends AA (Alcoholics Anonymous) meetings daily, and enjoys sober dances on the weekends. Aaron doesn't dance, but he observes the dancers and listens to the music. He does not disclose information about his life, but I hear things from my clients during drug treatment sessions. Clients talk more about Aaron than about themselves in their counseling sessions. It sounds as if Aaron is well respected in the hood.

"What is wrong with drug addicts?" is not the question to ask. People with addictions already feel shame. "What is right about drug addiction?" is a good question to ask addicts because they can open up without feeling judged and being defensive. I am not a typical addict. When I start working, people say I don't belong here. They don't know that I am a workaholic. My Japanese parents and society never wanted me, but at least my work here needs me. Before I know it, I'm working Japanese salaryman hours, providing group and individual sessions, talking on the phone with probation and parole officers and public defenders regarding clients' progress reports. Sometimes, judges call from courtrooms regarding clients' reports, and I try to help my clients avoid going to jail.

I'm usually in my office minding my own business and doing my job quietly. I've never expected any help from Aaron because he is usually not in our office. I advocate for my clients who have legal issues and the court dates, but they have to gain knowledge and skills to maintain sobriety. On many occasions, clients get upset about a positive drug tests when I confront them about it. Aaron and I never talk to each other except when I'm in a crisis situation, and he shows up out of nowhere when I need help with angry clients. In my first year of drug counseling, I've learned that relapse is part of recovery, and dealing with clients' relapses is my main job as a drug counselor.

Six months into my first job in America, with rap music playing in the dark room at the drug counseling office, I learn another important lesson. Before lunch, when all the group sessions are over, I notice my cell phone is not on my desk. It is hard to believe that someone stole my cell phone. I check my purse over and over again. I'm sure I must have misplaced it, I tell myself. I figure that I probably left it in my apartment. I spend the rest of the day without a cell phone. I cannot tell Aaron that I lost it because I don't want him to say "I told you so." Aaron has told me repeatedly not to leave my personal items on my desk and not to leave my toothbrush in the bathroom, but I still sometimes leave my purse and cell phone on my desk and step out. Every time Aaron reminds me not to do that, I say "OK, OK," I still forget. People who grew up in places like Hokkaido, where people never lock their front doors and car doors, have difficulty understanding the concept of protecting personal property.

At the end of the day, before I leave the office, Aaron tells me to look in a cabinet in our office. There is my cell phone. People like me don't get it unless we get a live experience. I never again place my personal belongings on my desk when I step out of my office. Not only Aaron protects me, but he protects my personal property. Aaron becomes my sensei in the hood.

Thursday afternoon, I attend weekly outpatient unit case conferences, where we all share the conflicts and struggles of our cases. Shelly, a social worker, usually starts with her case presentation because she is the most articulate and the one who is always prepared. I never fully understand Shelly's fancy words, so I usually pretend to listen without really understanding. Besides her fancy words, she has deep compassion for her clients, who struggle with drug addictions; she often protects her clients.

During one of Shelly's case presentations, Aaron starts saying, "Oh, no…" and rubs his shiny shaved head from back to front three times. That is the way he demonstrates his emotions, he is in deep thinking mode. He then strokes his goatee twice, top to bottom, which signifies that he is ready to explore his thoughts.

Aaron stops stroking his goatee and says, "That's bullshit. That cat is something else. You don't see it because of your own shit."

Shelly replies, "You don't know what you are talking about."

"That's shitty, you have to keep it real. You got to get your shit together."

"You got to get your shit together" is such a clear message. And it's true. We all have some unresolved issues that we need to work on, especially when we are treating clients who bring deep unresolved issues to us. Aaron often quickly picks up on clients' lies and dishonest behavior as well as counselors' unfinished business that we are unaware of.

"What are you talking about? Speak English!" Shelly says in an irritated tone.

I say, "You might want to consider countertransference when you are with a particular client, so that you don't collude with the client's issue," I say something I've heard in my clinical supervision.

Shelly replies, "What the heck are you talking about? Both of you, speak English."

Like most of Aaron and Shelly's discussions, this one ends with a deep sigh from both sides.

I usually take advantage of these situations to start presenting my cases, so I say "OK, moving right along," and I share my struggle with running group sessions, especially dealing with clients' aggression.

"This week, in a process group, clients were yelling at each other, so I had to call Security," I say shamefully.

"You got to kick them out. You can't keep a group like that," Aaron says impatiently.

"I can't kick them out of a group room."

"You got to cross the motherfuckers off of the group sheet."

"What? Are you crazy?" I turn to the other side of the table and look at Shelly.

She rolls her eyes and says, "See, that's what I'm talking about."

In the late afternoon, I facilitate a women's group. One of my clients and another group member start to argue in the middle of the group session. I tell them to stop, but they continue. My client stands up and shouts at the other woman.

"Please sit down," I say politely.

*- Trouble to be Loved -*

The two women keep shouting. To them, I don't exist.

"If you don't sit down, I'll have to dismiss you, I'll have to cross your name off the attendance sheet. It means you won't get credit for today. I don't want to do that because you've been doing well," I say with a firm voice as I grab my pen and the attendance sheet.

My client seems shocked. She slowly sits down on her black plastic chair and looks at me with her big round eyes.

"Sorry, Ms. Yay-sue-co, that was disrespectful," she says as she looks down.

Just like that, Aaron's non-colluding approach worked.

That night, I attend a weekly individual clinical supervision with Ralph, my clinical supervisor. I tell him about Aaron's recommendation to dismiss clients for the safety of the rest of the group, when group members violate group norms. Ralph never agrees with Aaron's tactics, but he always respects Aaron's point of view. Ralph is impressed with Aaron's ability to think analytically and with his understanding of psychology, though Aaron does not have an academic psychology background. Ralph seems to enjoy Aaron's great sense of humor without any judgment. I'm not afraid to explore my struggles in the sessions at work, but I do not tell Ralph that I almost crossed the motherfuckers' names off the attendance sheet. I try my best to keep Aaron's colorful language between us.

After five years, Aaron and I are still office mates. Despite our awkward relationship resulting from ignoring each other in the beginning and speaking foreign languages to each other, we end up completing each other's sentences like an elderly married couple. Aaron does not know that I am aware of how he recruits street teen gang members and introduces them to rap, teaching them not to fight, but to express themselves through music. Aaron continues his daily rituals that include cleaning his office compulsively and spraying water on his shaved head before he facilitates his group. He prays each time he goes into the group room for a session.

Sometimes, I see the orange light on Aaron's desk in our dark office when he is sitting. I see his shadow on the polished floor. Aaron's softness and vulnerability are not present in front of his shadow. My toughness and boldness, which I refuse to present in front is my shadow. Our common ground is our tendency to feel comfortable with people who ignore us and leave us alone. Aaron says that he does not like needy women. I don't like needy men. His needs are projected through his important duty of protecting clients and employees. My needs are to be protected. Our needs are met perfectly for quite a long time, yet it is far from happily ever after.

"Witnessing the power of healing and transformation has kept me going. My clients got better, I had hope. I saw a client's chaos, I felt chaos, but I felt safe there because Aaron protected me. I felt I belonged there."

"You might not feel safe here with me," Jay says.

"It's crazy. It's a crazy job."

"You say you're crazy and move on to another topic," Jay says.

## - Trouble to be Loved -

"I have a tendency to favor strong people. Perhaps I believe only certain people can protect me."

I pause and then go on, "While I was seeing Donna, I felt more love towards my mother. I don't know how I did that. I may have felt guilty because I betray my own mother by finding a more ideal one in Donna."

"You physically need Donna at this time and can't call upon her," Jay says as if he is talking to himself.

"Rationally, I understand that Donna lives within me. Everything I gain in my therapy is inside of me. Based on what I learned from books and lectures, I can think that all my mother did or didn't for me was counterproductive, but she did best she could given her knowledge and conditions. I get it, but this did not help me to live peacefully and feel worthy. I need to forgive her. I need to forgive myself. I want to forgive her so that I can move on. I often hear that forgiveness is the key to having a peaceful life."

"Why do you keep saying forgiveness?" Jay sounds ticked off that I am stuck in forgiveness.

I don't say anything, but I realize that I could forgive as long as I don't think I have to.

"Could you verbalize how you loved your mother when you were seeing Donna?" Jay asks.

I repeat what I learned in the session, "As my mother said, I have no musical talent, but so what, I'm good at many other things. I've accomplished something even though I partially failed. I'm able to connect with people I love, and they are there for me when I need them." My breathing becomes slower, then my hatred toward myself and Mother fades away.

"I'm glad you didn't get rid of me. I'm glad I am still here with you." I pause. "You are not a weak Batman, my mother is not a Joker, and I'm not a victim." I take a deep breath and ask Jay, "Then, who are you?" In my mind about Jay, who he is, is who I become. I keep looking at the white wall. It's a direction for me to become who I am. The past is over, what now?

"We have to end," Jay whispers.

## CHAPTER NINE
## Empty Stomach and Emtpy Mind
## 九

**Month 2: Small Head and Big Belly**

"I had an endoscopy last Friday. I have a stomach problem, caused by years of over eating with impunity – I didn't gain weight. My doctor told me to not over eat, but all I can think of is food. I'm hungry all day, every day. Even now, I'm thinking about going to the drive through at In-N-Out Burger and ordering a cheeseburger and fries with a large Sprite. Then, I'll go to the Starbucks next door and order a large frappuccino, a brownie, and a blueberry scone." I close my eyes and gulp.

Jay is listening.

"Today, when I was at a stop light, I saw a woman who was carrying a lot of takeout food and a Starbucks frappuccino with whipped cream. She was drinking her frappuccino while she was crossing the street. She easily looked to be 400 pounds. She has something I don't and can't have. Something, I really want, I'm envious."

"Your stomach problem is getting in the way of your reaching 400 pounds," Jay speaks softly.

"Why can other people get to 400 pounds and I can't? My fantasy – I can eat, eat, eat and never get sick. Everything I eat will stay with me until I get to 400 pounds." I pause. "Fantasy is not real. If my fantasy were real, I would be really crazy."

"For some people, there is no clear line between fantasy and reality," Jay says.

"Are you telling me that my fantasy of getting to 400 pounds is my reality?"

"We need to investigate."

I realize how ridiculous it sounds so I try to talk more rationally. "When I took the children and adolescent program, I read a paper about child eating disorders. It said something about separation from one's mother and oral aggression followed by the separation anxiety." I pause. "I remember I slept with chewing gum in my mouth as a child. I had to cut my hair because the gum got in it." I shake my head a few times. "No matter what I do, I can't get rid of my mother. My dog shakes the mud off his fur. Why can't I do that?"

"The bad ones stick with you," Jay speaks calmly.

"The more I try to get rid of it, the more it sticks. After all, my bad mother is still with me, and Donna, the good mom, is gone. I understand that I should be a good mother to myself, but it's not easy."

"I understand you might have physical issues and you're dealing with it, but I also wonder if there are things you are holding in that may influence your health."

"I'm obsessed. I can't let it go. I don't even know what I'm obsessed about, and what I have to let it go of. Women should not have a big mouth in my culture, they should not talk. I'm a fake gold Buddha with a small mouth on a small head with

# Empty Stomach and Emtpy Mind

a large belly. She does nothing but smile. I became an Obake because the bad one keeps sticking with me."

"Obake?"

"I once saw myself there, but I was afraid to do anything about it." I retrieve the memories of the city of Kamakura, where I lived during my early 30's when I worked in Tokyo. The day I was haunted by an Obake.

"I became friends with a physician who had spent many years in Mexico, because he was the only person who smiled at me among the professors and teachers at the college where I taught. The physician had a house in Tokyo, but his deceased parents had a house in Kamakura. He said his siblings were all deceased as well. But he kept his patents' house in Kamakura. I wanted to move out from my aunt's house in the noisy area of Ginza, so I decided to rent the house from him."

Jay sits behind me and keeps listening. I close my eyes to transport myself to 1999 in Tokyo.

It takes an hour and half to get to Kamakura from Tokyo by train. A one-hour or two-hour commute in Tokyo is not uncommon. After 90 minutes, the train stops at Kamakura station. Unlike train stations in Tokyo, the station in Kamakura is silent. Younger people move to Tokyo for convenience.

I'm walking on narrow streets lined with hundred-year-old pine trees and thousand-year-old ginkgo trees. All of the houses are surrounded by tall trees and high stone fences and sit on steep slopes with long stone steps to get to the front door. Large old houses are up on hills where nobody seems to be living. I can't see clearly from the street, but there seem to be no driveways and no cars. The city looks as if it hasn't changed much since medieval times.

There were constant wars and harakiri during the Kamakura era. If the person dies in a sudden or violent manner such as murder or harakiri, the spirit is thought to transform into an Obake, souls or spirits that don't have legs and are not grounded. Oftentimes, the lower the social rank of a person who died violently, or who was treated harshly during life, the more powerful Obake they would return. It's no surprise that powerful Obakes are in the silent city of Kamakura.

If the person who dies is influenced by powerful emotions such as a desire for revenge, love, jealously, hatred, or sorrow, the spirit is thought to transform into an Obake. Once a certain emotion or thought enters the mind of a dying person, his Obake will come back to complete the action or resolve the thought before returning to the cycle of reincarnation. If a conflict is left unresolved, the Obake will haunt the living.

It feels humid even though it's autumn, and no one else is walking on the streets after 5 pm. A block ahead of me, I see an elderly lady walking slowly and carrying grocery bags. I walk fast to catch up with her so that I won't be totally alone. Suddenly, she disappears. She must have turned onto another street. I am all alone again. It would not be surprising if lost samurai spirits are circling the town. They are everywhere as they are moving without legs.

When I turn left at the next block, I see what looks like a temple, an archway gate in front of an old building. Kamakura Elementary School is written in charcoal ink on an old wooden

## Empty Stomach and Emtpy Mind

board. Tall bricks wall around the building, I can't see or hear anything from the school – the children must be all gone.

I keep going to find the address, 111 West Mishima Road. I find a city library in front of the east gate of the house, but the gate is chained. The house is supposed to have four entrances, but I only see two. I walk around to the small rusty unlocked south gate. I touch the rusty knob with two fingers – it's wet. When I lean forward, the metal gate makes a low squeaking noise, and it echoes through the neighborhood. As I close the gate, I smell musky earthy an aroma from the wet soil, the stone steps are covered with moss. Past the gate, narrow stone steps on a steep slope are surrounded by skinny bamboo trees. Each step I take, I smell earthy subtle scents. The humidity makes my skin feel sticky. When I look up, the moss-covered steps seem endless. I carefully walk each step, so I don't kill moss; moss can live on lifeless objects, yet it can be easily killed by living objects. Moss grows on stones or metals, but fallen leaves could easily kill moss. As moss is rootless, as Obake is legless – as a rootless woman whose soul was stolen by living objects, my family, I sense I belong to this house and town.

At the end of the steps, a stone lantern appears in a zen garden – no flowers. A small red lacquered bamboo rocking fountain called Shishi odoshi (scare away deer and wild boar) is almost hidden in the garden; it combines sounds and motion to create a compelling water feature. The fountain's bamboo arm rocks forward when it fills with water, then rocks back to make a gentle "clacking" sound that will chase away any critters eating the garden. The back of the garden fades into a forest of

*- The Moon Home -*

towering trees that grow up the hillside. I don't see the next door neighbors. There are no lights.

I open the sliding glass entrance door to the house and step into a concrete entrance area, where I take off my shoes. I step up to a long wood floor hall, which connects to the kitchen. A living room and library on the right side, and a bathroom and stairs on the left side. A suit of samurai armor in a glass case in the hall dominates the entrance to the house.

The owner of the house asked me to break the glass case and take the helmet with horns outside in the event of a fire. The helmet costs half a million dollars, he said. Since the armor belonged to the owner's deceased parents, he did not insure it. I'm responsible for the half-million-dollar armor. If I had failed to protect this armor back in the Kamakura period, I would had to have performed harakiri in front of the Shogun. This armor costs more than my life. This single armor takes me all the way back to the Kamakura period; ancient voices echo and ancient shadows appear through the samurai armor.

Next to the living room is the library. I carefully touch a small antique piano with my fingers. I see a framed photo on the piano, and it looks like deceased family members from the 1970's. Past the library is a steep stairway to the second floor. At the top are three tatami rooms totaling about 1200 square feet, all empty except for five zafu cushions on tatami mats. In the largest tatami room, a small dim lamp shines on a recess known as tokonoma, which contains rustic and simple pottery items for a tea ceremony. The pottery shapes are not quite symmetrical, and the colors and textures are unrefined. A part of the tea cup seems chipped – it must be wabi-sabi.

## - Empty Stomach and Emtpy Mind -

In the evening, after the sun goes down, I don't hear anything except the old wall clock ticking. I feel as if I'm not the only one in the house. I reach a window that faces the back yard and slowly open the shoji screen in front of the window. The window looks as if it hasn't been opened for decades. I sense I'm been watched. I look out at the window, but see nothing but darkness. When I shove away this unknown sense, I see my reflection in the window. I keep having the feeling that something is lurking nearby and watching me from behind. They always see me before I see them. "Ali Ali out free." I turn, I look, I freeze in the empty room. I don't see anyone. I turn again and scan the tatami room once more. It is nothing, I tell myself. Questions keep coming back to mind. How did all family members die in this house? There are no mirrors in his house, not even in the bathroom. I start down the stairs. Suddenly, I see a small buddha in the corner of the glass case by the armor in the hall. Why didn't I see it when I came in? A small mouth on a small head with a large belly – she is smiling.

The emptiness is never fulfilled so she eats with a smile. The fantasy of continuous eating and never having to lose anything, all the things I eat stay with me forever. The long hallway looks like a lonely road, the silent town is falling below. The sound of the moving bamboo fountain in the zen garden rises and falls when water makes it full. The night is approaching quickly.

"I'm eating. I'm forcing food into my stomach so that every available space is filled until nothing more could possibly fit. My hunger never gets satisfied. I am a small head with an empty stomach. The emptiness can never be filled." I begin to withdraw, turning away from Jay.

"What does a small head mean to you?" Jay asks.

"Unable to think," I reply, "Do you think I miss my bad mother, so I eat bad food? Food always make me anxious. I can't eat good healthy food. Am I eating badly to punish myself and get sick?"

"You said that you yelled at your mother on the phone in May when you two were talking about your dad's illness, and you felt guilt and shame. Then, you stopped talking about your mother. I'm wondering if that may be affecting the way you work on your issues. Your missing and loving Grandma and Donna and your shame and guilt are interfering with and overriding your feelings of connecting, loving, and possibly living."

"I stopped calling my mother after May. I can't have a bad mother when I am good. That relationship cannot co-exist. I have to destroy one for me to have the other. I have to destroy the bad, but it has not been successful. I feel guilty by not talking to my mother and not getting any information about my father's illness. I punish myself by eating bad food and getting sick." I take a deep breath. "I still have the fantasy of having someone, hopefully you, Jay, help me when I say I DON'T KNOW." My voice becomes bold.

"How do you feel talking about this? What does it mean to you when I'm not giving you the answer?" Jay asks.

"Rationally speaking, I understand I have my answer within myself, but I still want someone to feed me. I feel happy when you give me the answer, and I feel sad when you don't give me the answer."

# Empty Stomach and Emtpy Mind

"Maybe it might be true both ways," Jay says in a voice so low that I almost miss his words.

"Giving up a fantasy is so painful. It seems true that there is no clear line between fantasy and reality," I say.

"What does it mean to you to give up a fantasy?" Jay asks.

"Hopeless… I don't want this to be the Jay effect. I don't want to lose all the happiness and goodness, one day when you leave, as Donna retired."

"You are worried because now you want to see yourself in your eyes, and you are anxious about finding out if you like the things you find out about yourself." His dry cough is coming out from his Adam's apple. The sounds of his dry cough go straight down into my esophagus, I swallow it with no way knowing whether I could digest it or not.

### Month 4: Body Speaks When Mind is Absent

"We have been talking about food recently, so I brought chocolate chip cookies and brownies. I hope you like them." I hand Jay a disposable plastic container. "My focus was on cookies and brownies and I forgot my pillow today." I pull the couch pillow to put my head on it and lie down.

"What does it mean to you if I like your cookies and brownies?" Jay asks.

"Sharing common thing means being connected. I wonder I'm asking you to digest things that I cannot digest."

Jay says, "Hmm."

"In my 30's, when I was dating actively, I would order a bottle of Budweiser with a cheeseburger and french fries. My dates would often say that most women order a small salad or cucumber sandwich. I would just order the same thing my date ordered. I can eat salad at my house, why should I go out and eat salad?"

Jay sniffs.

"Once my therapist said that eating and going to the bathroom are only things that can be controlled as a child. I don't seem to be able to control my over eating."

"Eating is having a relationship with food," Jay says.

"Love and hate," I say.

"Do you feel love?"

"No, it's not love. It might be hate. It's definitely hate. I put hate into my empty stomach because I'm nothing."

"Tell me about nothing."

"Not existing. My childhood is nothing, my life is nothing, nothing is bad so I eat to become something. Hate is better because I feel as if I exist."

"That might affect your struggle for existence.".

"I wish I could just say NO THANKS like one of teachers at the children's program that I've been attending. He says no thanks to sweets on the table when I offer them to him. I can't say no thanks to food. Would you be able to say no thanks?" I ask.

"How would you feel if I said no thanks for the brownies?" Jay asks.

"Rationally, I understand you have the right to say no, but I would get hurt and then I would never want to see brownies again, EVER!" I say.

"So, No is a powerful word," Jay says calmly.

"My Japanese mother and Japanese society have said NO to everything about me. Saying No has been an issue for most of my adult life. For me, it was work, exercise, and food. Food and work are connected, these I impulsively do."

"We could talk about how you do things excessively."

A year ago, I left the continually expanding galaxy that I call Los Angeles County. My Milky Way galaxy, the Department of Mental Health. While I worked in this galaxy, there was a particular orbit that made my body move itself and travel around it every day. The evolution of this galaxy can be affected by interactions and collisions, I learned in my science class. I move in its orbit in a regularly repeating trajectory as if I were a small planet moving around the sun. A small planet moves faster because of the smaller distance it needs to trace a greater arc to cover the same area. And there is a black hole – in a black hole, there is nothing, not even light can escape once it gets past the black hole's event horizon. In my case, it wasn't a horizon, but it was a perpendicular metal detector.

As I begin going through the metal detector by the county building entrance on a Monday, I say good morning to Dave, a county sheriff who is a retired veteran. It's 7:30 am. The morning sun shines on the waiting room through the large glass entrance doors behind me. Two security guards are checking clients' belongings before they get into the building. I use my county keycard to open the door to the work area from the waiting room. Passing the break room, I smell the refreshing scent of coffee brewing. I stop and peak at the break room as if I were a conditioned rat. Two dozen doughnuts on the table from Dr. Kaiser, a psychiatrist whose wife died a year ago. A vegetable plate next to the pink doughnut boxes from Nurse Anna, she always brings something healthy to compensate for the candies in her office. I take a cup of fresh coffee and a chocolate glazed doughnut to my office. I place my purse into my desk drawer and turn on the computer. Before the computer is ready, the chocolate glazed doughnut is gone. I come back to the break room and grab both a coconut cake and a powdered sugar doughnut. I return to my office and find that my computer is ready. The screen says I've been using the same passwords for 31 days and it won't let me get into the system unless I change the password. One more thing I have to do this busy Monday morning. I eat the coconut doughnut while I'm changing the password. There are 28 new emails. I eat the powdered sugar doughnut while I check my email. I scan the emails that list me on the "To" line and make notes on my to do list. I leave the other emails that were cc'd to me to check later when I have more time. I check my voicemail; there are 23 new voicemails from my clients. I listen to each message and make notes on my call back list. I hear a receptionist paging me over the loudspeaker from the front office. By 8 am, 25 walk-in clients are waiting for us to see them. They keep coming until 5 pm. I finish three doughnuts and a cup of coffee before 8:00. I'm full of energy and ready to see clients.

## – Empty Stomach and Emtpy Mind –

At 11:45 am, the hallway echoes with Cindy's announcement that training on bipolar symptoms and medication will start at noon in the conference room. I run to the lady's room before the training starts. I realize that the last time I went to the restroom was before I left my house at 6 am. A physician and a representative from a pharmaceutical company are getting ready for their presentation. I sit at a table with psychiatrists, nurses, and therapists. A lady from the pharmaceutical company distributes lunch boxes to all of us who attend the training during our lunch break. I open the lunch box to find a chicken sandwich with almonds and cranberries, potato chips, and a chocolate chip cookie that's the size of my palm. Pharmaceutical companies always bring us some fancy foods. Even when they bring sandwiches, they come with something extra like almonds and cranberries, or coconut and mango. My focus is on the food, not the training. By the time I finish my lunch, the training is over. At 1 pm, I'm ready to see more clients.

Later in the afternoon, Sharon, my supervisor, brings a red velvet cake to the break room. I open the freezer, take out a large container of ice cream, and eat the cake with two scoops of ice cream. Dr. Zaidel, a single female psychiatrist who maintains a raw vegetable diet is sitting at another table in the break room. I tell her that I don't know why I'm eating so much at work when I'm not hungry. She tells me that it is psychological, in that practitioners tend to take things in orally after their sessions because they feel pieces of them are taken away from their patients. The more I work, the more I eat so that I don't feel completely empty. Every time I finish a session, I return to the nurse station and grab three Milky Way candy bars from a plastic box on nurse Anna's desk.

At 5:30 pm, the clinic closes. I'm back in my office and begin completing my assessments and session notes for the day. I notice that it's getting dark outside, and I shut the blinds. At 6 pm, I get ready to leave the office. I pass the nurse station to find that nurse Anna is still in her office coordinating a medication training presentation by another pharmaceutical company for tonight. Anna asks me if I can attend the training. I have to eat dinner anyway, so I agree to attend. I have to be there at 7:00 for the two-hour training. "Are you leaving?" Jane asks from down the hallway. "Drug dealer dinner," I respond, "Have a safe drive."

I drive 45 minutes to get to the restaurant. There are not many people there on this Monday night. The training is in a private room, a presenter is already talking about a new antidepressant and its effects. I sneak into the room without making noise. I find Dr. Wing, he waves, so I sit next to him. The moment I sit down, a waiter brings appetizers: crab cakes, chips with a spinach dip, and large blackened shiitake mushrooms. A waitress comes and takes my order. In a whisper, I order a T-bone steak with an iceberg salad. After I finish every food in front of me, I order dark chocolate cake with Irish coffee. I feel as if my blood was sucked out by vampires during the day at work, but now I'm stuffed. All of the emotions that were taken away during the day are finally replaced through my stomach. I'm ready to work tomorrow.

Less than a month later, during our monthly staff meeting my boss suddenly asks me to give a 15 minute speech. I feel

## Empty Stomach and Emtpy Mind

extra pressure because I'm still in my probationary period and the District Chief has come to observe this meeting. I stand up immediately and walk toward the front without hesitation. When I reach the front, I ask my boss what I should talk about. "Anything... maybe about yourself?" He gives me an innocent look. Public speaking is not something that I am accustomed to or trained for. If I speak without preparation, my English might not be understandable, but this does not stop me because saying no to my boss is not acceptable in my culture. The story I decided to tell is about how I got to the US and why I picked California, my misunderstanding of customs and culture, and my mistakes and embarrassments as a foreigner. People in the office are kind enough to laugh instead of making faces. I complete my speech and sit down. The meeting continues.

The following week, my boss hires another foreigner. In the monthly staff meeting, my boss asks the new foreign employee to give a short speech. "No, thanks," the foreigner says without hesitation. "Oh, OK," my boss responds and moves on to another agenda. "What the heck," the speechless voice in my head says, then I give the new employee a mean look. Can she decline our boss's request? I could have just said no to his request? Where I come from, one cannot decline; if your boss asks you to do things, you just do them; if your boss asks you to sing at Karaoke, you sing; if your boss asks you to finish your drink, you finish it. No questions asked. By the time I pass my probationary period, I have learned that people can say no in this country.

Later that same week, I arrive at the office as usual and go to the kitchen to get my morning coffee and a Danish. Coming out from the kitchen, I see someone's dark shadow. It happens so quickly yet so slowly. The deputy lifts me up and quickly sets me down on the other side of hallway. I freeze, as I am in the air. The Danish falls from my right hand, but I'm still holding my cup. No part of my body can move, except my eyes. I'm frozen.

A man is choking a psychiatrist in front of a restroom. Two other deputies arrive from the other building. An angry man, in Batman cartoon pajamas, with no shoes on. A deputy officer in a brown uniform, with army boots on. The man is swinging his arms back and forth trying to run away. A deputy grabs him from behind and slams him to the ground. The another deputy holds the man's legs, but the man's feet and arms slip through and get away from the two deputies. The third deputy tackles the man. He swings, he bends, he quickly pulls himself along, and he finally gets away from the deputy. The man's body is a like slippery snake. His head moves from right to left and then makes circles. And now he straightens his whole as if to stretch himself out of his body. The deputies move toward the man, and two of them finally hold the man's arms and legs, which are moving spastically as he lies on the floor. The third deputy grabs the man's hands and pulls them behind him.

I'm still frozen while my eyes are glued to the scene. Two deputies hold the man on either side and take him away. I pick up the Danish on the floor. Half of my coffee is in my cup and the other half is on my jacket. Why am I still standing here? Why didn't I leave immediately? There is no way I could know or anticipate that the incident would leave me with my morning coffee and Danish in a mess on the floor. However, my reaction was neither fight nor flight. Instead, I simply froze, playing

## — Empty Stomach and Emtpy Mind —

dead, a primitive and powerful survival reaction as if I were a powerless rabbit in front of a lion. If I don't exist, they can't see me. Avoidant behavior does not cause fear. The incident did not happen in my head, so I continue to work.

Later in the morning, I find out that the psychiatrist did not prescribe the medication that the patient requested. When the psychiatrist began to escort his patient out of the office, the patient got angry and attacked. For months, I had seen the psychiatrist treat his patients thoughtfully and respectfully, with deep empathy and compassion. The chill comes afterward. Saying no could be a danger to our lives, even in this country.

In the afternoon, Alice, a single mother, comes in with a big smile. Her only son, Ben, was taken away from Alice by Child Protective Service two years ago. Ben was in a foster family for over two years, and a month ago, he finally returned to Alice. She says that she feels happy living with Ben, who is now three years old. Though she says she is very happy that she's getting child custody back, she has been complaining that Ben repeatedly says he loves his foster parents and wants to go back to them.

I ask Alice why Ben is not with her today. She says that Ben is in the waiting room with her sister. Alice says Ben fell off his bed and broke both legs. Something tells me to ask her to bring Ben into the office. She goes to the waiting room and brings back a baby bassinet that holds Ben. Both his legs are in casts, and he has no smile. His blue eyes turn gray, and then the gray turns to stone. I again ask Alice what really happened to him. She sticks with the story that Ben fell off his bed and broke his legs. When she looks me in the eyes and smiles, I can't quite pinpoint the look, but it seems to be either confidence or satisfaction. I'm confused about her facial expression, I feel sick to my stomach at the same time. A number of past sessions come back quickly into my mind: her story of becoming a mother as a result of being raped; her feeling of hatred for the man who raped her, Ben's father; her jealousy and envy; her hatred toward Ben's foster mother; and even Ben's words such as "I want to go home," or "I don't like you."

I must admit this uncontrollable feeling of hatred toward my client. I should not hate her, I'm here to help her. My mind is going one way, but my heart goes another. Ben's soul goes into the dark, so does mine, and eventually he will be taken away, and possibly will come back to her again.

Alice said that she wanted to have a child because she didn't want to be alone. There is a difference between having children and being a mother. I'm afraid if I tell her something out of my anger, she could become angrier and possibly hurt Ben even more. There is nothing more I can do to save this boy. In front of Alice, I call Child Protective Services to investigate Ben's injury. Alice is angry and says Child Protective Services is already investigating her. Ben looks powerless as I feel powerless. There is nothing more I can do.

For many years, in my substance recovery work, I helped parents get back custody of their children. I was a strong believer in helping parents who struggle with drug addictions or mental illness to get parental rights back. Seeing Ben in the bassinet with two broken legs makes me question what I have been doing and why am I doing this job for the past years. Everything I've done in the past 15 years became meaningless,

## Empty Stomach and Emtpy Mind

and I feel disgusted with myself for being incapable of saving Ben. The only idea that saves me is that a childless woman like me, whether by fate or by choice, at least harms no children but myself as a result of my failures.

After five years of working for Los Angeles County, my professional life appears to have hit a wall. Five years and 20 pounds heavier, with high cholesterol, prediabete, and a stomach ulcer, have not stopped me from being a public servant. When AB109 goes into effect, I transfer to the county Probation Department as a therapist. My new job consists of conducting assessments of people who are released from prison, to determine whether it appears to be safe enough for them to return to the community. It's my habit to change location when I feel stuck in life.

On my first day at the Probation Department, I walk in and see a Hollywood cop TV show crew shooting the stairs toward the main entrance. On the other side of the building, there are mountains of fruit, cakes that look like poppies, candies that look like emeralds, rubies, and sapphires, also a variety of drinks. Everywhere I go, there is plenty of food. I need to lose the 20 pounds, but it seems as if I just can't get away from food.

When I walk up to the second floor where my office is supposed to be, there are a bunch of offices with glass walls and doors, just like my repetitive dream of glass elevators. I notice women who look like the Kardashians, sexy bodies with shiny hair, walking in high heels. I hear the taps and clicks. They are not TV actresses, they are probation officers.

After the two weeks of training, I report to work at another probation office, in east Los Angeles. On my first day at the new office, I leave my home at 6:30 am to beat the traffic. When I

## – The Moon Home –

get to the gated parking lot, I show my badge to the camera at the parking gate, and they let me into the parking lot. As I'm parking my car, a large silver SUV comes in from behind and parks next me. A middle aged man in a gray suit and brown tie gets out of the SUV. I turn around, show my employee badge, introduce myself, and tell him that I don't have access to the building. He says he is one of the supervising officers. When I hold my hand out to shake his, my cell phone, lunch, and drink fall out of my pink Victoria's Secret paper bag. My tea had leaked from my mug and destroyed the bag. While I pick up my stuff from the ground, the supervisor appears awkward but remains silent. I carry my stuff I dropped in one hand, and a large black briefcase in the other hand, so I keep dropping things as I walk toward the building. He probably has never seen a dorky therapist. That's how I met Mr. Bunuel.

At the first entrance door, he enters a long code on a number pad, and opens the door and enters with me. He walks 60 feet, and at the second door he enters another code, which appears different from the first. Then he and I walk to a third door, and he enters one more code. Finally, we get into the open area where other people work. He shows me to my office, which is locked. While he is looking for the key to my office, I go to the lady's room, but it turns out that I need a code to get in. Mr. Bunuel says he does not know the code for the lady's room, so he will ask one of his subordinates to escort me there. So many codes in the Probation Department.

Mr. Bunuel never smiles, never participates in small talk; he walks straight to his destinations, point A to point B, never wandering around – he is efficient. His shoes look brand new,

## Empty Stomach and Emtpy Mind

his hair looks like newly mown grass – he appears shiny. He educates his subordinates about mental health and the purpose of collaboration between the Probation and Mental Health Departments. He treats therapists as partners.

In my new position, all assessments include suicidal and homicidal 5150 evaluations. I have to keep in mind a few things: I have to show a calm demeanor and respect, but I must also speak firmly and clearly. The key is whether the client is an imminent danger or not. For instance, a man tells me that he is suicidal. My question would be, does he have a plan to kill himself? If he does, when? Does he have a means by which he's going to do it?

OK, you are suicidal, when are you planning to kill yourself? OK, you want to kill yourself today, how will you kill yourself? OK, you want to kill yourself with a gun, do you have access to a gun? OK, you own a gun, where do you keep it? OK, you have your gun in your drawer in your closet, and want to kill yourself today when you get home. Now, I have to write a hold.

Providing assessments for people who come straight from prison is different from the other types of assessment I've done. The key is finding out whether it's safe to release these people into the public. Sometimes, the man I assess is handcuffed and has been transported from prison to my office by two officers with bulletproof vests and guns. I have to admit how difficult it is to do a great job as an assessor. I'm not a fortune teller or mind reader. Who is responsible if someone gets hurt? Where could people who were just released from prison possibly live and get a job to support themselves? I nevertheless felt that I wouldn't be comfortable working in the environment if Aaron at the drug treatment hadn't taught me about the prison mentality.

One Monday morning, at 7 am, I'm reading a client's 30-page prison file. I'm expecting the client at 8:30. The state prison considers releasing non-violent inmates early. A tall slender middle-aged man with an old white T-shirt and sweatpants walks into my office escorted by two officers. I introduce myself to the client, and explain what is going to happen in the next few hours. I ask him to sit in the chair in front of my desk. The client doesn't smile, and seems to avoid direct eye contact with me. I place a pen on my desk for the client to sign the informed consent and release forms. The client picks up the pen with both of his handcuffed hands and starts signing without reading carefully. He seems physically uncomfortable signing those forms with handcuffs on. I help move the forms so that he can sign more quickly. I remove the pen and put it into a desk drawer, leaving nothing on the desk. One officer uncuffs the client and leaves the room, but two officers resume their position outside my office.

I ask the client about his background and see if it matches his prison records. The client has a Ph.D. in physics. In my mind I call him $E=mc^2$. $E=mc^2$ was convicted of forgery, and he did most of his time in the Santa Barbara prison. When he talks about his educational background, his passion for physics is evident. While he speaks of his passion, I forget my role as a therapist and become a seven year old girl. I can't help asking him about $E=mc^2$ and why the stars shine and why the galaxy lights up. $E=mc^2$ says that 73 percent of the universe's energy is dark

## — Empty Stomach and Emtpy Mind —

energy, energy of nothing. According to the Big Bang Theory, that's what's blowing the galaxies farther and farther apart. After $E=mc^2$ finishes talking about his passion, I realize that I haven't been excited and passionate about anything for a long time. Am I missing something in my life? Follow the stars, $E=mc^2$ says before he leaves the office.

That night, when I get out of the office, I look up at the sky. It is hard to see stars from a huge, brightly lit city like Los Angeles. Polaris is always there in the same place day and night even though it cannot be seen. If I ever get lost, follow the Polaris, once Father told me. The powerful Polaris's spark keeps me going, so I've decided to stay in my Milky Way galaxy for a little longer.

A couple of weeks later, I have an allergic reaction that causes rashes all over my body. In the middle of the night, I'm transported to the Marina del Ray Hospital. Doctors test me for allergies to more than 200 foods, plants, and chemicals, but they can't find anything that I'm allergic to. One thing that the doctors haven't tested is my job. I might be allergic to my job.

By using the body to express itself, my mind transforms my body when my mind can do no more, and so my body takes over. I constantly worry about what I do and fail to focus on who I want to become. Lying in the hospital bed, I reflect on my professional direction and personal life and begin to realize that I need to molt and cast off my old shell to become who I really want to be in the next chapter of my life. In order to get rid of rashes, I have to get rid of my old shell and Los Angeles county jobs forever.

## - The Moon Home -

I'm staring at a ceiling fan in Jay's office, lying down on the couch.

"My county bosses gave me an opportunity to be a public servant, and I gained valuable friendships there. Their mentoring has been invaluable for my professional and personal life, and I always look back on my county work as an exciting and significant experience. As I lost my way in Japan, I found another way in America. This country gave me more than I gave to it." I pause.

"I'm not sure if I'm on the right path. I would have kept overeating and over working if I continued to stay there. So I quit, but I still keep eating because nothing fills me up." I don't know how to have a good relationship with food. Donna, my therapist once said to me that my saying no is the end of a relationship. I couldn't say no to the county so, my body had to say no."

"Your body must be very upset, and possibly sad," Jay says from behind.

"My body speaks when my mind is absent. To me, anger is more productive and sadness is unproductive."

"You might feel you can't get out of there once you're depressed."

"I won't allow myself to take care of my own health."

"I wonder if you let others do that."

"No, I would never do that. My husband asked why I was so mean to him when he was taking care of me."

"You might feel you are not worth being taken care of."

## Empty Stomach and Emtpy Mind

"When I was in the Marina del Ray Hospital, I thought I was going to die. I told my husband to put my corpse in the cheapest cardboard box and send it to Japan when I die, so my parents would burn it," I say expressionlessly.

"Then, my husband told me that he didn't want to do that because he loved me."

"It sounds like you can't take anything good without returning something."

"I refuse to take a good thing for free. I don't want to owe anyone. I have a tendency to think that people must have a bad motive if they want to give me something for free."

"For many years, you believed it was too much trouble for someone to love you. You believed loving someone and yourself were not worth it. The thing about being a therapist is that you tend to become your patients. The loving example is, as you know, your mother. You are not able to see your patients as your mother was not able to see. You became your mother with your patients, because having her was better than having no one." Jay speaks with a formal voice.

"I've been frightened of my patients, as my mother was frightened of me."

"Your mother was afraid of you because your spirit threatened her way of managing and being in the world, so, she limited herself from you. You inherited your mother's way of protecting herself."

"That was the only thing I was taught."

"In giving you one way to limit yourself, your mother also gave you the possibility of discovering another way." Jay pauses. "Years ago, you saw yourself through your mother's eyes, then you saw yourself through Donna's eyes. Now, you want to see yourself through your own eyes."

"Daughter, person, patient, and therapist…" My breath finally comes back. I change the subject when I look at the clock on the side table. "I didn't get last month's bill."

"I forgot again," Jay replies.

"I don't want you to feel uncomfortable billing me. Did I say something last week? Or a week before?"

"I have to think about why I have been forgetting," Jay says softly.

This time, Jay changes the subject. "What is the meaning of not bringing pillow today?"

I feel a welcoming sensation in my mouth, a safe source of nourishment from Jay, and it becomes an acceptance deep in my stomach. I am finally full.

# CHAPTER TEN
## Love

✝

I'm dreaming I'm in the airport. An unknown woman approaches me and whispers something. I see many people who just arrived from Kenya. They can speak English but they whisper in their language so that other people won't know what they are talking about. I don't understand their language. They give me a note but I don't understand their writing. I sense their tension, danger, and despair. I'm overwhelmed by their needs so I furtively move to another room. A large empty cage sits on the floor with its door wide open. I sense a fierce animal is free. How did it get out? I have to find and put it back in the cage, and lock the door so it won't come out again. I look around, but I don't see it. Suddenly, I feel a sensation on my calf and I look down. An orange-brown mane quickly swipes my calf. The animal's coat is soft, but a chill runs through my spine. I don't see the animal, but the fur reminds me of a large and powerfully built cat. A hairy tuft at the end of its tail passes through me and then disappears.

***Month 6: Agression and Libido***
Lying on the couch in front of Jay and talking about what comes to mind becomes a natural daily occurrence.

"Yesterday, Matt and I had an argument about a stupid thing as usual, it was one of thousands of meaningless arguments, then, last night, I had the dream." I pause. "I think the lion represents Matt. He is so aggressive and a danger to others. He needs to be in a cage and locked up." I sigh deeply. "Lions can't be domesticated like dogs and cats. They can't communicate with humans and co-exist. It's so sad. Lions are such beautiful animals, and they don't need to be in a cage. They need to be in the wild."

"I understand it's difficult to live with Matt, but what are your feelings when you are around Matt?" Jay's voice becomes firm.

"When Matt is angry, I get scared. When I'm scared, I attack." I make a claw with my left hand and scratch the air and hiss. "When I'm angry, I don't act civilized. Am I a lion too?"

Jay responds with a "hmm" and says nothing else.

"What?"

"If your alternative association, you as the lion, what does that mean to you?" Jay asks.

"When Matt becomes a lion, I become a lion too. I react to Matt's emotional engagement and expression of thoughts. I'm easily influenced by other people. When I become a lion, no one can touch me or control me." I turn my entire body away from Jay. "I don't want to be in a cage anymore. I grew up in a cage. I pause. "I hope I don't have 'beauty and the beast' syndrome." My mind skips around. "For many years, I believed I

# - Love -

could make unlovable violent beasts into loving and kind men. Giving up that fantasy is upsetting and disappointing, but I don't want to keep wishing that aggressive men can become loving and caring if I love them deeply enough."

"You mentioned you and your therapist talked about that years ago," Jay recalls and continues, "I wonder if it has something to do with your being hospitalized as a child."

"I was a sick child. I was in the hospital a lot." I look at the white wall in the office.

"It might not be that just physical illness was keeping you there. You might have believed that you needed to be in a cage."

"Am I afraid of my own madness? Or, is it narcissistic to believe that I could tame a wild and dangerous lion? I don't want to be controlled by men. I don't want to be controlled by my own obsessive mind."

"Months ago, when your mother criticized you on the phone, you became unable to think for days, and you said that you felt stupid and depressed."

"Is what happened between my mother and me the same thing that happens with Matt, and related to my dream?" I ask.

"We could talk about that."

"When I'm angry, I become terrified of my own anger. Growing up in my parents' house, I experienced how angry people seem idiotic and crazy. I didn't want to be like that, so I isolated myself from others without expressing it. Then, I became depressed by being unable to articulate my own thoughts and complicated feelings. Matt expresses his anger by just saying he is angry, that reminds me of my parents. I want to be able to communicate what is really going on and connect with those that I love, rather than just blowing up. But it is not easy."

Jay is still listening.

"I guess the lion could be me." That leaves me with another question. "Are you also suggesting that the unknown Kenyan woman is also me?"

"What do you think?"

"I always wanted to visit Africa. Africa is a mysterious and powerful place."

"There are many Africans in your dream, they must be very powerful, and even perhaps multi-dimensional," Jay says in a quiet voice.

I'm listening, thinking, and waiting.

"You said you were overwhelmed."

"It would be too much for me to handle what they would say if they spoke out loud or even wrote in a language that I actually understood, so instead, they whispered."

"But the cage was already opened. A powerful, aggressive, and confident lion is out of its cage and has been freed," Jay speaks.

"I've been rejecting the aggressive side of me. In my culture, women should not be aggressive and powerful, and they should be ashamed if they are. I become aggressive with Matt and I don't know why."

"I remember you talked generally about Matt, but I don't remember you talking about Matt in detail," Jay says.

"It was my midlife crisis," I chuckle.

Jay is listening so I continue to talk.

## - Love -

"We all keep having birthdays, some of us keep on going without really growing. That's why, on my 50th birthday, I decided to get analysis." I pause. "My 40th birthday didn't feel like for celebration, but more like midlife crisis. On my 40th birthday, Donna reminded me of the discussion that we had, shortly after I started seeing Donna, about babies." I think about the conversation that I had with Donna on my 40th birthday.

I said to Donna, "Today, I turned 40. My mother never remembers my birthday. I've never bothered expecting anything from her, and I thought I was fine. But I feel different this year, I feel I'm getting old, I don't have anybody in my life, I will never have children, I will become old and die alone."

Donna quickly replied, "Years ago, you said you didn't want to have children of your own."

Then the forgotten conversation returns. It was a few years earlier, I was in my late 30's, I told Donna that women I know, who are mothers, disappoint me, including my own mother. Some said they wanted to have children, some said there was no choice because having children is one of the responsibilities of married women. Having children and being a mother are two different things, but none of them said that they wanted to be a mother.

"I remember what I said in the session three years ago, why am I panicking today? Supposedly, being a parent is an extraordinary thing, so am I really missing that? If I really wanted to have a baby, wouldn't I have tried to have one by now?"

Donna asked, "There's more to life than having babies. What would life be like without babies?"

I responded, "A life of spontaneity, extraordinary adventures, being able to discover myself, to be able to live in a foreign country and fall in love, and to be deeply connected with someone I love and care for."

Donna smiled. "You have so much more."

After a long silence, when I'm staring at the ceiling and thinking about the conversation with Donna, Jay asks "Any thoughts?"

"I guess Donna prepared me a few years in advance and prevented me from being affected by a midlife crisis. After I spoke out loud about how my life would be, I realized I hadn't dated for a while. In the spring of my 40th birthday, I decided to attend a singles party at a Italian restaurant on Sunset Boulevard." I start talking about how I met Matt, my husband number three.

The cocktail bar in the Italian restaurant is dark, and the guys all look like nice enough, but I can't help wonder how many of them have criminal backgrounds. I'm always suspicious when it comes to men, especially after experiencing two divorces, on top of my many failed relationships. Tonight, I realize that I feel a bit self-conscious about being the only Asian in the room. Some just look at me and smile and some give me their business cards, which read attorney in criminal law, Hollywood actor, and a Ph.D. in something. At the age of 40, it is not easy to read these small-print business cards in a dark cocktail bar.

"Are you old enough to drink?" A guy looks at a Reidel scotch glass in my hand.

## - Love -

"I'm 39," I lie. After I lie about my age, I realize that wearing a green suede mini skirt with brown suede knee high boots is not even appropriate for 39. I look like a 21 year old who's trapped in a 40 year old midlife crisis Asian woman.

"Since you are a therapist, do you think you can play me like a puppet?" A guy standing beside me holds a green drink. Is that his pick up line? He is wearing a plain white cotton shirt, blue jeans, and white running shoes. I realize the guy was listening to my conversation with another guy. "Hi, I'm Matt." He holds his hand out to shake mine. Half of his dark hair is gone, but his blue eyes are shining through his glasses. He takes out his wallet to pay for his Mountain Dew, he has no business card. He holds his credit cards, driver's license, and cash together with a plain rubber band; that is his wallet. Matt who is in a state of no shame worships Adam Corolla, a podcaster who used to be a carpenter and boxer, and he quotes Adam Corolla as if he were referring to the Bible or Shakespeare. He never chuckles or giggles, but does laugh like a maniac. Matt appears to take a risk with the very thin line between insults and jokes. "What made you come to the US?" It's such an unoriginal question to a foreigner like me.

"I failed every university I applied to in Japan, and I also went through a divorce there. I'm a shameful member of my family, and I had nowhere else to go," I answer truthfully.

"What made you study psychology?" This is also unoriginal.

"My family is crazy, so I wanted to learn about craziness." I look at him.

Matt looks at me. "I was beaten." This is original.

## - The Moon Home -

After an hour of our conversation, Matt asks with his animated eyes, "What's the percentage chance that you think we'll end up together?" This is also original.

I laugh without any reason, but something tells me to pause instead. 30%, 50%... After I start to put numbers in my mind, I think about our cultural differences. From my observations, American people are romantic and praise others highly in public. When American men form relationships with women, they tend to fall in love dramatically, and share with their friends and family how the relationship is blooming, so I decided to say 70%. Matt becomes furious and offended that he gets only 70%. Matt and I just met, so receiving a 70% should be more than enough, but he was a math major, and numbers mean more to him than just numbers, they mean structure, relation and the truth. In my mind, 70% is a pass – both thumbs up. In Matt's mind, 70% is a C and that is not acceptable. For the future references, I can't give him numbers.

After years and years of dating happy and healthy people in the City of Angels, I am hopeless when it comes to keeping a relationship for more than six months. I find it refreshing to meet an outraged Bostonian who is deeply sarcastic, cynical, angry, and neurotic.

Matt is handsome and absolutely attractive in an extravagant intellectual way. He is punctual, prompt, and seldom makes mistakes, qualities that one can always depend upon. Although he doesn't display his considerable intellect unless I ask specific questions, being with him is like carrying around a calculator, dictionary, and newspaper all in one. I sense his confidence through his demeanor; he has no problem telling people

- *Love* -

what he thinks and wants. After many failed dates and marriages, this reliable, confident person begins to seem more valuable as my life partner.

One Saturday night, shortly after our meeting at the Italian restaurant, Matt invites me to his house for dinner. I'm very cautious about visiting a stranger's house after seeing the movie "Silence Of The Lambs." The movie was the first movie I watched in a theater in America, and it has deeply affected me. I let my girlfriends know Matt's home address in case I end up in his dungeon. My girlfriends tell me to make sure bottled beverages are sealed and opened in front of me.

Matt's house does not seem to have a dungeon, and his housekeeper keeps the house clean and organized. He cooks his deceased mother's recipes, chicken casserole and a frozen desert that contains frozen strawberries and bananas with whipped cream. His cooking ability and extremely domestic independence are very impressive. For hours, we talk about our past, present, and future.

After my visit to Matt's home, he sends me an email that says, "It was a magic..." In a romantic relationship, magic moments seem important. It seems as if we need magic or the memory of magic to carry our relationships.

The following weekend, I invite Matt to my apartment for dinner to reciprocate. He likes nothing else, but meat and potatoes, salt, and sugar. He tells me his favorite food and drink are pepperoni pizza and Mountain Dew. He also tells me that he does not eat organic foods, so I get a $5 frozen pepperoni pizza from Ralph's and arrive at my apartment on Tuesday night.

# - The Moon Home -

Matt lets himself into my apartment complex, and he is already waiting for me in front.

After I open the door for Matt, I drop everything and open the oven. As he places the colorful flowers on my kitchen table, I start to clean my oven, which is filled with pots and pans. I realize I haven't used the oven since I moved in two years ago. After I remove all pots and pans and to put the frozen pizza into the oven, Matt starts to dust the top of the oven door with paper towels. He asks me if I have ever used the oven, and reads me the directions on the box. It's just a frozen pizza, it should not be complicated, so I figure that it's not necessary to follow the directions. After a while, smoke starts coming out of the oven, so I know that the pizza is done. "Is your recipe just to keep cooking it until the smoke alarm goes off?" Matt asks. As he bites into the burned pizza, he asks with eyes wide open, "What kind of Japanese does not follow directions?"

"How about we not see anyone else but only each other?" Matt asks me to go steady. It seems that Matt's observation of my inability to complete domestic chores has not affected his decision about pursuing the relationship. Most Japanese men would freak out about the thick dust in the kitchen and burned frozen foods. Matt wants us to watch TV and go grocery shopping together; he wants me in his life, without me cooking and cleaning. It doesn't sound like a bad deal for a relationship, especially not having to pretend who I am.

Later that evening, I have to think about safe sex. Although I have never taken precautions to protect my emotional state, I always followed safe sex guidelines in order to protect myself from diseases. In 1990, when I arrived in this country, AIDS was not curable or even treatable. During the 1990's, unprotected sex could be dangerous. America taught me about safe sex, so I created a set of dating rules:

1. Men have to initiate the first date.
2. Accept dates with other men until I date someone exclusively.
3. Go on dates only on Friday or Saturday nights.
4. Google a man's name before dating him.
5. Let my girlfriends know the name of my date.
6. Make sure I can reach him on the phone.
7. Request an STD test with results before having sex with him.
8. Ask about his plans to introduce me to his family and friends.
9. Be ready to leave if he doesn't say "I love you" within six months.

"I ask boyfriends to take an STD test before I get intimate with them," I tell Matt.

"Do you think I have an STD?" Matt seems to be offended. "I don't have an STD."

"I need to see the written results of a blood test," I say kindly.

"Are you saying that I'm lying to you?" Matt's face becomes red and irritated.

"You said you've never taken an STD test, so you don't know. You are assuming or hoping that you don't have an STD. I can't trust a statement from someone who does not know," I say. I don't understand the point of this argument. We won't get intimate physically or emotionally anytime soon. This dialogue

# The Moon Home

leads me to feel suspicious about him. Matt finally gives me an result, but he complains that he is embarrassed by requesting STD tests to his physician. Matt feels that his physician thinks of Matt as a some kind of freak.

Before I become physically intimate with Matt, I want to make sure that he truly represents who he claims to be. "Do you think an omission is a lie?" I ask.

"What is the definition of omission?"

"Are you telling me that you don't know the meaning of omission?" I'm offended by a question like that, especially from people like him, an attorney.

"I think the definitions of omission and lie are different," Matt insists.

"I know what the dictionary says about those two words, but it doesn't' matter what it says. I'm curious about what you think," I say. This causes me to wonder about the direction of this relationship. Is he trying to get out of my question by talking about technicalities? Matt asks me to define everything, so I tell Matt, "I think an omission is not the truth. I think that an untruth and an omission are both lies."

Two days later, after Matt carefully looked up the definition of lie, he finally agrees with me, but I've forgotten the purpose of my question. While I'm listening to Matt's reasoning for not answering my simple question, I contemplate the failure of my first marriage because of my ex-husband's omission. For Matt, as an attorney, an omission seems to have a different definition from a lie. What is Matt's principle? For attorneys, the truth or untruth might not be a matter of subject, and there might not be a clear line between.

## - Love -

How much of myself should I be willing to sacrifice for my partner? For Matt, there is no compromise, compromise is settlement. It's never good for lawyers to settle for other people's benefit, so he's never compromised. He eats breakfast at 5 am, lunch at 10 am, and dinner at 3 pm. He goes to bed at 9:30 every night no matter what. He only takes me to restaurants where he likes to eat, and to places he enjoys for our vacation. Even on our vacation, he often withdraws into his work. There is no flexibility or compromise. As I become Matt's girlfriend, I start to lose my existence, my identity is tied to that of Matt's girlfriend.

Matt, a corporate attorney, mathematics in major who overvalues intellectual verbalization with a condescending elegant attitude, is focused on a strategy to win arguments. He objects to every reason I make and disputes my rationales. He believes that I know more tricks to relationships than other women because I am a therapist. If my sentences are incorrect, I must have the wrong intentions, my motives must be malicious. He pushes our talks into arguments, these arguments turn into fights. It is more than just an inability to maintain his emotions and hide his opinions, but conscious eagerness to show that his views are the correct ones. Mathematics is black and white, law is guilty or not guilty, but there are lots of gray areas in emotions. As a lawyer, if he doesn't win, he loses. As a therapist, there is no winning unless the other party wins. Attorneys and therapists are like oil and water, and therefore cannot be mixed.

Being in a relationship with Matt makes my issues flare up. Matt's passion for debate makes me question Confucianism, and that's another aspect that does not fit between us. It's the

*- The Moon Home -*

belief that there are qualities that make a good woman, which include obedience to parents, authorities, and husband. The ability to remain quiet is as important as being an attractive and intelligent woman. Matt does not allow me to follow the thousand years of Confucian moral obligations in the context of a woman's life, passed down from my ancestors, school, and society.

I, as a Japanese woman, am not supposed to argue or say no. Even after years of education in America, I could not entirely reject Confucius until I met Matt. Matt's eyes light up full of excitement when I say no to him. I realize that this is the way Matt connects with others. At the age of 40, I have to practice a new way of living. All I've experienced and practiced in my life was saying yes, now I have to reverse this life-long practice. I'm not accustomed to saying no, I have no idea when and how to say no, so I start to say no to everything just to please Matt. I then try to find some reason why I disagree. Figuring out a reason why I disagree after I actually disagree is not easy because I'd never practiced having opinions.

As much as I try to please Matt by saying no to everything, I find Matt impossible to live with. Matt's strategy is to pretend that he does not understand my rationale. His pretending to not see my points and his continuing to examine me makes me feel as if I'm standing on a rug that could be pulled out from under me at any moment. He takes information and twists it to give a completely negative connotation, and to hunt me into a corner until I can't think anymore. I get caught up explaining things over and over again until I'm exhausted and my mind is not functioning. And, on and on in a series of twisting

– Love –

questions as if I were being cross examined. There is no mercy in our arguments.

Matt gets very annoyed when I serve food to our guests after they say, "No thank you." In Japanese culture, no does not mean no, and Japanese insist on having company eat or drink even when they say "no thanks." Though the Japanese have a reputation of saying "sorry" quite often, Matt complains that I never apologize. Language is a tricky issue and involves complicated cultural barriers. The Japanese often confuse the word "sorry" for "thank you" because they empathize with people who do something for them, and feel bad about what people have to go through. The Japanese consider other people's efforts because they have empathy for other people who do something for them. Americans say similar things like "I am sorry to bother you, I hope this is not too much trouble for you, I hope you don't mind," but these are less common among Americans because Americans speak their minds and usually don't do things they don't want to.

Matt also complains I never say thank you. Although many Asians say "thank you" and "please" to strangers because they should not take strangers for granted, this does not apply to family members. Japanese don't thank family members. Among traditional Japanese couples, care and concern might be demonstrated by taking care of the other's physical needs, such as cooking, cleaning, fixing broken things in the household rather than by verbally expressing concerns and appreciation. For Japanese, love is an obligation, love is sacrifices and their relationships are based on depending on each other. Japanese couples take things for granted, which is considered to be part of normal and healthy lives.

In contrary to Japanese couples, many Americans believe that marriages are about togetherness that is 50-50, to be equals without dependency, and to love without obligation. American couples make sure they don't take anything for granted when it comes from their partner's gestures, they make sure that their partners know that they are not being taken for granted by expressing gratitude and appreciation. Therefore, saying "please," "thank you," and "I love you," are important for a couple.

Matt says "I love you" more than a few times a day. He hugs me for no reason; he is not afraid of expressing his affections. Japanese don't value verbal expression of emotion so they don't express their feelings verbally. Instead, they express their emotions by behaviors or services. Matt is not happy that I repeat "I love you" only after Matt says he loves me. He calls me a parrot and complains that I never say I love him spontaneously. However, he is never discouraged by my parroting behavior. After I've lived in America for so long, I still feel awkward about physical contact and still run away from him. What made me so scared about accepting love from him?

I'm afraid that this relationship will also become contaminated by my mother's concerns. Mother asks about Matt. "What does he do for a living?" When I tell her that Matt is an attorney, she does not quite understand. "How can you guys make a living?" In Japan, especially on the island of Hokkaido, attorneys and therapists are mystical occupations because no one uses their services. In my mother's mind, Matt and I have fictitious occupations and are unable to pay bills. My parents are losing face because of our occupations. In stead of translating the endless conversations about our cultural differences, I make up things that Matt will never know. Losing face is such a convenient phrase. Whenever I have difficulty explaining Japanese culture, I use this phrase for American people, and they seem to understand when I say it.

I find my relationship with Matt in turmoil when our work becomes extremely busy because of Obama's health care reforms in Matt's work place. Our challenges are triggered by our work stress and personality differences. Our frequent long-lasting, shameless arguments leave us overwhelming exhaustion. We talk about everything, anything about our past, present, and future. Our sleep deprivation, depression, depletion, and then feelings of abandonment take over our lives.

Countless talks, discussions, arguments, and fights confuse and compel Matt and me to the point where we are constantly over-sensitive to each other. The tension in this relationship is all about being preoccupied and obsessed with each other's thoughts and actions. The closer people get, the more issues come up. Neither of us is willing to change, so we wrestle with competitions and disappointments. When couples are in a fight, it is hard to stop because there is no referee. No one can tell us which comments are brutal. Matt and I haven't reached an understanding as to why winning in life is important. There is a never-ending torrent of words angry expressed, which I find depleting and suffocating. Matt and I are completely lost. What we are fighting for?

"My stage designer friend told me that people often take only a few minutes to decide whether to make an offer on a new house. People can fall in love with a house the moment they enter it, while the rest of the house does not matter," I tell Jay.

Jay sniffs.

"Matt was fixing his house to sell while we were attending couples therapy. We have to fix his house and our relationship before we move on with our lives. I was terrified that we would fall in love without getting to know each other, as if we were deciding to buy a house the moment we open the door without looking at the rest of the house. In order to avoid that, Matt and I decided to go to couples therapy."

"How did it go?" Jay asks.

"I liked Dr. B, but Matt said Dr. B was my advocate and attorney. Supposedly, Dr. B protected me from Matt, and I used Dr. B as my safety net, is that so bad?" Jay says nothing, so I continue, "If I used Dr. B as my safety net, whether consciously or subconsciously, I would not be proud of myself. My mother used me to protect herself from her mean and unloving husband." I pause again. "I became my mother."

"You could not have your own relationship with your father because of that," Jay says.

"I understand why Matt was upset about the dynamic with Dr. B," I say. After a long pause, I start telling Jay how Matt and I attended couples therapy.

## - Love -

In couples therapy, couples often start with very different levels of willingness to engage in the process. If one of them is no longer in love with the other, therapy is not going to bring them closer together. A couples therapist works with two clients who both bring the complexity of their lives into the therapy. Not many therapists take couples, and not many therapists are experts in couples therapy.

Matt and I have been invested in this relationship for a year and half. Before we invest more of our time, energy, and emotion, we need to re-evaluate our potentials. Matt and I agree to see a professional. Matt has a strange notion of a therapist's mind. He thinks therapists are puppet masters, and he has a fear of being controlled by therapists. For me to avoid failed therapy, I let him pick our therapist. That way, he can't say that intentionally I find a therapist who will favor me.

Arguments between Matt and me become out of control. We can't wait any longer, so Matt finds a therapist and schedules the first appointment within a week of our agreement. After work, Matt and I arrive at the therapist's office at 6:45 pm. We sit in separate couches in the waiting room, not talking or even looking at each other. Dr. B opens the door at 6:55 and hands each of us an eight-page intake packet. "Do you need pens?" Dr. B asks. "We got it," Matt and I say at the same time. It takes less than five minutes for us to complete the forms. Matt pushes a red button on the wall to call Dr. B. It's already 7:00. We don't want to waste our allotted time for this expensive session. Dr. B comes back immediately and takes us to his office.

Matt and I follow Dr. B's broad shoulders and enter his office. He has a gymnast's body and is not much taller than me.

## - The Moon Home -

As we enter, we see a dark wood antique desk and chair in a narrow rectangular office with walnut walls. We walk on the hardwood floor through the dimly lit room to the far end, where there's a couch and chair. I feel as if we walked for miles. Beyond the couch is a sliding glass door, and outside there is a spacious outdoor garden made up of distinctive sections where the plants and herbs are lit by warm yellow garden lights. The antique wooden furniture and the green plants from the outdoor garden create a mindful atmosphere. This unexpected oasis brings me a detachment from our relationship problems. For a moment, I've forgotten the imbalance of my mind.

Matt and I sit on the brown couch side by side avoiding each other's gaze. Matt tenses up and moves away from me when I speak. The distance of our seating arrangement reflects our lack of emotional closeness. What is getting in our way?

Before Dr. B speaks, he looks at Matt, then at me, and then both of us together. I glance at Dr. B's salt and pepper hair, his thick beard, and then his sparkling brown eyes behind his reading glasses. Dr. B starts talking to us, expresses how he is impressed by Matt's and my speedy completion of the intake forms. "You must be smart," Dr. B looks at Matt. "Not emotionally," I say, the veins in my left temple standing out. "There is competition in the relationship." Dr. B gives a sudden, wry smile, and the strong line of his jaw softens.

Dr. B seems particularly curious about our sex life, examining frequency and libido very carefully as he clicks his brown pen on and off with his thumb. I failed many marriages and relationships, but they were never destroyed over sex, and sex was the furthest thing on my mind when I thought about our therapy. I understand that many American couples see Dr. B concerning intimacy issues, and sex may be a major problem for many couples. So, he tries to reinforce our sex lives as a natural therapeutic process.

In our first session, like other many couples, we start to speak of what we do not want from our partner. "I don't want her yelling so much," Matt tells Dr. B. Dr. B looks at me with a surprised face and asks, "Do you yell?" I have been quiet so far, and Dr. B is apparently wondering whether this quiet person really yells.

"I don't usually yell at people, but Matt is impossible. I can't feel like myself while I'm with him. My therapist told me that I react to Matt's critical comments, and I find it very difficult to respond calmly to his criticism and sarcasm. Matt won't stop until I raise my voice."

Dr. B looks at both of us and says, "I'm wondering if that's what Matt has practiced in his previous relationships. You guys have a divorce history, with underlying conflicts, hurts, and disappointments that must be addressed, understood, and repaired before you move on to marriage. I'd like to help you guys to move from criticism and sarcasm about each other and to be able to communicate differently so that you can have an intimate relationship."

We have unresolved trauma that is yet to be discovered. There is a lot of tension and distance between us because our traumas have not been healed, and we are stuck in our past relationships. It is easier for us to blame and be angry at the other rather than admitting our fear or hurt. As we take that path, the tension manifests and there is no more emotional intimacy.

Both of us are so focused on winning over the other that we end up as losers in the relationship. However, we are both willing to invest time, energy, and money in therapy, and this shows that we really want to heal. That's what I heard from Dr. B.

It seems obvious to Dr. B that there are injuries from past failed marriages, and from family relationships. Who are our shadows? Shadows that get shorter and longer in the morning and afternoon, shadows that neither of us can catch, shadows that finally get beyond our control. Dr. B seems willing to be a shadow buster. It is clear to me that Dr. B has diligent patience, warm empathy, and strong leadership skills. The first meeting with him convinces me that something can be achieved by his counsel. However, Matt and I leave our first session without any solutions.

Dr. B tells us that therapy is not something that is needed, it's something that is wanted. We don't need to be in therapy, we want to have a loving, caring, and long lasting relationship. I never had an equal-status relationship where there is respect and love, but this time I want to be an equal. I realize that when I feel powerless, I become invisible; when I feel invisible, I become angry; when I become angry, I sabotage myself and become powerless again. I get stuck in a dark spiral. When we are fighting, we are not listening to or understanding each other. Our pattern of communication has been to blame the other and defend ourselves rather than to take responsibility for our own actions.

"How was your week?" Dr. B starts the second session, and this initiates tension. Matt and I both wait for another to say something, but neither of us talks. "What about saying what you see and think," Dr. B says.

I look at Matt with mean eyes. "Our arguments and fights are not at that level, our arguments are at a primitive level. We fight over Pearl Harbor, Yoko Ono, Hitler's team because Matt brings those topics up every chance he gets."

Matt's eyes become shifty, he hates me saying this in front of an audience. I keep looking straight at Dr. B. "You told on me?" Matt gives a nervous laugh, he seems to be embarrassed, as he should be. He is not expecting me to tell Dr. B about the ridiculous things he says.

Matt has a passion for perfection, and he's frustrated by, rather than enjoying, our cultural and personality differences. Matt likes to poke me when he is bored, for example asking me, "This is the American way, that is the Japanese way, which one is better?" In therapy, I don't feel shame anymore, so I tell Dr. B how Matt interacts me in the primitive level. When I accept one aspect of myself, I must sacrifice the other one. I feel I have to chose either the American way or the Japanese way. As I anticipate losing an argument by giving up on the part that I own, I react to Matt with anger.

"It is not about Yoko Ono, it's about something underneath that Matt has not addressed." Dr. B looks at Matt and me. Matt defends himself and moves to another topic that doesn't involve his issues, he is a professional. Dr. B figures out Matt's other strategy, which is to find a way to get someone angry and to point out the person's anger and label the individual as an angry person so that the other person cannot touch Matt's issues – a typical lawyer strategy. Matt becomes more defensive and verbally aggressive when Dr. B pushes the bottom of his issues.

It is especially difficult for Matt and me to identify our own behaviors that have contributed to the problem because in our mind, doing so means we were "wrong." To Matt, he has be right, because wrong means losing not winning. For me, being wrong means shame, losing face. Matt and I continue to struggle.

Most of Matt's pre-college classes were for "gifted" children, and he never had the experience of interacting with kids who were not academically inclined. When we argue, he would get ferociously upset if I didn't understand what he meant, or I spoke unclearly. He is not capable of comprehending that different types of human beings exist in this world. In his mind, if I make mistakes or if I don't understand something, I am deliberately making mistakes to confuse him or pretending to be dumb to cause him trouble maliciously. As far as I can remember, there is no "gifted" class in school in the island I grew up. At an early age, I learned that there are many different types of people. My experience of failure in every aspect of life was in contrast to Matt's "gifted" experience; this difference becomes a deep gap between us more than East vs. West or men vs. women.

Dr. B encourages me to offer a positive tone and strokes in my interaction with Matt, and also to display appreciation if I feel I have been heard. When one of us becomes angry, the other has to reinforce our learning. Matt is good in reaching out, often apologizing and making the effort to heal. Admitting our own mistakes is important, but "cheap sorry" and "quick forgiveness" create mistrust. Dr. B makes a request to Matt to make amends because Matt apologizes quickly, but he goes back and behaves the same. "Observe your own behaviors and attribute it, own them. Don't spin and play with the truth and attempt to defend yourself." Dr. B looks at Matt. "You are an attorney, you can argue any position. You've been practicing that for most of your life." In Matt's mind, you're either guilty or not guilty, and he always has to win, he can never lose or be guilty, therefore he never changes or improves. For the first time in many years, I thought about the Gabacho seat in elementary school and its concept of shame and guilt. If you're not guilty, then there's nothing to be ashamed of, but if you are guilty, and you want to know what to do about your guilt, then you've got to embrace the information shame brings to you. Matt should be in the Gabacho's seat to learn to welcome and honor his wrong doing and shame so that he won't continually do the same things.

Dr. B feels very bad about how Matt treats me with verbal aggression. Dr. B expresses empathy toward me and criticism of Matt. Dr. B explains that he understands my cultural background and upbringing, and that makes Matt uneasy and apprehensive. Matt begins to distance himself from Dr. B, saying that Dr. B acts as my advocate. Matt provokes Dr. B as the result of Dr. B's emotional impact on Matt, while Dr. B recognizes and amplifies those qualities in Matt. Dr. B stands up for his beliefs and Matt aggressively challenges him. At one of our sessions, those two men make me feel terrified. Then, I begin to withdraw, turning away from critical moments.

After being worn out by months and months of arguments both inside and outside of therapy, I consider quitting. If Dr. B can't change Matt, I'll be left troubled and hopeless. Today, I want to give up on Matt, give up on this relationship, and give up on therapy. Dr. B looks at me and says, "Old dogs can learn new tricks." I say nothing but smile with my mouth closed. I know that won't change my mind. Dr. B looks at both of us and says, "You understand people don't just change. It will take time." As a therapist, I understand. Dr. B looks at me and continues, "I understand you might be losing hope because Matt does not seem to change. But do you think Matt keeps paying three hundred dollars every week to just come here to be blamed day after day? You don't think he is that much of an idiot, do you?" Dr. B says with a serious face. I laugh out loud unintentionally. Throwing money away is not something Matt would do. Dr. B and I know it because of the way Matt accounts for everything and the fact that Matt has created a 50-page prenuptial agreement to make sure I cannot steal anything, not even one penny. After Dr. B cracks me up, he quickly realizes that that the prenuptial agreement is a dent on our relationship. Dr. B says that it is not just about the unfairness of the agreement, it's about Matt's capacity to visibly see who I am, and therefore to project his mistrust and anger towards me. Money can't buy love, but money can be an expression of love and a reflection of hope. I begin to realize that people like Matt keep spending a lot of money on therapy and attorney fees for a reason, so this relationship must mean something for him. It might be some form of love or a glimmer of hope. Matt and I keep sitting on the couch, not saying anything. After a few minutes of silence, the fresh breeze comes through the open window. When I look out into the garden, for first time in many months, I realize that I've forgotten that there are sparkling shinny lights that illuminate the healthy green plants. I inhale the breeze and close my eyes to focus on something other than this relationship.

There are many reasons why Matt and I should split up, but one reason to be hopeful is our mutual respect for Dr. B. Matt and I have quite distinct memories and we try to reinforce what Dr. B suggests regardless of our likes and dislikes. Matt and I believe our arguments can be softened into conversations, and we must follow Dr. B's advice if we want to have a long-lasting and loving relationship.

Matt uses certain words to intimidate me such as "You ruined my day," or "You deliberately did that." I become impatient with his blaming communication style used in every conversation, so I announce that he is not allowed to use those harmful and meaningless words anymore if he wants to pursue this relationship. He is no longer allowed to do the followings if he wants this relationship to work: 1) roll his eyes when he thinks my thoughts are irrational, 2) pretend to playing the violin when he observes my feelings are hurt, 3) snap his fingers when he wants me to respond quickly, 4) snort through his nose when he wants to ignore my opinions. Surprisingly, he agrees not do these things anymore. But I let him keep using "What's the verdict?" and "How say you?" For Matt, simple questions are allowed.

I understand my announcements are not really therapeutic strategies, but I believe setting some ground rules are important in any relationship. I've learned this from Caesar Millan's T.V. Show "The Dog Whisperer." After Matt and I start to live with my ground rules, we begin to be able to think deeply about ourselves and communicate differently.

*- The Moon Home -*

After many sessions, Matt realizes that it was his mother who had not given him credit for his accomplishments. People don't decide to go to rigorous schools when they turn 17, they know that even at an early age, the place they are going is not average but indeed special. In Matt's mind, his mother never give him a credit as a child, she wasn't even proud of him for graduating cum laude from the prestigious school where he'd earned his J.D. Not giving Matt credit provokes an emotional response. His eagerness to receive credit from a woman who does not speak proper English and failed every university in Japan tells me that Matt's credit-seeking behaviors are not from his rational mind, but from his deep emotional needs. In Matt's mind, it was not only that he wanted recognition from his mother but that he also wanted to be loved by her, he wanted to earn her love.

Matt slowly recognizes that his anger toward his mother and the mistrust from his past failed relationships are being projected onto me. At the same time, I become aware that Matt's criticism reminds me of my mother. I remember that it was my mother who was critical and fearful of me when I was growing up. I recognize an emotional reaction toward Matt that originated from my mother's criticism. "In a marriage, it is OK to give partners things that we did not receive as a child," Dr. B says. This also makes clear the importance of giving credit to Matt that his mother didn't provide.

Dr. B repeatedly reminds Matt that neither of us win using a blaming communication style. Every day, we practice the following: 1) We have to be able to bring up an issue in a calm and respectful manner; 2) We need to be able to avoid blaming or making accusations and ask questions with a curious state of mind; 3) We have to listen and respond with empathy. Matt and I have to practice these things over and over again until we consistently do them without thinking. If we are half as intelligent as we think, these concepts should be common sense, but we need to understand this not only intellectually, but also at an emotional level. For us, that is challenging.

Dr. B introduces us to a very simple idea: it is not worth it for us to fight unless it is a life-threatening situation. For us to do that, we need to be able to recognize our own desires and consider what is important for us, and why it is important, so that we can negotiate our requests. Matt and I practice thinking about whether the issue at hand is life-threatening, so that we can decide whether to make a big deal out of our concerns. Some of the messages that Matt and I have received in therapy are complicated concepts, but some are very simple, common sense ideas, and they help Matt and me become less threatening and more creative and authentic to each other. For Matt to modify his behaviors, he must learn that his self-protective aggression can often becomes harmful to our relationship. He also gains meaningful insight in order to become willing to take a risk to change his approach for his own happiness. For me, my responses are more owned. My expression of my love for Matt has grown over the years. We learn a variety of ways to communicate, instead of attacking each other. By the time Matt completes the renovation of his house, Matt and I have grown as individuals and as a couple.

Human connections are many and varied. Some couples share their passion, some have common interests or backgrounds.

## - The Moon Home -

Matt and I are seldom involved in each other's life. An attorney and a therapist, oil and water, East meets West, we don't have anything in common but each other. Through couples therapy, Matt and I win the curiosity of having the strength to open our hearts and trust each other despite our differences.

Communication does not require sophisticated language. Whether it's humans or monkey babies, their mothers notice that they have needs and provide for them with care and love. One sign that a female gorilla is in love is that she can be seeing picking nits off of a male companion, grooming is one form of primate's showing care and love. Matt is a self-sufficient man, he prepares his own meals, and has a house keeper he trusts. The only activity that Matt asks me to perform is cutting his hair. His hair turns out a different style every time, but the haircut ritual is the only time he feels like receiving care from me. My first attempt made his hair look like Hitler's, and he expressed anger. After my skills improved, his hair turned out like that of Steven Spielberg or Steve Jobs, and only then did Matt expresses satisfaction. Our communications are softening and we are expressing vulnerable feelings.

Matt and I take two steps forward and one step back. Our experience of failed relationships made us take this opportunity to figure out why our past relationships failed, rather than falling into the "this time will be different" spiral. That is what I wanted.

After a year and half of couples therapy, our level of tolerance and attachment has grown. We are not sure how much is from our intellect and how much is from emotion, but we have come to accept that it was our hurts and disappointments that

## - Love -

became our shadows and turned us against each other. Those scars will never disappear, but now we are able to see each other's scars in our minds and hearts, and we find compassion for one another. Finally, Matt and I feel more secure about ourselves and our relationship. We learn that rather than being fearful, we are able to express our truths to each other.

I feel different this time: no romantic gestures, no getting down on one knee, no big diamond, no ostentatious wedding. Just two adults deciding to make a commitment to take care of and love each other. We married at the Beverly Hills City Hall, not because we lived in Beverly Hills but because the city hall was the only place that provided ceremonies on the weekends. Matt and I worked even harder right before Matt's early retirement. I saw clients at my private practice after our wedding ceremony. I feel the wedding was like the renewal of a driver's license or paying taxes at a government office.

Soon after Matt's retirement, we moved to the beach. Throughout the year, the beaches in Los Angeles are sunny and clear, but the breezes become cooler as the sun sets. Matt and I walk on the beach, where the sunlight plays on the waves. There is no crowd at the beach on a weekday. Under the wave going off forever into the horizon, the silver lines of the wave reflect the orange calm sun as it moves slowly toward the horizon. Above the horizon, there are soothing sounds of waves crashing on the beach rhythmically and timelessly. I can see miles of water, and the constant moving waves tell me that I've moved 3,000 miles from the other land. I keep reminding myself that there was a time I struggled with existence, and wanted to disappear. At the moment, the deep Pacific ocean absorbs every noise on the beach and every disbelief in my mind.

Seagulls are flapping their wings as they soar in serene circles above the ocean. The sun is no longer beating on me as it moves closer to the horizon. I take off my sunglasses and walking shoes. When my bare feet sink into the warm wet sand, a dark gray rock on the dry sand catches my eye. I bend over to pick it up, and I feel the weight of the gray rock – it feels prickly. I put the rock down on the wet sand and it's gently removed from my hand into the warm water. The wave carries the rock back to the ocean, and it rolls as if it's bumping one rock after another.

I sit on the dry warm sand in front of the water. Next to me, I see a little flat oval stone on the sand. I reach for the stone and rub the smooth surface with my fingers. On the beach, most of the stones are no longer prickly. It probably took hundreds of years to smooth these prickly rocks. As I hold the smooth gray stone in my hand, I think of Matt. Matt swims every day in order to smoothen his prickliness, the same way carvings on stones are worn down by water. While I'm rolling the smooth stone in my hand, Matt sits beside me.

"If my college friends find out that I married an Asian, they will be shocked. I was famous for not eating foreign foods, and for not visiting other countries. I love American food and culture." Matt does not lose his ability to display a strange mixture of prickliness and a charming demeanor. "I love you so much," Matt looks at me straight in the eyes and tells me. This is another thing Matt has not changed. "We are in love, after 12 years of togetherness in hell, we are still unbelievably in love," Matt says

- *Love* -

that when he consumes excessive amounts of Mountain Dew. "We are two damaged people who try to make the best of it together. I'm glad we met." Matt smiles. Twelve years later, there is no more debate, no more explanations, no more translations. We are finally able to speak the same language – the language of unspoken words called insight, connection, and healing.

In the matter of love, we weren't soul mates, it wasn't magic. We found each other and didn't give up on love. While I'm experiencing the power of water, I'm listening to the silence of my mind. When Matt expresses his belief in magic, I'm still skeptical. True magic might be that we're still alive and are sitting next to each other. Matt calls me a plant serial killer because I kill all the live plants in the entire house and yard. Despite our craziness and differences, Matt and I miraculously managed to not kill each other's spirits. That is magic.

The rest of the evening is slow, watching black and white movies is our reward at the end of the day. My complicated life becomes very simple, and my unpredictable days become predictable. We are sitting on the couch and watching a black and white version of "The Wizard of Oz" on a 52-inch television placed on the wall in the living room. "I love that you're not afraid of me." Matt's bold words are transforming into vulnerable ones. With two divorces and numerous failed relationships, I was left alone every time. All my life, I felt relief when people left me. People leaving me made me feel empty, and it gives me long lasting melancholia, but alone always felt right for me. This is the first relationship where I don't have to hide the aggression inside of me and where I feel no need to be courteous. When I look at Matt sitting beside me, for the first time in my life, not being alone feels right. There is nothing much to say about our daily lives, we'd already covered everything.

On the screen, the lion lies down on his bed of straw and Dorothy lies beside him and places her head on his soft shaggy mane, while they talk of their troubles and try to plan some way to escape. Lions are meant to be untamed, just like how some people are meant to be. I lie beside Matt and put my head on his soft shaggy mane. After all those years of our adventures and learning of lives, his shaggy mane has softened like the prickly rock smoothened in the water.

## CHAPTER ELEVEN
## Cuckoo's Nest
+−

***Month 12: Life Energy***

It hasn't occurred to me that Father will die until he is actually really dying. I started to see Jay because I began having strange dreams shortly after Father was diagnosed with liver cancer. But I'm still not sure how much I'm aware of his death. For most of his life, Father's lifestyle consisted of heavy drinking at a Geisha bar, smoking like a chimney, eating red meat for every meal, consuming huge amounts of salt and sugar, and sleeping four hours a day. He is lucky that he didn't die in his 40's and 50's. He should be grateful that he lived until 80 with that kind of lifestyle, which can cause any kind of cancer at any age.

"Other than his liver cancer, my father's physical health is fine, and his cholesterol, blood sugar, and blood pressure are all normal. He still eats red meet with lots of salt and desserts with lots of sugar. He smokes continuously every chance he gets. He doesn't seem close to dying anytime soon, but I'm thinking about taking some time off to see him. My bosses tell me to see my father before it's too late. Liver cancer seems to have fewer symptoms than other cancers, but when it progresses, it's rapid and sudden. My bosses are both retired surgeons, so I should consider their advice."

"You are considering it because you are told to," Jay says.

"I might be in denial, but it's hard to believe my father will die. He has such a powerful life energy, which I didn't inherit. He doesn't sound as if he believes he is going to die, but I should not ignore my bosses' advice."

"Life energy," Jay emphasizes.

"Most of my life, I've had death energy. I wish I could live, really live in the moment. None of my colleagues likes working with surgeons, but I find it very comfortable. Sometimes, I wonder what makes me feel so comfortable being with them. Maybe I chose surgeons because I wanted to live. Maybe I believe that surgeons have some secrets about life and death."

"Hmm," Jay is still listening and waiting for me to continue.

"After Matt decided to retire early, we moved to the west side. Matt stays home and focuses on his hobbies and exercising. Aside from taking a course on children and adolescents, I feel disconnected from therapy after leaving my therapist position at L.A. County. I left the past in order to pursue new life objectives, a new chapter of my life, but I have no idea what I want to do next."

Jay doesn't respond to every statement and question, and I begin to feel OK with not being fed by him every time, because I know he is listening and with me even when he doesn't give me a word. I continue to talk about whatever comes to my mind, about another chapter of my life.

## Cuckoo's Nest

I don't mean to permanently quit being a therapist. After I think about the next chapter of my professional life, instead of practicing at another mental health facility, I return to working as a therapist at medical clinics. Two retired surgeons who have their own general medical practices give me an opportunity to work with Japanese-speaking patients who suffer from psychological symptoms. Years ago, when I was an intern, I remember that I would become nauseated when I saw Japanese patients. Back then, their issues and problems were too raw for me to deal with. After many years of my own personal therapy, now I can't imagine a better place for me to start learning about who I am and who I can become.

For the first time in my life, I consult with surgeons on my clients' cases. I see fearless confident quality in both of surgeons. They have an exceeding sensitivity and urgency for illnesses and disorders, so they want me to fix their patients' symptoms quickly. The first thing I have to do is let them know that therapy takes time, but that it will work for many people. Surgeons are intuitive, and they expect others to be. They don't like to listen to narratives, so I think twice before I open my mouth. I must think about how I can describe complicated situations in a few simple sentences. Many people think surgeons and therapists speak different languages, and we are different people, but surgeons and therapists have one commonality, which is an in-the-moment interaction, in contrast to being prepared by having written content. Very often, we must decide what to do immediately, in the patient's presence. Therapy sessions cannot be choreographed, and neither can surgery. Though two surgeons seem not to get overly involved in my work, I am very lucky to have bosses who respect therapy.

As the months pass, the awkwardness I feel for providing sessions in my native language with my own people is gone. Many of my clients say things like, "I don't cry because I don't want people to think I'm crazy. I don't want to show my emotions because people may think I'm mental." Another time, they say, "Teachers tell me that I use the word 'maybe' too often." Japanese girls are comfortable with ambivalence, but confused about cultural differences. I sense that their American teachers struggle to teach these girls who do not express their own opinions. They are physically separated from their ordinary home life, but their minds continue to reflect their upbringing.

In my two new practices, I begin to feel comfortable and even confident with Japanese female patients who came to America because their own society rejected them. Most of them live in America but their minds are still in Japan. This causes stress, and they express this stress through their bodies because they don't express their emotions. They want to be treated for skin rashes and digestive problems, but they hesitate to be treated for anxiety and depression. However, once a physician tells Japanese patients that their physical symptoms might be caused by stress because there is no evidence of physical causes, many of those patients can welcome the help provided by their therapist.

Those young women struggle with new expectations in a new land, and this reminds me of when I arrived in America without knowing who I was and who I could become. While I'm trying to figure out who I really am and focusing on my clients, I also think about my bosses, the two retired surgeons, their views on life and death, their way of thinking and beliefs. They don't seem to care about money, and they never express concerns or interest in money. People who are facing life and death situations so often in their lives might become less interested in money. "Everything we own in this life, we are borrowing. We return everything we owe when we die." Grandpa told me that when I was a little girl. I think of the magazine I had to read: statistically, most people leave 90% of their assets behind when they die. Why do people obsess about money?

On the day of Christmas, Matt and I are invited to a dinner party. As friends and colleagues start to arrive, Bruce, my boss, is bringing out a steaming chunk of sizzling meat from one of the large ovens. People are greeting each other and socializing, but my eyes are glued to the whole animal on the large kitchen island. There is plenty of other food on the table, but I pay special attention to the chunk of prime rib, not because I like prime rib, but because I don't want to miss an opportunity to observe how my boss, a surgeon, cuts it with a knife.

Bruce pulls up his tuxedo sleeves and grabs a large sharpened silver knife. He holds it in his right hand as if he were an orchestra conductor. A large fork in his left hand sticks into the perfect juicy prime rib that still sits in a large aluminum pan on the kitchen island. Bruce is left-handed, but he holds the knife in his right hand because hospitals seldom have left-handed scalpels, so he trained to use a surgical scalpel in his right hand. When I tell Bruce that it must be hard to use a non-dominant hand for something that needs fine motor skills, he says that cutting is a small portion of surgery and that the majority of surgery doesn't involve cutting. He also mentions that he finds it convenient to use a scalpel with his right hand so that he can use his dominant hand to do the majority of the work.

Bruce shows his skills by penetrating the tip of the knife into the meat as he gives a gentle push with his right index finger. Slowly, the knife sinks deep into the golden colored ribs. Quickly, the bloody juice comes out with small bubbles from the incision, then the blood runs into the sizzling aluminum pan when he pulls the knife out. He cuts the second slice, and this time, the knife reaches the tendons. He carefully removes the tendons with the other side of the knife, so the knife won't cut them. For surgeons, cutting tendons is prohibited.

He cuts a chunk of prime rib into steak sized slices, and then he places each piece onto fine silver china. The slices of prime rib on the plates are neither flat nor the same shape. Some pieces have a bone sticking out, some include tendon wiring, and some are just meat. He serves ribs like detached objects, they all have unique shapes on the china. I stand there mutely and keep watching Bruce's right hand and the cut up meat.

The Christmas dinner is beautifully displayed on the huge wooden dining table. Bruce grabs a roll and cuts it in half, then adds a piece of butter that's bigger than the half roll. Slowly, he bites a large chuck of the butter with the roll; quickly, the butter melts into his mouth. Bruce, a surgeon, an attorney, and a farmer, eats butter as a appetizer. When I tell him that his brain might be made out of butter, he responds with biological facts: the human brain is nearly 60% fat, and fatty acids are the most crucial molecules that determine our brain's integrity and ability to perform. I learned in biology class that the human brain weights about 3 pounds, so his brain must contain 12 sticks of butter.

While Matt is getting a second helping of juicy prime rib, I get up and leave the table. I walk around to the living room, which has a large sliding glass door access to the backyard. It's not yet completely dark outside, so I can still see wild farmland. One of Bruce's colleagues told me that Bruce destroyed a beautiful swimming pool in order to create small farmland in his backyard in Bel Air. I step outside, yellow begonias and orange kalanchoe on the bottom of the slope catch my eye. As I walk up the stone steps toward the slope, I see three cherry blossom trees on the side of the slope. The garden is unorganized: plants are all over, scallions are mixed among mints, and mints are mixed among basil herbs. They look wild, they seem alive, they are coexisting in this wild land. I walk closer to these herbs and bend over. When I get close, I realize that mints have lavender flowers. It looks like that mint season is over, but the area still smells like minty gum.

I hear a noise behind me. Bruce and Matt are following me to the garden. I turn around and say to Bruce, "I wish I had your talent of raising vegetables."

"Anybody can do it," he quickly replies.

"I can't even keep my pets alive." I wrinkle my forehead.

"Turtles are not easy to kill." Bruce is not smiling.

"Yasuko is a plant serial killer. She kills every plant in the house," Matt tells Bruce with a childish smile.

"It's hard to kill succulents," Bruce says enthusiastically as his fingers touch the sharp end of the aloe vera. He looks further into the garden as he walks toward it.

## The Moon Home

There is a knife on the ground, and then another knife; he keeps a knife every three feet because he does not like to look for a knife when he needs one. Surgeons and knives, there is something between them like samurai and swords. Bruce bends over and cuts up portulacaria and haworthia from the dirt as he holds the shaft of the plants with his right hand. He becomes natural and wild when he is in his garden. Bruce gives some succulents for me to take. "I want to have plants in the dirt, not just on a plate or vase," I tell Bruce. "The roots will grow if you put them in soil. That's what plants are about," Bruce says with confidence. While I am holding the rootless haworthia in my hand, I realize that I probably need desert animals and plants in my house. They are strong enough to survive in a tough climate. Thick surface desert plants can live in the desert, where it's both extremely hot and cold. Their prickly surfaces protect them from predators. Rootless plants could even grow roots in the soil on their own. The moment the prickly desert plant pokes my hand, I think about a woman who is running around two lands with rootless legs, looking for soil to settle in and for someone to nurture her.

That night, I take the spiky haworthia home and decide to nurture it in the pot until it develops roots.

After the holidays, on one hot winter day in west Los Angeles, I get out from the office and walk across the street. Los Angeles is a peculiar place, with many buildings, busy stores, and loud construction sites, and among all this is a place that does not seem to belong in the area. It's a place named Hashimoto Nursery. In the time between two clients' sessions, I swing by and look for pots for my growing spiky succulents and some pesticide for sickly ficus trees.

A large area of the nursery is enclosed by a fence to create division between greenery and busy streets. The left side of the entrance is the pots area, which includes gray, beige, white, red, black, and green pots. They come in many sizes, square, rectangular, round, and some are large enough to fit my entire body inside. Hundreds of them face the busy street, and they seem to protect plants and flowers from the noise and dust from the busy street. As I look at the colorful pots, I think of the ceramic class I took as a child. I remember it took weeks to complete a small piece; for these large pieces in the nursery, it would probably take months. I never had a special talent for anything, but to work diligently and steadily and to keep making a small effort is something I can do. Making pottery is something for which I can use my strengths.

As I enter through the main entrance, I smell greens and clean air from trees and plants in the nursery. This patch of nature cleanses everything from city noise and carbon dioxide. The breeze from Santa Monica allows me to sniff the flowers; some have a sweet scent, while others have an almost sour or bitter scent. The sunlight throughout the nursery makes the colors of the plants and flowers bright and quite distinctive.

After passing the pots, I see a cashier and a barn. Pothos, areca palm, and other familiar indoor plants are displayed on a tiered stand. The barn has a shaded glass wall so that the plants don't face direct sunlight. They live in the shaded barn among many small succulents. As I breathe in through my nose and exhale slowly, I realize that my body has been forgetting to do deep breathing ever since I've lived in Los Angeles. When I open my eyes, the plants' colors seem clearer than before. Having enough oxygen in my brain might affect my eyesight.

I circle around to explore the other side of the nursery, where there are flower beds on top of wooden pedestals, they cover every inch of the large south side of nursery. Yellow, purple, and white pansies are next to bright orange marigolds; my eyes can't catch up with countless bright colorful flowers. Who creates a canvas for the arrangement and nurturing of thousands of flowers? Suddenly, a lady appears from nowhere; she is bending over the narrow walkway between the flower beds. Her pastel colored apron on top of her pink cotton long sleeve T-shirt camouflage her among the colorful flowers. She is placing young flowers on the wooden shelves near the street, behind the fence.

I stand next to her and watch her moves, in order to steal some plant care secrets from her. She inspects every flower and removes the brown petals. When I peek at her face through her straw hat, sweat is dripping from her forehead. It's 2:30 in the afternoon, and the sun is still high. I move behind her to avoid direct sunlight. I squat and reach the yellow mocca St. johns and pretend to look at the flower bed. When the lady pulls her long sleeve over her elbow and wipes her sweat with her white gloves, I see her gray hair. Here is my chance to get her attention. "Excuse me," I interrupt. She keeps patting the dirt without looking at me. "Excuse me." My voice gets a little loud. The movement of her hands finally stops. There is small clump of gray dirt that falls off into dust as she brushes the dirt from her hands and stands up. She does not look happy that I interrupted her work. I pull an infected ficus leaf from a ziplock bag, and tell her about my ficus trees that have been infected recently. She grabs the leaf and lifts gently into her eye level. "This is pee," she says. "Pee?" I look at her. "Yes, insects' pee." She nods. I'd never heard about about insects' pee, and I can't tell insects not to pee on my plants, so I ask her how I can keep my plants away from insects' pee. At the same time, I show her the pesticide that I had just grabbed from a shelf. "When do you spray this?" The lady asks. Before I answer her question, she says I should spray in the morning when the sun is not so strong and that I should water the plants before I spray pesticide. There is a time for everything. She also explains the reason for this method. Strong chemicals can easily burn plant skin, especially under the strong sun in southern California. When it comes to pesticide, water and mild sunlight can protect plants from pesticide burns. I open my right palm so that she can hand me back the leaf. I don't want her to feel as if I'm asking her to get rid of the leaf. "That's OK, I'll take care of it," she says.

I already feel relief from finding out what caused the ficus problem. When I take a deep breath and raise my head, a section of tall outdoor plants in the far back of the nursery catches my eye. As I walk toward and get close to them, I clearly see some delicate, graceful ficus trees. I turn around and see the Hashimoto lady behind me. She and I are both looking at the ficus trees. "My ficus trees look so different from these healthy ficuses here," I say as if I were talking to myself. "They are sensitive to being rotated. They don't like changes," the lady replies. "But make sure they get sunlight from all directions." Ficuses are delicate and complicated plants.

*- The Moon Home -*

When I am about to leave the nursery, I hear a cuckoo bird from the back of the nursery where they keep tall plants and small trees. I start walking as if summoned by the bird's call. Carefully, I walk down the dirt walkway, balancing my body so that I don't touch any plants on either side. As I reach the far back of the nursery, I stop and look up. Shafts of sunlight appear, only partially filtered through the leaves of ficus trees.

"On the island of Hokkaido, people call cuckoos 'planting birds,' because hearing the sound of the cuckoo is a sign to begin planting beans. Farmers do not plant any beans before they hear cuckoos because it's too cold for beans to grow. Cuckoos must have complicated inner clocks. Farmers in Hokkaido don't farm by the time of month, they farm by the call of nature," I tell the lady.

"It is rare that we hear cuckoos at this time of day. Cuckoos are rare birds anyway. They eat caterpillars that eat plants, but the majority of birds don't eat woolly bears, you know, those hairy caterpillars, no other birds eat those except the cuckoos." When I turn around, she is no longer looking at me. She is replanting podocarpus, a relatively short tree that would fit in a small garden.

Cuckoos are peculiar birds, they eat things other birds won't, they don't raise their own young, but let other birds raise their young by laying their eggs in another bird's nest. A cuckoo's body temperature is too low to hatch its own eggs, which is probably the reason Cuckoos let other birds hatch their eggs. Interestingly, when a baby cuckoo has grown and the time comes for them to lay their own eggs, they choose the nest of their foster parents, the one they were raised in.

## - Cuckoo's Nest -

As I'm paying for the pesticide, the cashier says that the lady who took care of me is the owner of the nursery. Her name is Hashimoto. The owner hires people to handle money in the shade, while she is out there under the sun all day, every day, and takes care of the flowers and plants.

When I reach the gate to leave the nursery, I feel the breeze from the Santa Monica beach. My sweaty forehead is finally starting to dry in the cool breeze. It's 3:15 pm, time for me to leave the nursery and cross the busy street. I start running. I have to get back to the office to see another client at 3:30. As I begin waiving to the Hashimoto lady who is focusing on digging into the soil, I am only now, digging into whatever it is I am out here to do in my therapy office.

"I saw three clients this afternoon. The sessions were filled with a lot of emotions. It's nice to be taken care of after I take care of others." I take a deep breath as I lie down on the couch.

"When it comes to life energy, the secret is to have a passion and to enjoy nurturing. For many years I wondered why some people had life energy and I didn't, why some people could keep plants alive and I couldn't. It was not a secret. I could enjoy taking care of my clients because I had been taken care of by you, and you didn't seem to be bothered by it. I know how to take care of others because I've been taken care of. My life energy comes back after I've been taken care of either by you or by myself, and then I want to do something I like or enjoy. Painting, writing, or doing something creative, even planting, something nurturing. People say psychology is science;

we therapists think psychotherapy is an art that reflects clients' deepest emotions, a way to articulate their circumstances, and a path to understand the inside of their worlds. This, I think, is why I'm fascinated by this field.

"I've been able to dream at night for the past few weeks. They are strange dreams, but I'm well rested. When I'm able to dream, I can sleep. My consciousness and unconsciousness have been balanced."

"Sometimes, I still feel my death energy come back, and then I have no energy to do anything. When that happens, I think to myself, why do I have to change? Why don't I just stay where I was and be comfortable. I don't paint or write when I feel like that."

After a long pause, Jay speaks, "A part of you might believe that if you change, you will lose everything about yourself. You won't exist. All would be gone."

"Do I believe everything is so bad that if I were to change, I would be completely gone? That's crazy."

"What you call crazy could be your unconscious."

"It has a name, so I don't have to use the word 'crazy' anymore. What about the word 'stupid' that I frequently use?"

"What do you think?"

"Denial, unable to think, unable to verbalize my thoughts…"

Jay is listening.

"Tell me, Jay, am I right?"

"Do you have to know now?"

"It's like puzzles or paintings. I need to figure out where this piece goes, I want to figure out what color I should use."

Everything is unpredictable as a client, and my voice becomes desperate.

"Do you want to complete your puzzle today?"

I laugh in agreement, then there is silence.

"Our time's up," Jay whispers, as usual.

Once, I thought that I left the troubles of my old self behind when I arrived in America, but my memories of Japan and its customs and habits never completely faded away. At one point in my journey, I became more aware that nothing can separate my two lands and identities. Instead of trying to get rid of some parts, I've learned to accept all aspects of myself and integrate. In our hours together in his office, Jay helped me to open up my senses and memories in order to extend the roots of my rootless mind into the soil of my unconscious to reveal a fascination with the structure of thoughts, thoughts that were out of order and full of chaos.

Jay's gentle push helped me to find ways to articulate my mind, and formed my overwrought thoughts and undesirable language into something meaningful. During our sessions, I felt chills when I was terrified, but my arms and legs were relaxed when my feelings were contained. Those experiences are hard to forget. I was given an opportunity to grow in my ability to associate between the sensations of my body, feelings, ideas, memories, and dreams, and this led to a feeling of my existence.

I realize that there are two aspects of learning. "Learning about" is an intellectual activity such as reading books, and "learning from experience," such as talking about feelings and thoughts while I undergo analysis with Jay. Learning from experience probably takes a lot longer than reading books and listening to lectures, but the newly created sense of who I am lives in my body, not just my mind.

I notice there is one commonality between psychoanalysis and zen practice; the significance of both is to experience rather than understand intellectually. Originally, I thought analysis was for learning and understanding our mind's deep desires. Gradually, I learned that analysis is not just about analyzing minds, it is also about development and maturation, even love. When I look back on my entire life, I see myself eager to connect with someone deeply. Through my experience of being connected with Jay, I also experienced being connected with myself, and it was the most exciting and powerful passage of my life. Doing that brought me back to life again.

One spring day, on my way to the airport in a taxicab, I look outside. As an airplane in the sky becomes larger and begins its descent to the runway, the prolonged roaring sound follows overhead. When the sun light hits the airplane, a spark of silver light travels through me. I keep looking in the distance letting the silver light fill the sky.

I've traveled back and forth between those two lands many times before, but today, I remember when my world had split in two. Running away or running toward my problems seemed like my only options, so I continued to run. I chose my own path rather than the one already given, the path of no direction, no footprints. For many years, I thought I lived in two separate homes, two separate worlds, and I was two separate people. The two different homes, worlds, and people were so far apart, and my feelings for both lands were painfully ambivalent. In either home, with my polarized mind, I felt so far from myself that it felt as if a black hole had consumed my identity and destroyed my existence; but not long ago, the black hole released something that was new and alive.

The ever-shinning sun is setting, transforming from a blazing red to a calm orange. I don't close my eyes because I want to remember. As the air cools down, the wispy clouds become puffy depths in the sky, and the cotton-like clouds around the sun turn elegant golden orange. The white moon appears on the other side of the sky and floats in the air. Since the white moon is still not quite round and clear, I take little notice of its existence. The moon is neither a planet nor a star as I am neither an American nor an Japanese. For most of my life, I believed the moon was directly opposite the sun in the sky. For the first time, I notice that the sun and the moon can exist at the same time in the same sky. When I continue to stare at the space between the sun and moon, the space between appears to narrow.

"Where are you going?" the cab driver asks while looking at me through the rear view mirror. "Home. I'm going home." I look at his eyes in the mirror and smile.

As the cab approaches the airport, the sun is getting closer to the horizon. The peaceful orange sun is reflecting off the golden yellow clouds, and the sky is becoming purple-pink. The tenderness of the purple-pink light turns magenta and silently reflects off the city. When I look at the sky through the window, a white light around the moon fades away into the atmosphere.

## - The Moon Home -

Then, the clouds move slowly toward the horizon. Suddenly the sun is no longer there. All is slowly becoming a deep midnight blue. As the sky has darkened and the yellow airport lights start to glow, the white moon becomes clear golden yellow as it shines in the sky. Night fades to day, day fades to night, and a new day slowly approaches. In ten hours, when I get to the other land, I will see the sun again. When I board the airplane that takes me home, either home, there is peace within me.

> Where ever you live
> Whomever you're with
> Whether you plan or are guided by fate,
> Your endless path will take
> Whoever you want to be

# Acknowledgments

Many friends and family were generous with advice and support: Petra W., Lisa L., Suzan C., Michael F., Melanie A., Lynn Y., Richard N., Shiral T., Stacy D., and Katie M. This project would never have become a book without you.

A profound thank you to my mentors and friends who guided, supported, and encouraged me in my career and personal life. The nonprofit organization that supported my work visa; I wouldn't be in this country without you. Throughout my career, my managers and colleagues, too numerous to name; I've treasured your guidance, support, and friendship. A deep bow to my teachers and classmates at the New Center for Psychoanalysis, for your wise counsel, knowledge, and kindness while I was in the Child and Adolescent Psychoanalytic Training Program. Last but not least, I'm deeply indebted to my therapist, couples therapist, and analyst, who didn't give up on me; you brought me back to life.

www.ingramcontent.com/pod-product-compliance
Lightning Source LLC
Chambersburg PA
CBHW022353040426
42450CB00005B/159